THE SACRAMENTS

Historical Foundations and
Liturgical Theology

KEVIN W. IRWIN

Paulist Press
New York / Mahwah, NJ

Library of Congress Cataloging-in-Publication Data

Irwin, Kevin W.
    The sacraments : historical foundations and liturgical theology / Kevin W. Irwin.
        pages cm
    ISBN 978-0-8091-4955-1 (pbk. : alk. paper) — ISBN 978-1-58768-554-5 (ebook)
    1. Sacraments—Catholic Church. 2. Catholic Church—Liturgy. I. Title.
    BX2200.I79 2016
    234´.16—dc23
                                                                        2015023577

ISBN 978-0-8091-4955-1 (paperback)
ISBN 978-1-58768-554-5 (e-book)

Published by Paulist Press
997 Macarthur Boulevard
Mahwah, New Jersey 07430

www.paulistpress.com

Printed and bound in the United States of America

TABLE OF CONTENTS

CONTENTS

I
_____

PREFACE

For three decades now, I have taught courses in liturgy and sacraments at The Catholic University of America. My methodological premise has been that the church's liturgy grounds what we believe about the sacraments and how God acts among us through them. I learned this from beginning with summer school courses in liturgy at the University of Notre Dame in the late 1960s at the feet of Aidan Kavanagh and Thomas Talley, among others, and when continuing to my doctoral work in sacraments at Sant'Anselmo, Rome, at the feet of such giants as Cipriano Vagaggini, Burkhard Neunheuser, Gerhard Bekes, Salvatore Marsili, and others.

The modest aim of this book is to explore how the liturgy of sacraments can inform and form our understanding of the sacraments and our participation in nothing less than the reality of the living God through them.

Part 1 sketches out what has been said by theological giants in the constellation of the Catholic theological tradition from the Scriptures through Vatican II—theologians, saints, and the magisterium. My intention here is to be informative, thorough, clear, and dispassionate.

Part 2 sketches out in summary form a methodology of how I understand the liturgy to be the basis on which we can engage in doing sacramental theology.

Part 3 sketches out eight elements that, taken together, comprise what I regard as a theology of sacramental liturgy to flesh out the methodology presented in part 2. Here I intend to offer what may well be new insights about the theology of the liturgy and how theology can be derived from the liturgy.

At The Catholic University of America, I have directed eighteen doctoral dissertations, been a reader for over fifty more, directed forty licentiate theses, and been a reader for two dozen more. I have taught some eighteen different courses, mostly at the graduate level. It has been and is an honor to work with such students in a variety of mentoring, classroom, and seminar settings. Not infrequently, I have urged them to "sharpen the pencil" on the wording and rhetoric of their questions and comments in class discussions and in their written work. Not infrequently, they have done me the honor of helping me to do the same.

I offer this book in deep thanks to the students whom I have had the privilege to teach at the North American College in Rome, at Fordham University, St. Anselm's College, in the summer program at The University of Notre Dame, as visiting professor at the Gregorian University and Sant'Anselmo, Rome, and at CUA. Each day as I set about to write this book, the faces of those students came to mind and heart. It is my hope and prayer that other students and readers will find this book helpful in welcoming and experiencing God's always amazing grace and life-changing power through the sacramental liturgy of the church.

The Solemnity of the Epiphany, 2015
Washington, DC

INTRODUCTION

How to Understand the Sacraments

The purpose of this book is to offer an overview of what sacraments are and what they do. Part 1 concerns the historical evolution of sacraments and sacramental practice from their biblical foundations through the liturgical reforms of the Second Vatican Council. Part 2 is a methodological bridge that describes the sources and method that will be applied in part 3 concerning the liturgy as a major and firm foundation for understanding the theology of the sacraments today.

Notice that I began by talking about what sacraments are and do. The heart of this book is about the ways in which the liturgy of the sacraments has been celebrated and understood in history and the ways in which the liturgy can (and should) influence how we understand the sacraments today.

The term *liturgy* means all the public rites of the church's prayer (more on the meaning of this term toward the end of this chapter). Two Jesuit scholars who have had a great impact on my study of sacramental liturgy are Robert Taft, SJ, and Edward Kilmartin, SJ. From among the many profound insights they have given us about these sacred realities, I want to begin this book by noting two in particular.

Robert Taft, SJ, said that "liturgy is like a top, you can't understand it unless you spin it." If you google the words *top, spin top,* and *spinner top,* you will invariably be directed to the Wikipedia source that discusses briefly what a top is, with illustrations. But an article with words and pictures can only describe and show you what a top is in terms of shape, design, size, color, and so on. A video of a top being spun shows what a top really is. A top is meant to be spun. The

1

spinning of the top makes a top a top. It cannot be understood without being spun.

Edward Kilmartin, SJ, said that understanding liturgy is like understanding what the term *dance* means. He said, "The dancer dancing is the dance." A Wikipedia article defines *choreography* as the art of designing sequences of movements and specifying how they are to be performed. But it is when dancers dance the movements they are assigned that it is really "the dance." Choreography is really choreography when it is performed. Then it is really dance.

I begin with these two seemingly simple statements because, in reality, it is the celebration (the "doing," the "enactment") of the sacraments that is the basis for the kind of theological explanation of them contained in this book. The celebration of the sacraments contains the church's agreed-upon and time-tested signs, symbols, gestures, words, and the context in which these are enacted, all of which comprise what sacraments are and do. Words will always fail to describe adequately and fully what sacraments are and do. But like any other kind of theological writing, we rely on words to assist us in what is really an impossible task—to describe God and the things of and about God when God is really a mystery and the supreme being who always invites us into a relationship, an embrace. Writing about the sacraments is meant to assist in understanding, appreciating, and ultimately, immersing ourselves more and more fully, richly, and deeply in their enactment. But writing is no substitute for celebrating sacraments and, through them, being embraced again and again by God— Father, Son, and Holy Spirit—to be sanctified and to be more and more fully who we are as those who celebrate sacraments and who grow in the life of faith through them.

LITURGY AND SACRAMENTS

My professional training in the study of liturgy and sacraments has been from the historical and theological perspectives, both of which are reflected in this book. Part 1 aims to be a theologically informed historical study of sacramental liturgy. Parts 2 and 3 aim to combine what are often two separate disciplines—liturgy and sacramental theology—and to argue on the basis of the liturgy what sacraments are and do. More often than not, courses in liturgy concern the historical evolution of the public rites of the church and how to perform them. And courses in sacramental theology have come to be theological explanations of what sacraments do. In my thinking, these "separate" disciplines should be one.

What I hope will become evident in this book is that explanations about the sacraments in the early church were first based on the experience of the actual celebration of the sacraments in the church's liturgy, especially in the patristic era (see chapter 3). Then the theological study of the sacraments became separated from understanding the liturgy of the sacraments for a number of understandable reasons, beginning with what I call the "early medieval period" (see chapter 4). In addition, the church's canon law on the correct celebration of sacraments became part of what comprised "sacramental theology."

This book is about the historical evolution and theological understanding of the liturgy of the sacraments. Throughout the book, I will make explicit reference to the church's sacramental rites as celebrated at various times and places throughout its history and as celebrated today. Parts 2 and 3 will emphasize the present rites of the church's sacramental liturgy that we celebrate today (usually in the vernacular) and that were issued as a result of the Second Vatican Council's decision to revise all of the church's liturgical rites.

These sacramental liturgical rites as revised after Vatican II invite us to study sacraments with special attention to what we hear and say in the prayers, Scripture readings, and other texts, and what we do in the gestures and the sacramental signs and symbols in the sacramental liturgies themselves. The saying "What we pray is what we believe" is from the Latin *lex orandi, lex credendi,* which literally means "the law of praying, the law of believing." Underlying this phrase is the presumption and assertion that every prayer text, biblical reading, and scriptural allusion, action, gesture, and symbol used in the liturgy of the sacraments has a theological meaning that deserves to be understood, reflected on, and made a part of our lives. The maxim "What we pray is what we believe" grounds this study of the history and theology of the sacraments with the liturgy as a basic foundation.

The church's prayer and belief as celebrated in the liturgies, and therefore the celebration of sacraments, have implications for how we act and how we live our lives in the marketplace of life, and we should reflect on those implications for proper Christian living. For me, the adage *lex orandi, lex credendi* is therefore expanded to read *lex orandi, lex credendi, lex vivendi* (literally, "the law of living" for the last phrase) so that a proper understanding of sacraments comes from both what we pray (*orandi*) and from what we believe as derived from the liturgy (*credendi*). Together these should shape how, sustained by the sacraments, we lead lives ever more fully converted to the gospel of Jesus Christ (*vivendi*).

THE CATHOLIC INTELLECTUAL TRADITION

At many Catholic colleges and universities today, an important revival in the concept of Catholic identity is taking place. Some campuses offer programs called "Catholic Studies." Among other things, these include courses in Catholic philosophy and theology as well as an emphasis on campus ministry programs involving the careful celebration of the liturgy and a variety of other prayer experiences, retreats, and services. On an academic level, this revival means reclaiming "the Catholic intellectual tradition" and raising up the writings of representative authors from different eras whose works give breadth and depth to what Catholic faith and practice mean.

Catholicism is a theological tradition; it is not a fundamentalist religion. This means that for over two thousand years, men and women of faith have grappled with what the Scriptures and our faith believe, teach, and mean through the works of scholars (like St. Augustine, St. Bonaventure, St. Thomas Aquinas, among many, many others) as well as what the church teaches officially—called the magisterium. We are not a "one-size-fits-all" religion based on the Scriptures alone. Different eras, including today, have required different emphases and explanations of the gospel and what the celebration of sacraments means as celebrated and enacted in the liturgy. Different eras require different emphases as explained in the church's official teaching; hence, the evolution of the church's official magisterium. Part 1 recommends important treatises about sacraments and official church teaching from a variety of authors and in different periods of the church's history; it also offers a study guide. My experience in university classrooms and seminar rooms is that when students (re)discover the monuments of our theological tradition from the primary sources, they are awed by them and learn to experience through them something of the breadth of the Catholic theological tradition.

ONE BOOK ON SACRAMENTS?

One thing I have learned in teaching about sacraments is that there is no such thing as one book about them. There have been numerous books on what was often referred to as "sacraments in general" (explaining concepts such as "sign," when and how the sacraments were instituted, what they do, etc.) and on each of the individual sacraments. This approach is exemplified in the *Summa Theologiae* of St. Thomas Aquinas, in which he treats "sacraments in general" as well as the sacraments individually. But St. Thomas wrote during the thirteenth century when the rediscovery of Aristotelian philosophy provided a framework for him to help explain the Catholic faith. We do Aquinas a great service when we study his ideas (as we will do especially in chapter 5) in relation to what preceded him, what followed him, and who was contemporary with him (for example, St. Bonaventure). Catholic theology always deals with what we hold in doctrine and practice and adapts its presentation to contemporary needs. Hence the eight chapters in part 1 of this book offer an overview of ways in which sacraments have been treated and understood from the biblical witness to the present. All that any one book on sacraments can do is scratch the surface of the range of issues involved and lead the reader to more study and prayer about what theologians, the church's official teaching, and the actual celebration of the sacraments say and effect.

REPRESENTATIVE VOICES

In part 1 of this book, I offer commentary on a number of authors, with special emphasis given to five individuals who represent, in turn, what I call the church of the martyrs, the patristic era, the early medieval period, the Scholastic period, and the Reformation. Roman Catholicism has existed for over two thousand years. As essentially a theological tradition, this means that scholars and teachers in every age have grappled with what the Sacred Scriptures reveal, what the liturgy celebrates, and what sacraments are and do in a variety of ways in the several epochs that make up Catholicism. The authors in part 1 represent different eras and, in the case of the patristic era (chapter 3), the church both in the West and in the East. (As Pope John Paul II famously said, in the church "we breathe with two lungs"—East and West.) We need to respect both East and West for what they say and how they say it, even as this book is intended to reflect the Roman Catholic ("Western") liturgical and theological traditions. This means that the authors reflect different interests and concerns. Appreciating their contexts helps to uncover the meaning of their texts. In a sense, what follows is a selection of authors from the breadth of the Catholic intellectual tradition whom I judge to be important in comprising the mosaic of Catholic theology and teaching—a veritable "who's who" of authors in context.

CHURCH TEACHING

This book stands solidly within the Catholic theological and magisterial tradition. Notice that in the last sentence, I distinguished *theological* from *magisterial*. I did so purposefully in order to say that "Catholic teaching" is more than what is proclaimed by the official teachings of the church—the magisterium. For two thousand years,

Introduction

Catholic teaching on the sacraments has been informed by a variety of complementary voices who have tried to give shape and structure to what Catholics believe, say, and do in and through the celebration of the sacraments. These include, for example, the people whose treatises on sacraments are referred to in part 1, such as Sts. Augustine, Cyril of Jerusalem, and Thomas Aquinas. At times, some other voices about the sacraments and church life have been discordant; these include some of the writings of the sixteenth-century Reformers, such as Martin Luther, John Calvin, and Henry VIII. At those particular times in its history, the church's official teaching has been used to correct errors and restate orthodoxy, which means "correct teaching" or "correct praying" (more on this in chapters 3, 6, and 8). That the church's prayer had to be correct in terms of the theology it articulated (*lex orandi, lex credendi*) was crucial simply because a liturgy that was in any way defective or deficient could mislead and misinform those who celebrated those liturgies. Liturgical prayer always needs to be "orthodox"—correct words in prayers that reflect correct teaching. Up through the Council of Trent in the sixteenth century, there was a great deal of variation in the church's *lex orandi*, as the liturgy of the sacraments was celebrated in different cultural and historical settings. Because of the controversies at the time of the Reformation, the fathers at the Council of Trent decided to call for the editing and publication of the first Roman Missal (in 1570) and Roman Breviary (in 1568) that reflected correct beliefs and were to be used in the Western church. At the same time, there were exceptions to this universal rule, such as a religious community that had used its own Missal for at least two hundred years—the Dominicans, for example—or a geographical area that had a similar use—for example, the "Ambrosian" Missal of the archdiocese of Milan and its surrounding area. (The Roman Missal of 1570 is the original form of what we now call "the extraordinary form" of the Mass, so termed by Pope Emeritus Benedict XVI. The last version of this so-called Tridentine Missal to appear before the Missal as revised after Vatican II, now called "the ordinary form" of the Mass, was published in 1962.)

At the Second Vatican Council, the church was able to offer more expansive descriptions of its beliefs and practices because it was not dealing with explicit heresy and because Pope John XXIII, who convoked the Council, wanted the church to present its teachings and to reflect on its structures in order to make the church more pastorally accessible to people of our day, as well as its teachings and practices (including the liturgy). But again Catholic teaching is not limited to the magisterium. Catholic teaching has also always relied on the insights (and hard work) of teachers of Catholic doctrine in every age. Such teachers and the magisterium will concern us throughout this book, but especially in part 1.

TEXTS IN CONTEXT

The term *theology* derives from two Greek words: *theos* ("God") and *logos* (a "word" or "words" about God). The evolution of the Catholic theological tradition involves the evolution of how words about God came to be used and what their meanings meant and mean. One of the tasks of theologians and the magisterium is to seek to craft the best words possible for God and the things about God. But in a real sense, this is always an impossible task! What might more properly be asserted is that theologians have sought to develop the least inadequate words to describe God and the things of God. Words matter. Theological words matter a great deal. But understanding the evolution of theological words and their meanings also matters. Words can change their meanings over time and in different cultural contexts, so much so that the evolution of Catholic thought requires that we be attentive to the meaning of words in their particular contexts. In what follows, the texts under review will be placed in their historical context, noting, for example, how certain rituals are emphasized, how specific words are used, and why some Scripture readings are used in the celebration of sacraments. At other times, some texts under review will be compared and contrasted with those that have preceded or followed in order to determine both continuity and change. It is important to avoid anachronism, that is, presuming that a term in the past meant something that it did not or that the same term used in different eras meant or means the same thing at all times. For example, the

English word *priest* is a translation of the Latin word *sacerdos*, which carries with it the notion of offering sacrifice by one who is ordained by the bishop. But in fact another meaning of "priest" as *sacerdos* refers to the bishop himself as the priest who offers sacrifice on behalf of the church. This usage of "bishop as priest" is largely found in the documents up to and through the patristic era. The bishop was the priest of his diocese who offered the sacrifice of the Mass for the needs of the church. Those who assisted him were originally called "presbyters" (from the Greek word *presbyteros*), who assisted the bishop and, when necessary, took his place in offering the sacrifice of the Mass, and thus they also came to be called "priests."

AN ECUMENICAL CATHOLIC ORTHODOXY

The word *ecumenical* can be used in a number of ways—for example, "universal," as in ecumenical councils (such as Vatican II), where bishops and others from around the world gather to debate correct Catholic teaching and practices and to promulgate them in the light of contemporary controversies (for example, the Reformation) or to present them in new ways to the people of a new time and place (Vatican II). At the same time, *ecumenical* can also refer to a number of religions, with the phrase *ecumenical dialogue* meaning official discussions between and among religions aimed to foster mutual respect, mutual understanding, and eventually, reunion. Especially after the Second Vatican Council, the Roman Catholic Church set itself on an "ecumenical" journey with fellow believers in areas upon which we agree and in dialogue about areas on which we have different positions and teachings.

One area in which there is broad ecumenical agreement and consensus today is on the way the present sacramental liturgies of a number of Christian churches are structured, what they contain (words, signs, symbols, gestures), and how they are celebrated. Sometimes this even involves the proclamation of the same Scripture readings at the Eucharist on a given Sunday (for example, the Episcopalians, Lutherans, Presbyterians, and so forth), praying some of the same prayers during the liturgy (for example, some of the eucharistic prayers in use in the Catholic Church today are used in many Episcopalian, Lutheran, and Presbyterian Churches), and engaging in the same rituals (for example, at baptism or the Eucharist) in those same churches. Therefore what is offered in this book is meant to reflect and respect this breadth of "ecumenical" consensus on liturgical structures as well as to be respectful of an "ecumenical" readership from a number of Christian churches. At the same time, one of the fruits of ongoing ecumenical dialogue among the churches is that while we may use the same words when celebrating liturgy or when engaged in a theological conversation, in fact we dialogue partners may well mean different things. This means that "word swapping" and quoting the same phrases may well not reflect a common belief. This is another reason why we need to be very attentive to what texts actually say and mean, crafted, as they were and are, at particular times and places in the church's life.

WHAT IS A SACRAMENT?

The church's magisterium has never given a definitive and therefore binding definition of the term *sacrament*, but many church teachers and theologians have done so, as we will see. In its teaching at the Councils of Trent and Vatican II, the church has insisted on certain essential characteristics of *sacraments* but not offered an authentic binding definition.

At the risk of oversimplification, yet by way of an introduction to what follows, I would like to suggest the following definition of *sacrament*:

Sacraments are visible signs and effective means chosen by Christ and celebrated ritually in the community of the church to draw the church into an experience of Christ's paschal mystery by means of liturgical actions enacted through the power of the Holy Spirit with the active participation of the gathered assembly of faithful believers presided over by the church's ordained ministers using the sacred word of the Bible, rites, and actions accompanied by prayer texts that describe the saving act of God that is occurring through them.

Etymologically, the Latin word for "sacrament," *sacramentum*, derives from the Latin word *sacrare*—"to make or be holy." This word itself carries a number of meanings, among which are the following: a person or thing constituted holy by divine right, a function reserved for public authority to "consecrate," the one who performs the consecration, the consecration itself, the person or thing consecrated, and the means used to effect it. The oath taken by Roman soldiers, for example, was a *sacramentum*, as they called upon the gods in binding themselves to service. In pagan writings, *sacramentum* was applied to the rites of Christian initiation (baptism, chrismation/confirmation, and Eucharist) but by no means exclusively. *Sacramentum* could also refer to the money placed in a sacred place by litigants. (See chapter 2, when we discuss the writings of Tertullian, and in chapter 3, when we discuss the writings of St. Augustine.)

The word *sacrament* also has its origins in the Greek term for "mystery," *mysterion*. The sense of the term *mystery* is something unfathomable, something so extraordinary and overwhelming that we can never fully comprehend it. Sacraments are often called "sacred mysteries," not in the sense of problems to be solved, but rather in terms of sacred realities to be immersed in and to be experienced again and again—the "mystery" of the reality and revelation of God among us—experiences so rich and profound that the only way to describe them is to call them "mysteries."

WHAT IS SACRAMENTAL THEOLOGY?

There are a number of possible definitions and descriptions of sacramental theology. Allow me to offer the following:

Sacramental theology may be understood to be the systematic study of the sacraments based on a prayerful reflection

11

on the liturgical celebration of these rites throughout history, and on the insights of theologians and other teachers in light of the church's magisterium. At given historical periods, certain theological points came to be emphasized, sometimes to clarify correct Catholic teaching whereby assertions of the magisterium clarified issues of conflict.

What follows in part 1 is divided into historical periods. Each section gives attention to those aspects of the ritual enactment of the sacraments in the liturgy during that period that required particular theological reflection and (in the latter chapters) the assertions of the magisterium.

Part 2 offers a summary of the precedents in our tradition for basing the study of sacraments on the liturgy (chapter 9) and the specific method and agenda that follows in part 3. Part 3 offers an exploration of four things that comprise every celebration of the sacraments—sacramentality, human work, the word enacted, and prayer events—and four theological realities in which we are always engaged when celebrating sacraments—the Trinity, paschal memorial, *communio*, and the "already and not yet-ness" of sacramental liturgy. For more information on specific rites, recourse should be made to books and articles on particular sacraments and to the historical evolution of the liturgy of each of those sacraments.

PRINCIPLES OF SACRAMENTAL THEOLOGY

Just as I judge that there is no "one" book on sacraments and sacramental theology, I would also argue that there is no one agreed upon set of "principles" for sacramental theology. At the same time, in part 3, I offer eight theological themes that run through the repertoire of the revised liturgies of the sacraments that, taken together, are meant to comprise a helpful way of looking at and appreciating the sacraments. All of these themes can be said to be traditional in the sense that they derive from the church's experience of the liturgy of the sacraments throughout the ages. At the same time, these principles are also very contemporary since they are based both on a two-thousand-year tradition of the experience of the celebration of sacraments, and also those things that we can readily recognize as we celebrate the revised sacramental liturgies today.

MAKING DISTINCTIONS: LITURGY, LITURGIES, SACRAMENTS, WORSHIP

LITURGY

In what follows, the word *liturgy* will be used in a number of ways. A familiar definition from the Greek term *leitourgia* is that liturgy is a "public act." Because we are dealing with a faith-filled action of the baptized people of God, *liturgy* will refer to the public work done in faith by the believing assemblies as established and endorsed in rituals promulgated as the church's "official prayer." But what the gathered assembly does in celebrating the liturgy is always initiated, sustained, and supported by the fact that God in Christ himself is the principal agent acting in and through the liturgy and is inviting us to do this in his memory. When one speaks of liturgy, one should always think of an action, an event, an occurrence. To define *liturgy* as a noun is really impossible. What is really preferable is to describe what communities of faith "do" in response to God's initiative when they celebrate the liturgy.

LITURGIES

The use of the plural here, *liturgies*, is important in order to indicate the variety of the different kinds of liturgies in which we can engage. This includes a number of things, starting with the fact that all the sacraments are liturgies. But then, in addition to the liturgies of the sacraments, there is the Liturgy of the Hours, which are structured prayers prayed as many as seven times a day using psalms, Scripture readings, and prayers—for example, Morning Prayer and Evening Prayer. Other kinds of liturgy include the Order for Christian Marriage when this is not celebrated at a Eucharist (for example, when one of the parties is not a Catholic or not baptized), the Order for Christian Burial when this is not celebrated at a Eucharist or "Funeral Mass," or rites for religious and monastic profession, which, however, are almost always celebrated at a Eucharist. Other liturgies include the rites associated with the Order for the Christian Initiation of Adults, specifically the Rite of Election, which is often celebrated by the bishop on the First Sunday of Lent in diocesan cathedrals, and the subsequent handing over of the Creed and the Lord's Prayer, which are part of the rites for Christian initiation. As will be stated several times in this book, the Constitution on the Sacred Liturgy of the Second Vatican Council stated that the liturgy is the "summit and source" of the church's life. It is as simple and complex as that.

[handwritten margin note: Sacraments are liturgies but not all are Sacraments ex. Blessings ↓↓↓]

SACRAMENTS

All sacraments are liturgies. But not all liturgies are "sacraments" in the way we commonly talk of the seven sacraments. It was in the thirteenth century that church teachers started to talk about seven sacraments as distinguished from the other kinds of liturgies that the church celebrated. At a much earlier stage, in what is called the patristic era (chapter 3), a number of things and sacred actions were called "sacraments"—for example, blessings and the use of such things as holy water and ashes. In the patristic period, it was not uncommon for authors to speak of the season of Lent as a "sacrament." But from the thirteenth century on and as taught explicitly at the Council of Trent in the sixteenth century (chapter 6), the Catholic Church has taught that there are seven sacraments. All seven of these sacraments are liturgies. As Pope St. Leo the Great stated, "What was visible in our Savior has passed over into his mysteries" (*Sermo* 74; PL 54:398)—that is, the sacraments.

WORSHIP

The word *worship* derives from an old English term that means to give "worth" to something or to someone (closely allied with the word *worthy*). For example, he or she is "worth" or "worthy of" something. Here *worship* will often be used interchangeably with *liturgy* as a "rite" or a "service" that shows honor to God (God is "worth" this "worship") in such a public event. God is really the only being that is "worth" our worship. In fact, that is what the first commandment is all about. Not having other gods before us means that no one and nothing other than God is "adorable" and worthy of our "worship."

WHO MIGHT BENEFIT FROM THIS BOOK?

I have three "publics" in mind as I write this book.

The first "public" are upper division college and university students who might use the written text "as is," noting especially the discussion questions at the end of the chapters.

A second "public" who also might want to use the book "as is" are laity who could read it on their own or as part of a parish or other kinds of study groups, again with the study questions at the end of the chapters.

A third "public" are graduate students—including those training for lay ecclesial ministry, or priests, deacons, seminarians, religious, and teachers in Catholic schools or in the variety of faith formation programs operative today—who would use the text "as is," but who would then work through the treatises and church documents referenced in each of the chapters in part 1 for reading, study, reflection, and discussion. This audience will also want to make generous use of the discussion questions at the end of each chapter and the bibliographical sources at the end of this book.

HOW TO USE THIS BOOK

I would suggest that anyone reading this book should have at hand a copy of the Roman Missal and the liturgical rituals of the sacraments as revised after Vatican II. These come in a number of editions, especially the Missal, but a very convenient two-volume set of the other sacraments is entitled *The Rites of the Catholic Church*, 2 vols., prepared by the International Commission on English in the Liturgy (Collegeville, MN: The Liturgical Press, 1980, 1990).

The reader will notice that there are no footnotes in the text. That is deliberate in order to make the text as easily accessible as possible. The sources for any authors quoted are found in the bibliographies.

PARTICIPATION AND PRAYERFUL REFLECTION

Before concluding this introduction, I want to address two issues in particular that may well make the study of sacraments and sacramental theology different from other courses in theology.

First, we celebrate the liturgy of sacraments for God's sake and for our sakes. In the more precise language of church teaching, in and through the liturgy of the sacraments, we glorify God and we grow in holiness. One of the ways we sometimes describe this phenomenon is by using the phrase *active participation*. Especially today, with the comparative clarity of the revised sacramental liturgies after Vatican II and their celebration in the vernacular, we can readily understand and appropriate the meaning of what we celebrate. This kind of comprehension also facilitates the way we "participate"—literally "take part in"—the mystery that is God "actively"—that is, with our minds, hearts, and all our senses. The means we use to do this in the liturgy of the sacraments (Scriptures, prayers, signs, symbols, gestures, and so forth) matter a great deal because they are the church's unique means of inviting and enabling us to "take part in" the very reality of God. The study of the liturgy of the sacraments should help us experience God more and more fully, more and more deeply, in the community that is the church through these central and saving celebrations. (Much more on this in chapters 15 to 18.)

Second, we are to reflect on what we read, say, and do in the liturgy of the sacraments so that what we pray becomes more and more what we believe and that praying and believing shape how we look at life and how we live our lives. The liturgies of the sacraments are not "time outs" from the world and everyday life. They are special "times apart" so that through celebrating them we can work to put life, with all its joys, hopes, successes, and yes, failures, into proper perspective—the perspective of faith from and in Christ's paschal mystery (his dying and rising for us and our salvation). In other words, if the paschal mystery is the mystery of our faith, as we acclaim at each and every Mass in which we participate, then one result of celebrating sacraments should be that we view our daily lives through the lens of the paschal mystery. It is like putting on and seeing through a pair of eyeglasses. Glasses help us see better and more accurately. The spiritual "glasses or lenses" that the church's liturgy provides for us is the paschal mystery, through which we view all the joys, sorrows, successes, and failures of our lives. These spiritual glasses or lenses are not rose-colored glasses that deceive; they are the clearest glass possible— glass that helps sharpen our vision through the eyes of faith.

The study of the sacraments should be as rigorous theologically and academically as possible. But it should also be as pastoral as possible, meaning that sacraments are always celebrations of the people God calls and sustains in life as his very own. Prayerful reflection on what we say, hear, and do in the liturgy of the sacraments (sometimes called *lectio divina*) before and after the celebration can and should foster an ever deeper and richer appreciation of what we do in and through the liturgy. This should be one of the indispensable bases on which the liturgy is founded and that can continually foster in us an ever richer experience of God.

Part One

HISTORY

I

SCRIPTURAL FOUNDATIONS

The biblical authors have written about aspects of *liturgy* and *sacraments*, either directly in describing liturgical rites (for example, the Passover in Exodus, the baptism of John the Baptist, and the Last Supper in the Gospels) or indirectly when emphasizing aspects of the biblical experience of God and the chosen people. This follows from the very nature of revelation itself as the intervention of God in human history. The fulfillment of the entirety of the event of revelation is Christ toward whom the Old Testament leads. The following seven themes offer essential and foundational aspects of the biblical witness that grounds the church's experience of this revelation and salvation in sacramental liturgy.

A COVENANTED PEOPLE

God repeatedly called the people of Israel and, to this day, still calls Jews and Christians to a covenant relationship with him at different times, in different settings, for different purposes, and with different partners. In the Old Testament, the covenant with Noah and his family (Gen 9:8–15) promises never again to destroy the living things on the earth. There is the covenant with Abraham and Sarah and their descendants, ourselves included, through which they and their descendants will become a great nation (Gen 12–17). Through the covenant with Moses (Exod 19–24), the chosen people of God receive the commandments in order to experience God's direct revelation and guidance on how to live in fidelity to the covenant. The prophet Jeremiah announces and promises a "new covenant" (Jer 31:30–33) that Christians believe is the coming among us in the flesh of the Incarnate

Word of the Father, Jesus Christ. It is he who invites us into a covenant relationship now in the communion of the church. The pertinent assertion of Jesus in the Gospel of Matthew 18:20, "Where two or three are gathered in my name there I am in the midst of them," summarizes this fundamental aspect of biblical religion. Each day, we refer to the covenant relationship between God and the chosen people (and, by extension, ourselves) at our morning prayer in the Liturgy of the Hours in the canticle of Zechariah (Luke 1:46–55):

> He promised to show mercy to our fathers
> And to remember his holy covenant.
> > [Breviary translation]

In biblical religion, we are part of one another, and we go to God together at God's gracious invitation and sustaining love. This is the essence of a *covenant*. It is not a *contract* of equal parties (which is never possible because God is God and we are humans). Rather, a *covenant* relationship is always a relationship that God offers and to which we respond. It is a relationship forged with God and one another in faith and in love. This sense of belonging to one another is a basic foundation for all Jewish and Christian liturgy. It is absolutely fundamental for our celebration of liturgy and sacraments. We are members of one another in this covenant relationship, which is always an invitational and sustaining relationship from, with, and in God. When we ask God to "remember" the covenant, we are asking not for a mental recollection (something God does not need) but, rather, that he give our covenant relationship new vitality and ourselves (literally) new life (see "An Act of Memory" below).

This covenant relationship is articulated in the fourth Eucharistic Prayer at Mass:

> Time and again you offered them covenants
> and through the prophets
> taught them to look forward to salvation.
> > [ICEL translation]

The corporate nature of God's revelation to a chosen people and the corporate response of that people to God through conversion to biblical faith, ritualized in liturgy and in what we have come to call sacraments, derives from the fundamental communal experience of faith found in the biblical witness. Israel's and the church's nature as corporate entities is an essential principle for understanding sacraments. We experience God together. We go to God together. We bear one another's burdens because we are in this privileged, covenant relationship together.

AN EXPERIENCE OF SALVATION AND REDEMPTION

The words *salvation* and *redemption* are used regularly in the Bible and in the prayer texts of the liturgy and sacraments. These words refer to our need for God and, by extension, to our need to celebrate the sacraments. We find and experience both salvation and redemption in the celebration of liturgy and sacraments.

Salvation has its roots in a healing metaphor. It comes from the Latin *salus*, meaning "health, welfare, salvation." *Redemption* has its roots in an economic metaphor; it means "to buy back."

One of the ways to understand the meaning of these terms is to look to familiar stories from the Book of Genesis (chapters 1–3) that provide a narrative of the human condition and our need for Jesus Christ. In the first chapter of Genesis, we learn that, like all of creation, we male and female human beings are made "good" in God's image and likeness (1:26–28). But it also means that, like our ancestors in the faith, Adam and Eve, we share a certain distance and separation from God (Gen 3). They disobeyed God, and ever since, humanity has inherited this separation, sometimes called "original sin."

This means that we needed a Savior and a Redeemer to mend that separation and reconcile us with God the Father by "healing us" (salvation) or by "buying back" (redemption) what was lost through the sin of our first parents, Adam and Eve. This is who Jesus Christ is. We call him "the second Adam" because he overcame what we inherited from sinful Adam (and Eve). We receive salvation from him, the second or "new" Adam. The words *disobey* and *obey* are very important terms in this narrative in Genesis. Adam and Eve *disobeyed* God's command not to eat of the tree of the knowledge of good and evil as exemplified in the garden of Eden narrative. The proper response by the chosen people to God, however, is *obedience* to God's will. Each of us knows well that sometimes we do this successfully, and sometimes not so successfully. The supreme example of obedience is Christ. As we pray in the New Testament Canticle about Christ at Evening Prayer:

> He was known to be of human estate,
> and it was thus that he humbled himself,
> obediently accepting even death,
> death on a cross.
>
> (Phil 2:8) [Breviary translation]

Christ's obedience is the antidote to the disobedience of Adam and Eve. What was lost through them has been restored in and through Christ. This means that the covenants of biblical religion lead to our experience of the new covenant in and through Christ, the new and second Adam, our Savior and Redeemer.

One of the reasons we need sacramental liturgy is that in the sacraments, we experience again and again the fullness of God's salvation and redemption for us in Christ. All of this presumes that we are a part of a covenanted people, chosen by God, who together respond to God's plan both to save and redeem us.

AN ACT OF MEMORY

Throughout the Bible and in the texts we use in the liturgy and sacraments, the word *remember* is pivotal (as noted above about the covenant). At the Last Supper, when Jesus said, "Do this in memory of me" (Luke 22:19, 1 Cor 11:24–25), he articulated a number of things that are inherent in biblical ritual that come to us today in our liturgy and sacraments. While we hear the command to "do this" in

"Remembering"

the Eucharist specifically, this same ad[] characterizes all the acts of liturgy and sacraments in wh[ich we engage. All liturgy and] sacraments are essentially acts of mem[ory. When we "make memory"] or engage in an "act of remembrance" [in the sacraments, we are ask]ing something specific of God. We are asking God to *act* kindly toward us. Two phrases from the tradition of Jewish rabbis about the word *remember* are helpful here. One is "to remember is to give life, to forget is to let die." The other is "remembering is in the doing." The Hebrew notion of "making memory" is not about thinking or mental recall; rather, to ask God "to remember" means that we are asking God to *do* something for us out of his love and mercy. For example, we ask God to "remember us in your mercy," meaning that we ask him to act mercifully toward us. The Psalmist prays,

> In you I hope all day long
> because of your goodness, O Lord.
> Remember your mercy, Lord,
> and the love you have shown from of old.
> Do not remember the sins of my youth.
> In your love remember me.
> (Ps 25:6–7) [Breviary translation]

The Hebrew word *zikkaron* is behind the biblical term *anamnesis*, which is Greek for "memorial." Every liturgy is an act of this kind of "memorial." For the Jews, the central act of their salvation was and is the Passover (Exod 12:1–8, 11–14). For Christians, the central act of salvation is the entire event of Christ's obedient life, death, resurrection, and ascension to his Father's right hand in glory. What is unique about liturgy and sacraments—and, we might say, what makes them so important in our religion—is a biblical notion of time that is operative here. It concerns how a saving event in the past (the Exodus Passover and the "new" Passover in Christ) can also be a saving event in the present.

This is to say that these saving events happened in historical, chronological time. We have, at least, very good approximations of dates and locations to indicate when and where the Exodus and Christ's death and resurrection happened "once for all" (see Heb 7:27;

9:12; 10:10). But because these are unique and God-initiated events, they are not confined to the past. Rather, we experience these saving and redeeming "acts of memory" still here and now because they are "perpetuated" through the sacred rituals of Passover and the sacred rituals of Christian liturgy and sacraments. The term *perpetuated* is a very important and nuanced word. It is used in the Constitution on the Sacred Liturgy from Vatican II:

> At the Last Supper, on the night when He was betrayed, our Saviour instituted the eucharistic sacrifice of His Body and Blood. He did this in order to perpetuate the sacrifice of the Cross throughout the centuries until He should come again, and so to entrust to His beloved spouse, the Church, a memorial of His death and resurrection: a sacrament of love, a sign of unity, a bond of charity, a paschal banquet in which Christ is eaten, the mind is filled with grace, and a pledge of future glory is given to us. (no. 47)

Notice that it does not say that it is "*re*peated," or "*re*enacted," or "*re*done." (More on this in chapter 16.) The reason for this is that these terms indicate doing something again, whereas "perpetuate" means that by their nature, these saving actions of God on our behalf are not over and done with in the past, but that they continue and can be experienced again and again in the present.

The last aspect of how time is understood in liturgy and sacraments is that our present experience of salvation and redemption through these acts of memory leads us to yearning for their fulfillment in the future. Toward the end of the Passover, the Jewish people say, "Next year in Jerusalem," which is a prayerful plea for the coming of the Messiah, in effect the fulfillment of all Jewish liturgy and ritual, especially the Passover. In all Christian liturgy and sacraments, we pray, "Thy kingdom come" to indicate that we await when God will bring time to an end and we will enter the kingdom of heaven forever. The combination of past, present, and future (see chapter 18) is summarized in almost all of the Eucharistic Prayers we hear at Mass and in the acclamations we sing (or say) during the Eucharistic Prayers:

We proclaim your Death, O Lord,
and profess your Resurrection,
until you come again.
When we eat this Bread and drink this Cup,
we proclaim your Death, O Lord,
until you come again.

[Missal translations]

In sum, this means that the covenants of biblical religion lead to our experience of the new covenant in and through Christ, our Savior and Redeemer, through corporate ritual acts of memorial in which we recall God's intervention in saving history as recounted in the Scriptures, as centered on the Exodus and Christ's dying and rising (that is, his paschal mystery; see "Sacraments and the Paschal Mystery" below), as we experience dying and rising in our own lives here and now, and as we await our call from this life to life eternal.

WORDS DO SOMETHING

The three central pillars of Jewish piety and ritual are the synagogue (focused on the proclamation of the word), the home (the experience of "sacred" meals and dining rituals), and the temple (the offering of sacrifice). In this section, we are concerned with the proclamation of the word in every act of Christian liturgy and sacraments as derived from the synagogue service. (Meals and temple will be treated in the next section.)

God spoke and acted among the chosen people of Israel through his proclaimed and revealed word. This is at the center of the daily synagogue services in Judaism. The repeated proclamation of God's word through the Scriptures characterizes both the services of the word in Jewish synagogues and every act of Christian liturgy and sacrament. In every such act, the proclamation of the word and engagement in it is a major part of the celebration—for example, the proclamation of Scripture readings from the Lectionary for all the sacraments and the singing of psalms, hymns, and listening to God's word at the Liturgy of the Hours. The people of the Jewish and

Christian traditions are people of the Bible. The Jewish daily morning and evening prayer begins with "Hear, O Israel: the LORD is our God, the LORD is one" (Deut 6:4). This text is so important that it may be said many times a day by those of Jewish faith. It extols God as the Lord of Israel's covenant. The devout Jew hopes to die with this prayer on his or her lips. A small copy of this prayer is inserted into the *mezuzah* (literally "doorpost"), an ornamental container attached to the doorposts of the homes of every devout Jewish believer. It is displayed for personal veneration when entering and leaving the home.

The invitation to "hear" is at the heart of biblical religion. We are to listen and be attentive to what God says and does through his word. In religions based on the scriptures, words matter a great deal. In fact, words *do* something. In the Book of Genesis, God speaks and Creation happens, starting with the familiar text, "And God said 'let there be light' and there was light" (1:3). It is no wonder that Jesus is called the "Incarnate Word of the Father" (based on the Prologue to the Gospel of John 1:1–14), meaning that he is the summation of the creative and redemptive acts of God among us through his words (and actions). The first words of the Gospel of John are, "In the beginning was the Word, and the Word was with God, and the Word was God. He was in the beginning with God; all things were made through him and without him nothing was made" (1:1–3). Resonances with the very first words of the Bible in the Book of Genesis are deliberate: "In the beginning God created the heavens and the earth" (1:1). Words matter because words do something; they are creative, salvific, and redemptive. (More on this in chapter 13.)

Biblical commentators tell us that in the account of creation in the Book of Genesis (1:1—2:3), the real story is that God took what was there "in chaos" and put it in proper order. In a sense, we can say that we who are baptized and are believers come to the liturgy (especially through the Liturgy of the Word) to have our lives put in proper order by means of God's revelation. The Bible is God's word and it reveals the way God wants us to see and experience life. It is often about paradoxes, seeming contradictions that are really the bedrock of our faith. Among the central and foundational paradoxes of Christian revelation is that suffering leads to healing, death leads to resurrection, humiliation leads to glorification, defeat leads to vindication. At the same time that these profound paradoxes are proclaimed again and again in and through the Scriptures, we also realize that trying to live these paradoxes takes a lifetime. The word of God sets us in proper order. Its repetition and our frequent experiencing of it in and through the liturgy (that is, "listening" to it as fully as possible) attest to our need for continued conversion. It is never accomplished "all at once" or "once and for all."

One of the advantages of the reform of the liturgy after Vatican II is that the structure of the liturgy of the sacraments always involves the proclamation of the word of God (see chapter 13). The proclamation of these texts is paradigmatic in the sense that they are meant to join us, now, with what happened from the dawn of creation through all of God's dealings with his chosen people, beginning with the Exodus event and continuing in all Israel's history through the coming of Christ among us and his redemptive death and resurrection. The proclamation of the Scriptures read in a sacramental liturgy allow the same saving events to occur among us now. Words do something.

SACRED RITES

As noted above, the three central pillars of Jewish piety and ritual are in the synagogue (proclamation of the word), at home (meals and dining rituals), and in the temple (sacrifice). Throughout the Scriptures, these three locations and the actions that take place in them are central to Jewish liturgy and are the foundation of Christian liturgy and sacraments. In effect, what the early Christians did was to *adopt* and *adapt* the Jewish rituals of the word, dining, and sacrifice and thereby shape the rudimentary elements of Christian liturgy and sacraments. For example, in a summary way, we can say that the structure of the Christian Eucharist—in the Roman Catholic and all the other liturgical churches, such as the Episcopalian, Lutheran, Methodist, and Presbyterian—came from combining the synagogue service of the proclamation of the word with the Passover *seder* (annual) and Sabbath (weekly) meals as the structure of the Eucharist: the combination of the Liturgy of the Word (synagogue) and the Liturgy of the Eucharist (meals). The temple rituals also influence the structure of the Eucharist because we believe that Christ's once for all sacrifice of his death and resurrection, which fulfills the daily temple sacrifices, is made present, effective, and real through word and Eucharist.

When each and every sacred ritual was performed in the Old Testament, as they are performed today in Jewish synagogues and households, prayer texts are said or sung that, along with the proclamation of the word, also matter a great deal. Most often they interpret what is happening in and through the sacred actions. These texts recount God's saving and miraculous actions (*mirabilia Dei*) and, in their recounting, the same saving actions, such as the Passover, are made present. (Recall "An Act of Memory" above, and see chapters 14 and 15.)

Among other texts at the Passover, the toasts proclaimed over (four) cups of wine and the recitation of the *haggadah* (a Hebrew word meaning "telling" the story), which features a narrative of the Exodus events, matter a great deal because through hearing them and sharing in the Passover foods, generations of faithful Jews have participated in the same Passover in every day and age. Respect for and attentiveness to the words we use in our Christian rituals of liturgy and sacraments are important because in and through them, we take part in Christ's act of redemption for our sakes again and again.

Sacramental liturgy combines the proclamation of the word and the observation of sacred rites with prayers in order that we, as the covenanted people of Christ, can share in divine actions of salvation and redemption through Christ's death, resurrection, ascension, and exaltation to the Father's right hand in glory, where he lives to intercede for us, as stated in the Letter to the Hebrews (7:25).

SACRED MYSTERY

The word *mystery* carries a number of meanings: for example, a puzzle to be solved or something beyond our usual ability to comprehend. Among the several senses in which *mystery* was used in the Old Testament, two are especially important for our purpose. In the Bible, *mystery* refers to

> the divine plan for the salvation and redemption of the human race, and
>
> the revelation of this plan to Israel, leading to its accomplishment.

As used in the Gospels, *mystery* refers to the coming of the messianic kingdom in Christ. The Gospel parables of the kingdom furnish some indications about what this divine reality is. For example, the Gospel of Matthew, chapter 13, deals successively with two parables of a sower and how they apply to our hearing of the sacred word of God (13:1–23, 24–30, and 36–43). These verses taken together provide important insights into how we should appreciate the meaning of the mystery of the "kingdom of God" as expressed and experienced in the proclamation of the word in liturgy and sacraments. These parables present the paradox of how the mustard seed, the smallest of seeds, when planted becomes a giant tree (13:31–32). They employ the imagery of leaven that acts on the dough to make it rise (13:33–34), "buried" treasure in a field (13:45–46), and a net thrown into the sea (13:47–50). They are "folksy" ways in which Jesus reveals the paradoxical reality of the "kingdom of God," or the ways in which we should live the reality of God's revelation among us. The kingdom of God is not one locality; rather, it is anywhere that the way God's will is carried out for how things are to be and life is to be lived. Wherever peace, mercy, justice, forgiveness, reconciliation, healing, salvation, and redemption are experienced is where the kingdom of God occurs.

The meaning of *mystery* is most fully developed in the writings of St. Paul. For him the notion of mystery includes the following:

> the divine plan of salvation in Christ hidden from before creation,
>
> its manifestation by the Spirit through the prophets and apostles,
>
> then Christ himself, who is the mystery manifested in his incarnation and glorification,

31

finally (and perhaps most fully) it is Christ in us through whom
we receive salvation here and now
which salvation is to be completed at the end of time.

Writers in the early church both presumed and retained the various meanings of *mystery* found in Scripture.

While what we have come to call liturgy and sacraments have
many meanings and references in Scripture and in early church writings, the two interrelated concepts of (1) God's constant desire for our
"salvation" and "redemption" and his working to achieve it (sometimes called a "secret" that was "hidden" and is now revealed in Christ
and is experienced by us in liturgy and sacraments) and (2) its manifestation in our world for all time are central. We experience this now
revealed mystery of salvation in and through liturgy and sacraments.
In sum, *mystery* means that God's plan of salvation was established
even before the world began, was fully revealed and manifested in and
through Christ, and continues among us as a "sacred mystery" until
the end of time.

SACRAMENTS AND THE PASCHAL MYSTERY

From the moment of the incarnation, Christ the priest offered
all he did in honor of his Father for the salvation of the human race.
This priestly work includes his sacrificial death and glorious resurrection. He gave his life as an act of worship to God his Father. The notion
of Christ's priesthood (the one who offers sacrifice) and the description of him as the eternal High Priest are fully set out in the (New
Testament) Letter to the Hebrews. All that Christ did while on earth
pointed to the "hour" of his specific act of dying and rising—his act of
redeeming and saving us. Jesus' "hour" was accomplished at the end
of his life by his passion, death, and resurrection. For example, in the
Gospel of John at the wedding feast at Cana (2:1–11), Jesus told his
mother that "his hour" had not yet come (2:4). This hour was to be
the "pasch" of Christ (thus the term *paschal*, meaning "passage" or
"Passover"), that is, his passing over from mortal life through death to

resurrection and glory. This was the summit of his redeeming work. It is what we experience daily through liturgy and sacraments. Christ's dying and rising is the fullness of the mystery of God's saving action on our behalf.

As noted in the introduction, St. Leo the Great once said, "What was visible in our Savior has passed over into his mysteries." What was visible in Christ was his loving worship of his Father, in view of which the Father raised him from the dead, and in so doing brought into existence a race of which Christ, the second Adam, is Head. This is the church, the community of the redeemed. The greatest evidence of Christ's loving worship was his pasch. This event was the birth of the church of the new covenant. From the time of Christ's resurrection, what had been accomplished in his mortal body continues in his body, the church. The visible church is thus the sign of Christ in our day. What eyewitnesses saw in him while on earth is now manifested in the church. Just as the dominant note of Christ's life was his worship of the Father, so the dominant note of the church is likewise the worship of the Father through the Son in the Holy Spirit, especially and principally through liturgy and sacraments. In these acts, Christ's redemptive work of worship continues to render salvation and redemption present and active in our lives and is experienced, as always, in the communion of the church.

Having been raised from the dead and seated at the right hand of the Father, Christ is the accepted sacrifice, the lamb, immolated and glorified, the heavenly sacrifice. Christ in heaven is ever making intercession for us (Heb 7:25). Since we must come into contact with this accomplished salvation if we are to be part of the race of the second Adam, this heavenly worship becomes visibly present in the church through the sacraments. They are the means by which people are drawn into the pasch of Christ, once and for all accepted by the Father, operating among us through the power and work of the Holy Spirit. They are the means by which the church brings to fulfillment the redemption and salvation accomplished in Christ.

DISCUSSION QUESTIONS

1. Explain the importance of understanding the Jewish background to Christian liturgy and sacraments.
2. Name some examples of terms that are used in the Bible and the liturgy that need particular definitions and descriptions as distinct from our usual use of those terms.
3. What is the understanding and experience of "time" in liturgy and sacraments?

FURTHER READING

The Scripture readings, prayers, and rites for the Evening Mass of the Lord's Supper on Holy Thursday night are contained in the Roman Missal, the book used at Mass containing Scripture readings, prayers, and directions for how to conduct the liturgy. *Give Us This Day*, a monthly booklet published by Liturgical Press and available in print or online, is a handy resource for the actual texts. See www.litpress.org. (These texts will be referred to again in part 3.)

From the Scripture readings assigned for this Mass, pay special attention to the references to "memorial" in the reading from Exodus (12:1–8, 11–14), the institution of the Eucharist and "memorial" in the First Letter to the Corinthians (11:23–26), and the "high priestly prayer" of Jesus in the Gospel from John (13:1–15).

In the Mass prayers, note the references to the following words and phrases:

participate and *sacred supper* in the Collect,
the work of our redemption in the Prayer over the Offerings,
eternal Priest, everlasting Sacrifice, saving Victim, this offering as his memorial, eat and *drink* in the Preface,
present age and *for all eternity* in the Prayer after Communion.

2

AGE OF THE MARTYRS

This chapter will provide an overview of the way the early Christians from the postresurrection era to the early fourth century began to experience and explain the liturgical rites we have come to call sacraments. This era is known as the "age of martyrs" because conversion to Christ often led to the martyrdom of early followers for their newly held beliefs. The chapter begins with a summary of key New Testament insights about rituals that form part of the basis for the sacraments. This is followed by several other documents from this period that begin to give shape to the ways in which sacraments were celebrated and their meanings.

NEW TESTAMENT DATA

BAPTISM

Water baptism as a rite of purification and baptism "in the Holy Spirit" or in the name of the Trinity (they are not the same) occur in several places in the New Testament. That water baptism was a rite of purification done by St. John the Baptist is attested in the Gospels, which specifically describe how John administered it to Jesus at the beginning of Jesus' public ministry (Matt 3:13–17; Mark 1:7–11; Luke 3:15–16, 21–22). In the Gospel of Matthew, after his resurrection and just before he ascends to the Father's right hand in glory, Jesus commissions his disciples (*disciple* is an important term for the Gospel of Matthew, since the word for "disciple" in Greek is the same as "Matthew") to "make disciples of all nations, baptizing them in the name of the Father and of the Son and of the Holy Spirit, teaching them to observe all that I have commanded you; and lo, I am with you always, to the close of the age" (Matt 28:19–20, RSV Catholic ed.). Baptism as a result of the Holy Spirit's presence and work in the early Christian church is evidenced, among other places, in the Acts of the Apostles. There it states that three thousand were baptized on Pentecost in Jerusalem (2:41); further, Samaritans (8:12–13), the Ethiopian eunuch (8:36–40), Saul of Tarsus (9:18; 22:16), Cornelius and his household (10:47–48), members of Lydia's household (16:15), the household of the Philippi jailer (16:33), and many Corinthians (18:8) were also baptized. In his Letter to the Romans (6:3–11), St. Paul delineates a rich theology of baptism in relation to having died to sin and now living in Christ Jesus.

EUCHARIST

Jesus' early disciples enjoyed being at table with him—to learn from him and to dine with him. In Judaism, to be "at table" was a mark of intimacy and belonging, and was presumed to be for family and the closest of friends. For example, the Gospel of Luke offers us a number of instances of "table fellowship" with Jesus during his earthly life and after his resurrection. The bookends of that Gospel are when the shepherds find Jesus in a manger, the place where animals eat their food (Luke 2:7), and when the risen Lord appears to the disciples on the road to Emmaus discussing the Scriptures (Luke 24:28–35) and then sat "at table" (24:30), where they came to know who he was in the breaking of the bread (24:35).

The Gospel accounts of the Last Supper, set in the context of the Jewish Passover (Matt 26:17–29; Mark 14:17–25; Luke 22:7–23; John 13:1–30), and in St. Paul (1 Cor 11:23–26) should be read with these meals with the earthly Jesus in mind. What occurred at all of these meals set the stage for the early Christians to perpetuate the memory of the risen Lord through the early structure and ritual of the (sacrament of the) Eucharist.

OTHER RITES AND PRACTICES

That the liturgy of the sacraments uses gestures, signs, and words is clear. Exactly where they came from in the Scriptures is not that clear. Among the rites and practices in the Scriptures that are later found in the liturgy of the sacraments are the following:

1. Laying on of hands

   The "laying on of hands," referred to earlier in the Gospels, often concerns healings (for example, Matt 9:18; Mark 5:23; 6:5; 8:22–25; Luke 4:40; 13:13). Later, this practice came to be associated with the rites to designate and ordain those who would succeed the apostles and St. Paul in carrying on their work in the (official) ministry of leading and shepherding the infant church (see Acts 13:1–13; 1 Tim 4:14; 5:22; and 2 Tim 1:6).

2. Oils

   The uses of oil in the New Testament (for example, Mark 6:13) ground the use of oils in the sacraments, such as in initiation (baptism and chrismation/confirmation) and the anointing of the sick.

3. Assemblies for sacraments

   The practices of assembling for the synagogue services, attending to temple sacrifices, and sharing family meals for religious reasons all continued in the New Testament. That the early Christians came to both *adopt* and *adapt* these practices for their own use (as noted in the previous chapter) to reflect their belief in Christ's Passover from death to new life in heaven is also clear.

4. Offering sacrifice

   The early Christians professed faith in the sacrifice of Jesus offered once and for all (Heb 9:1–18) for the salvation of all humankind. Thus no additional temple sacrifice was necessary. The Jewish service of the word in the synagogue became the Liturgy of the Word in Christian liturgy and sacraments. The table fellowship in Judaism at the weekly Sabbath meal on Friday nights and the annual Passover seder were combined with the "once for all" sacrifice of Christ to become the table fellowship with the explicit sacrificial meaning of commemorating Jesus' sacrifice. The combination of word and table fellowship, which includes the sacrifice of Christ, forms the sacrament we call the Eucharist.

POST–NEW TESTAMENT DEVELOPMENTS

The earliest ecclesiastical writers were guided by the needs of their times, principally people's preparation for the acceptance of Christ and the refutation of errors. Not surprisingly, the rites for baptism and chrismation (later termed *confirmation*) and their completion in the Eucharist were their main subject. The earliest of these writers include Justin Martyr, Irenaeus, the Shepherd of Hermas, and the authors of the *Didache* and the *Apostolic Tradition* (the latter usually ascribed to Hippolytus of Rome). Some of these writings were principally apologetic (that is, they explained the reasonableness of the faith or the rituals used to express faith)—for example, the defense of the church's use of material creation in sacraments as opposed to those Gnostics or Manichees who shunned such usage of and respect for created things. Tertullian wrote on baptism and penance, and the *Apostolic Tradition* furnishes information regarding Christian practices, especially initiation (baptism and chrismation/confirmation) and the Eucharist. This work furnished the Catholic Church and many other Christian churches with historical precedents for revised rites for initiation and the eucharistic prayers used today. These early church documents often describe the meaning of the sacraments and the way the liturgy of the sacraments was conducted in general terms. At other times, for example in the *Apostolic Tradition*, the descriptions of the liturgical rites and preparation for them are rather detailed. One advantage of placing the descriptions of the liturgies and sacraments within larger treatises on several other related issues (for example, the *Didache*) is to remind ourselves that liturgy and sacraments are always to be understood as communal responses to conversion to Christ and the gospel, and that in them, we use things derived from creation and our human lives and that we use our bodies in the worship of God. Sacraments are meant to be high points in our experience of God's grace that then return us to live the graced life each day. As a genre of literature, an apology (such as that by Justin Martyr) is often based on contemporary philosophical principles and terms used by the author to base his arguments about the reasonableness of the Christian faith.

During this period, the terminology for "sacraments" was still fluid, with the Greek *mysterion* sometimes used alongside of or instead of the Latin *sacramentum*. *Mysterion* sometimes refers to God's plan of salvation, first "hidden" and then "revealed" and accomplished in Christ's paschal mystery. *Sacramentum* most often refers to these sacred rites through which we experience God's mysterious plan of salvation.

Among the authors and documents in this period, the following deserve particular attention.

IGNATIUS OF ANTIOCH (98–117)

Often considered to be a disciple of the Apostle St. John, Ignatius wrote seven important letters (to the Ephesians, the Magnesians, the Trallians, the Romans, the Philadelphians, the Smyrneans, and to Polycarp, the bishop of Smyra) about the developing Christian understanding of the church and the sacraments. He is often considered one of the Apostolic Fathers who followed in the tradition of the first apostles of the New Testament. Ignatius met his death through martyrdom, which he welcomed and about which he wrote in several of his letters. He called the Eucharist the "medicine of immortality" (*Ephesians* 20:2), which established an important precedent for the sacraments to be seen as "medicines" containing healing. One of his contributions was to sort out terminology and job descriptions for Christian ministers in the early second century. Many regard his comment in his *Letter to the Romans* to be among his most important: "I am writing to all the Churches and I enjoin all, that I am dying willingly for God's sake, if only you do not prevent it. I beg you, do not do me an untimely kindness. Allow me to be eaten by the beasts, which are my way of reaching to God. I am God's wheat, and I am to be ground by the teeth of wild beasts, so that I may become the pure bread of Christ" (*Letter to the Romans* 4:2).

One of the contributions for which Ignatius is noted is the way he delineated the church's leaders, especially because of the varied ways in which they were described in the New Testament. The terms that refer to the followers of Jesus (e.g., *disciples, apostles,* and *follow-ers*) and the leadership of the early church (such as *bishops, presbyters, deacons*) were varied and not always interchangeable among the New Testament books. Since there is no (high) priest so designated in the New Testament except for Christ himself as the High Priest (in the Letter to the Hebrews), there are no "priests" so designated as minis-ters in the New Testament. The term *presbyter* is used (regularly but differently depending on the particular NT book) to refer to a group of what we might call "elders" or "advisors" to the local bishop. In effect, "presbyters" are the forerunners of those whom today we call "priests" (that is, those who preach and preside at the liturgy in the absence of the bishop). One of the contributions of Ignatius to this dis-cussion is the way he organizes second-century Christian ministers and places deacons and presbyters under a single bishop of a diocese.

JUSTIN MARTYR (100–165)

Justin joined several other church authors in this period who pre-sented explanations about the reasonableness of the Christian faith. His *First Apology* (155–57) contains sixty-eight chapters, two of which deal with the emerging practices of baptism (chapters 61 and 65) and three of which deal with the Eucharist (chapters 65–67).

In his comments on baptism (chapters 61 and 65), Justin states that through this sacrament, we are "made new through Christ," that we are "regenerated" (literally "born again," as seen in the Gospel of John 3), and that we are "illuminated" (made sharers in the "light" of Christ) in our understanding of the world through our Christian faith. He refers to being "washed" as well as "baptized," which he then asso-ciates immediately with being an "illuminated person."

After water baptism, the newly baptized are brought to where "the brethren are assembled" (chapter 65). From this period on, the Greek term *synaxis* is used to describe those assembled for worship. It shares the Greek prefix *syn,* meaning "together," with the word *syna-gogue.* What follows is the Liturgy of the Eucharist starting at what today we call the Universal Prayer or the Prayer of the Faithful and ending with the dismissal. Particular features of Justin's description include the fact that the sign of peace—which is taken from the admonition in Matthew 5:23–24, "If you are offering your gift at the altar, and there remember that your brother has something against you, leave your gift there before the altar and go; first be reconciled to your brother, and then come and offer your gift"—follows the prayers of the faithful. This is a compelling ritual action reflecting the presumed harmony and reconciliation that should mark the Christian liturgical assembly prior to its worship. Justin outlines the eucharistic prayer and emphasizes that the (Great) "Amen" at the end is the assembly's very important affirmation of all that has been said and done at the altar; "amen" means "so be it." Those Christians who cannot gather with the liturgical assembly (for example, the old or infirm) receive the eucharistic bread from the "deacons" who serve at the liturgy and outside of the liturgy.

In this *Apology* (chapter 66), Justin calls this sacrament the *Eucharist* (Greek term for "thanksgiving") and understands that those who have professed faith in "Jesus Christ our Savior" can participate in it. The eucharistic "food" is "both flesh and blood for our salvation." He contrasts this food with that eaten in the "mysteries of Mithras," a (pagan) belief system that shares some of the same external rituals with Christianity but whose object of worship is the god Mithras, not Jesus Christ. In chapter 67, he summarizes the weekly eucharistic *synaxis* on Sunday, the Lord's Day (as opposed to Saturday, the day of the god Saturn and the Jewish Sabbath), by indicating that during the first part of the liturgy, "the memoirs of the apostles or the writings of the prophets are read as long as time permits" by the "reader" and that "the president verbally instructs" those present about those readings. Here we see the evidence of various liturgical roles: deacons, readers, and "the president" who eventually becomes the ordained bishop or priest (the one who offers sacrifice, meaning either the "bishop" or "presbyter"). Justin also indicates that those who are well off give what they think fit to care for those in need, specifically the orphans, widows, those who are ill, and any others who are in want.

DIDACHE (MID TO LATE FIRST CENTURY–EARLY SECOND CENTURY, PERHAPS FROM SYRIA)

The title of this (brief) document comes from the Greek term meaning "teaching." Its first line states that it is "the teaching of the Twelve Apostles." While this is only indirectly true—the twelve apostles did not actually write this document—the claim, nonetheless, invites the reader to take it very seriously. The *Didache* consists of three main parts. Chapters 1—6 deal with living according to the ethics prescribed in the document in order to choose between "the two ways—life and death." Chapters 7—10 treat baptism and the background to the Eucharist. Ministry is the topic of chapters 11—15. Chapter 16 concludes the work.

The section on baptism (chapter 7) logically flows from the description of the kind of life one should lead as a result of conversion to Christ and as a member of the Christian community (chapters 1—6). Baptism is explicitly to be rendered by invoking the Trinity, "in the Name of the Father, Son and Holy Spirit" in (running) water. Chapter 9, on the Eucharist, contains prayers that are to be said over the cup and the broken bread, in that order. Here the memorable and important assertion is made that as the bread was made into one from many grains, so may the church from the corners of the earth be made one by the Eucharist (9:8). Scholars debate whether, in fact, these are prayers for what we call the sacrament of the Eucharist or are blessing prayers said at table, as in the Jewish Sabbath meal or the annual seder. Whatever position one takes, it is clear that these texts are rich in their theology, in the kind of "thanksgiving" they offer, and in their influence on later liturgical documents.

In chapter 10, these prayers are a bit more elaborate, thanking God the Father for Christ (called "the child," from the Greek *pais*, meaning "servant" or "child") and for the church. This chapter ends with a reference to the "prophets" who preside and say these prayers—another attestation to the fluidity of terms for those we have come to call the "presiders" at the sacrament of the Eucharist. Chapter 14 contains a brief description of the Sunday Eucharist (starting specifically with reference to "the Lord's Day").

APOSTOLIC TRADITION (VARIOUSLY DATED, OFTEN EARLY THIRD CENTURY, ROME)

Part 1 of the *Apostolic Tradition* contains the most complete description of the rites to date to be used for the ordination of bishop, presbyter, and deacon (chapters 2, 7, and 8). These texts are extremely valuable because of their antiquity and because they are used in contemporary liturgies of ordination in many Christian churches today. Within the rite for the ordination of a bishop, the *Apostolic Tradition* contains a fairly complete outline for the eucharistic prayer that the newly ordained bishop would proclaim at the ordination Eucharist (chapter 4). Notably, this text is the source for the second eucharistic prayer used today in the Catholic Mass and used as a eucharistic prayer in a number of other Christian churches. The structure of the prayer is also notable: a prayer of praise and thanks to God the Father for His Son (also called the "servant" of the Father) informed by the way the Gospel of John refers to him as the "Word." That Jesus freely accepted his death also reflects St. John's Gospel, which contains no agony in the garden scene in which Jesus asks that the cup pass him by (Matt 26:36–46; Mark 14:32–42; Luke 22:39–46). The references to the bread and cup, with the phrases "broken *for you*" and "shed *for you*," are explicitly sacrificial.

What follows is very important because its explicit reference to the death and resurrection of Christ is preceded by the phrase *having in memory*. This section of the eucharistic prayer is designated by the Greek term *anamnesis*, meaning that this is specifically where we acknowledge that what we do here is to "make memory together." We "do this in memory" of the Lord. This is followed by a prayer, called the "invocation" from the Greek *epiclesis* (more on this in chapter 15), asking God the Father to send the Holy Spirit on the offerings and on the assembly. There are also blessings for other kinds of foodstuffs, such

43

as oil, and other ministers are consecrated or designated as such (for example, confessor, widow, reader, virgin).

Part 2 of the *Apostolic Tradition* contains a very complete description of the three-year preparation of catechumens for baptism and chrismation and the celebration of initiation itself (chapter 21). The catechumens are set apart from the "faithful," who are already initiated. They are examined on their conduct, often specifically about charity and doing good for others (widows, the sick, and so forth). This (vigil) liturgy of sacramental initiation contains many of the elements included today in the celebration of adult initiation: exorcism of evil spirits, profession of faith, immersion in water, use of oil before and chrism after water baptism, followed by the celebration of the Eucharist. "At cockcrow," they first pray over the water, which preferably is flowing in a fountain or down into it. The candidates then remove their clothing. The presbyter anoints the candidates (who are nude) with the "oil of exorcism." They are then immersed in the baptismal water three times while professing faith in the Trinity. After coming out of the baptismal water, the newly baptized are anointed with the "oil of thanksgiving"; they put on their clothes and enter the church for the imposition of hands by the bishop. The oils and water are used generously so that their entire bodies feel the oils and water, and the prayer said by the bishop refers to forgiveness of sin "by the bath of regeneration" (literally being "born again," as in the dialogue of Jesus with Nicodemus in John 3). The newly baptized now join the "faithful" for the first time in offering prayers ("prayer of the faithful" or "universal prayer"). This is followed by the sign of peace, which leads to the celebration of the Eucharist and the reception of what the bishop calls "the bread of heaven in Christ Jesus." The bishop presents the eucharistic bread to the newly baptized and they respond, "Amen." They drink from a cup containing the eucharistic wine and a cup with "milk and honey,...to indicate the accomplishment of the promise made to our fathers, in which God speaks of the earth flowing with milk and honey, in which Christ gave his flesh." [Texts from *Worship in the Early Church*, ed. Lawrence J. Johnson, vol. 1, 207.]

TERTULLIAN (160–225)

Tertullian, from Carthage in the Roman section of Africa, was a distinguished early church apologist. He became a Christian around 190 and later became interested in the movement called Montanism, which placed a new emphasis on private revelation by the Holy Spirit and was eventually deemed a heresy. Tertullian, it is argued, was attracted to Montanism's rigorous ethical standards, which reflected his own native stance on these issues. From the perspective of sacraments, three of his many treatises—he was a prolific author—stand out: *On the Flesh of Christ, On Penance,* and *On Baptism.*

Tertullian is credited with having been the first to use the term *sacramentum* ("sacrament") to translate the Greek *mysterion* ("mystery"), and he linked it to a military metaphor in the way soldiers took "a sacred oath"—the oath of allegiance required of Roman soldiers. For Tertullian, *sacramentum* referred to the mystery of God's salvation, the church rites associated with salvation as important signs of Christian commitment and loyalty, and more broadly the Trinity and Christ's paschal mystery.

His assertion that "the flesh is the instrument of salvation" is crucially important for the sacraments because it refers to the fact that Jesus Christ took on our flesh ("the Word was made flesh," John 1:14) and that this establishes the principle that we worship God by using our bodies (see chapter 12).

That Tertullian wrestled with the forgiveness of sins indicates that the church was not or ever could be for the perfect alone. He distinguishes two kinds of penance: one in preparation for baptism (which takes away all sins) and penance for major sins committed after baptism, including apostasy, murder, and adultery. He taught that these sins could be forgiven only once after baptism, and thereby asserted that the church could forgive postbaptismal sins.

In his treatise *On Baptism,* Tertullian goes to great lengths to explore the meaning of water and the way it is used in baptism. This is a clear defense of the church's practice in the face of other philosophical currents and practices that denied the appropriateness of using the things of this world (that is, water) for sacred rituals. The four main points in *On Baptism* are the following:

1. The elements used in sacraments, that is water, are themselves effective—they effect what they intend to effect.
2. Sacraments accomplish what the Scriptures tell us about the use of elements—for example, the water of the pool of Bethsaida (John 5:1–18).
3. In the sacraments, we use things from human life that have spiritual effects.
4. The sacraments derive their effectiveness from the command and action of God.

DISCUSSION QUESTIONS

1. Discuss the similarities and differences between the structure of the Mass as described by Justin Martyr and the Mass today.
2. Read and discuss St. Paul's Letter to the Romans, chapter 6, about baptism and its implications for the Christian life.
3. Discuss the properties of water. Why is it used for Christian baptism?

PRIMARY SOURCE: TERTULLIAN—*ON BAPTISM*

Critical edition: *De baptismo*. Edited by J. W. Ph. Borleffs. Corpus Christianorum Series Latina. Vol. 1, 275–95. Turnhout: Brepols, 1954.

English translation: Ernest Evans, *Tertullian's Homily on Baptism*. London: SPCK, 1964.

This particular edition contains a wealth of information in the helpful introduction and "Notes and Commentary" at the end.

On Baptism is rich in scriptural content. The footnotes of the critical edition and English translation identify important sources for the scriptural evidence on which Tertullian's argument is largely based. Among other things, *On Baptism* is an apologetic against Manichaeism and argues that the elements, including water, are good, not evil. The text is divided into two parts.

The following references are of particular note about the understanding of baptism, for sacraments and for liturgy in general.

PART ONE

I–II: Introduction

The reference to "little fishes" concerns those baptized into Christ, who is called the *ichthus* (the "fish"), a word that comes from joining together the first letters in Greek for the title "Jesus Christ Son of God Savior."

The phrase "by bathing death is washed away" refers to the theology of baptism present in St. Paul's Letter to the Romans, chapter 6.

III–VI: Symbolism of Water and the Baptismal Ceremony

This section contains a rich description of "that substance" or "this material substance" used for baptism and the reason why baptism is necessary for salvation.

The word *type* (§ 4) is a very important term used to describe sacraments and their relationship to Old Testament and New Testament events or teachings that serve as a basis for the use of material elements in the sacraments. The Greek term *typos* is rendered as *figura* in Latin. These are more fully described and used in § 9.

The balance of § 4 contains a solid anti-Manichaean theology on the value of water in baptism.

The description of the rite of baptism contains a reference to anointing with *chrism*. This term, from the Greek *Christos*, meaning "the anointed" or "the Anointed One," most often means Christ himself.

The description of the liturgical rite continues in § 8 about the imposition of the hand in blessing ("benediction").

The references in § 9 about Christ's baptism and biblical references are extraordinarily rich and important theologically.

PART TWO

X–XVI: *Theological Questions*

Several important theological issues are treated here: that baptism is done by another, that without baptism there is no salvation, and that preaching (and conversion) precede baptism.

XVII–XX: *Disciplinary and Liturgical Issues*

The issues raised here include the important role of the bishop in commissioning the baptism and the Christian *pasch* as an ideal time for baptism. The *pasch* is celebrated uniquely in the Paschal Triduum (the "three days" from the Evening Mass of the Lord's Supper to Easter day). The ceremony is described as containing prayer with frequent supplications, fastings, bending of the knee, and all-night vigils.

The treatise concludes by another reference to water when the baptized "come up from that most sacred washing."

3

PATRISTIC PERIOD

This chapter provides a very brief overview of the period from after the "age of the fathers" to the end of the fourth century as it affected the church's liturgy and sacramental practice. It will then describe St. Augustine's and St. Cyril of Jerusalem's contributions to understanding the sacraments and will outline and provide a commentary on St. Cyril's *Mystagogic Catecheses*.

OVERVIEW

By way of introducing this chapter, it is important to state that technically speaking the study of the early Christian writers, whom we call the "church fathers" in the "patristic" period (from the Latin term *pater* for "father"), is generally considered to span from the end of New Testament times to either 451 (the date of the First Council of Chalcedon) or to the end of the eighth century (the second Council of Nicea in 787). But for the purposes of this book, we have divided this timeframe into two chapters: the preceding one ("Age of the Martyrs") and this one. The primary reason is that after the Edict of Milan (c. 313), the Emperor Constantine agreed to treat Christianity benevolently. This was in contrast to the persecution the early church often experienced. This also allowed the church to grow and develop in new and uncharted ways, especially compared to the era of persecutions that preceded it. For our purposes, the patristic era is particularly important because a number of practices that shape our post–Vatican II liturgy— including prayer texts, the selection of Scripture readings, and the shape of the rites—come from this period, as do a number of terms that we use to describe sacraments and the sacramental action.

The patristic period is also a time in which the church's bishops and other teachers refined church teachings at synods and councils in order to clarify what was and what was not "orthodox" (from the Greek terms *ortho* and *doxa,* meaning "correct praise" and "correct teaching"). Often positions that were considered orthodox were clarified and refined because of controversies. The great catechetical works (from the Greek word *katechesis,* meaning "instruction on the faith") of Sts. Gregory of Nyssa (d. 395), Cyril of Jerusalem (d. 387), and Ambrose of Milan (d. 397) are devoted mainly to initiation (baptism, chrismation/confirmation, Eucharist). Like other writers in this period, these authors do not present specialized or systematic works on the sacraments, but reflect contemporary teaching and practice, largely through homilies and catechesis on the rites as then celebrated in both West and East. These instructions are often called "mystagogical catecheses" (from a combination of the Greek *mystagogia,* "to lead through the mysteries," and *katachesis*).

There are so many authors whose works are important in this period that it would be hard to offer a summary of them all. Therefore we have chosen to focus on two whose writings on sacraments have been very influential on subsequent teaching and writing, one from the Christian West, St. Augustine, and the other from the East, St. Cyril of Jerusalem. Clearly, the terminology and overall approach to sacramental practice place St. Augustine in a pivotal place in this era, and he has had significant influence on subsequent Catholic teaching. Among the contributions of St. Cyril of Jerusalem and his contemporaries are the structure and contents of much of the revised Order for the Christian Initiation of Adults. Therefore our treatment of his mystagogical catecheses is offered in some detail to help in appreciating this revised Order, which has had such an important impact on the life of the church today.

ST. AUGUSTINE (354–430)

A chief exemplar of the kind of teaching on sacraments we have received from the patristic era comes from St. Augustine. Many of the positions taken by church teachers at this time were the result of the need to specify correct teaching. One example of the kind of controversies that marked this period concerned those who declared themselves heretics or who followed the teachings of heretics but then decided to rejoin and be reconciled with the church. Did they have to be rebaptized? This controversy is addressed in St. Augustine's treatise *De Baptismo* ("On Baptism"), whose subtitle is often noted as "against the Donatists."

In his conflict with the Donatists, St. Augustine delineated aspects of baptismal theology that had not caught the attention of previous writers. The primary disagreement between Donatists and the rest of the early Christian church was over the treatment of those who renounced their (newly found and professed) Christian faith during the persecution under the Roman emperor Diocletian (303–5). This severe disagreement had implications both for the church's understanding of the sacrament of penance (recall Tertullian's teaching on forgiveness of sin in the previous chapter) and of the other sacraments in general.

The rest of the church was far more forgiving of these people than were the Donatists. The Donatists refused to accept the sacraments celebrated by the presbyters and the spiritual authority of the presbyters and bishops who had fallen away from the faith during the persecution. During the persecution, some church leaders had gone so far as to turn Christians over to Roman authorities and had handed over religious texts to be publicly burned. These people were called *traditores* ("people who had handed over"). These *traditores* had returned to positions of authority under Constantine I, and the Donatists proclaimed that any sacraments celebrated by these priests and bishops were invalid—in other words, that they did not "work." (More on the question of "valid" and "invalid" sacraments in chapters 4 and 5.)

The first question, therefore, was whether the sacrament of penance can effect a reconciliation whereby the apostate (someone who denies the orthodox Catholic faith), or in some cases specifically the *traditor*, may be returned to full communion with the community of the church. The orthodox Catholic position was that the sacrament of penance was for precisely such cases, in an extended process called "public penance." According to this process, a penitent guilty of such a grievous offense would spend years, even decades, first outside the doors of the church begging for the prayers of those entering, then kneeling inside the church building during services, then standing with the congregation, and finally receiving the Eucharist. This long process toward full reconciliation indicated that serious sins, such as apostasy, heresy, murder, and so on needed to be taken very seriously. They were the cause of church disunity. In this process, such a penitent was "excommunicated," which literally means outside the community of the church that celebrates its communion at the Eucharist (with *holy communion* being one of the terms we use to describe the Eucharist). The Donatists held that such a crime, after the forgiveness of baptism, disqualified one for leadership in the church, a position of extreme rigorism.

The second question was the validity of sacraments celebrated by bishops and presbyters who had been apostates under the persecution. While the term *validity* is really anachronistic, since it was several centuries before Catholic teaching distinguished validity and invalidity, it is a helpful shorthand term meaning that the church recognizes that God acts in and through such sacraments. If a sacrament is termed "invalid," that means that the church believes and teaches that God does not act in such a sacrament. The Donatists held that all sacraments celebrated by bishops and presbyters who had been apostates were invalid. By their sinful act of apostasy, such clerics had rendered themselves incapable of celebrating valid sacraments. Hence, to the Donatists, a priest who had been an apostate but who repented could speak the words of consecration forever, but he could no longer confect the Eucharist (really make it effective, or "work"). But to the rest of Catholics, a person who received the Eucharist from the hands of even an unrepentant sinning priest still received Christ's body and blood, their own sacramental life being undamaged by the priest's faults. The Catholic position, according to St. Augustine, was that the validity of the sacrament depends upon the holiness of God, the minister being a mere instrument of God's work, so that any bishop or presbyter, even one in a state of mortal sin, who speaks the formula of the sacrament with the requisite material element (for example, water for baptism, bread and wine for the Eucharist) and the intent of causing the sacrament to occur, acts validly. (This last statement deserves more explanation, which will follow in this and subsequent chapters.)

The underlying issue throughout this debate is the unity of the church and the danger of schism whereby a portion of the community that comprises the church takes a position that sets itself apart from the rest of it. The reality of schism damaged the church in St. Augustine's time, and he repeatedly worked to heal it. He wanted to be faithful to the fundamentally ecclesial ("church" or "community") reality of sacraments and emphasize that they are always celebrations of the whole church, which he terms "head and members," meaning Christ and his church (see Col 1:18; 2:19; 3:15). One of the reasons why St. Augustine and his colleagues addressed the errors of heretics is because of the "scandal of schism." Schism harms, if it does not destroy, the unity of the church. Hence St. Augustine is passionate in his defense of church unity.

In other writings, St. Augustine coined phrases and used terms that influenced authors in subsequent periods. In one of his homilies on the Gospel of John, St. Augustine writes, referring to baptism, "Let us rejoice and give thanks. We have not only become Christians but Christ himself....Stand in awe and rejoice: we have become Christ" (*Tractatus in evangelium Ioannis*, 21,8). As startling as this might sound, what St. Augustine reflects here is the importance and permanent effect of baptism. "We have become Christ." We also have become members of the Body of Christ, the church.

For St. Augustine, the term *sacrament* is used in a variety of ways, and three classes of things are called sacraments: (1) religious rites of both the Old and New Testaments and rites of paganism, (2) symbols or figures, and (3) revealed teachings of the Christian religion. These meanings are not mutually exclusive; the rites of the Old Testament are said to be symbols of those of the New. At this juncture, it is important to note that for St. Augustine, and for many other authors in this period, the number of things and sacred realities called "sacraments" were in the hundreds—for example, the imposition of hands, ordination, religious profession, the Lord's Prayer, feasts, and the word *Amen*.

THE SACRAMENTS

One of the customary ways for the church to speak of the sacramental rites (especially from the Middle Ages on) is that they are comprised of two elements—matter and form. But the roots of this terminology are in the patristic era. Attention is often drawn to scriptural references to these two elements used in the sacraments (Eph 5:26; John 3:5; Matt 26:26–28; 28:19; Acts 6:6; 8:14–17; Jas 5:14; 1 Tim 4:14). Reflecting on these passages and on the sacramental rites themselves, theologians have observed the use of material creation (matter) and human speech (form) as parallel realities in the visible rites we call sacraments. The early fathers before Augustine distinguished these two elements as objects (they used the Latin word *res*—"thing"—for material realities such as water, oil, bread). In sacraments, these objects are accompanied by prayers (words) that sanctify them. Later this distinction was expressed in the terms *matter* and *form*.

The other thing that St. Augustine asserted is that one needs to have the intention that the sacrament is to occur. The word *intention* is very important for our understanding of sacraments since it means that sacraments do not "work" automatically or, as some would say, "magically," even if one says the right words over the prescribed material elements. This is because the doing of sacraments involves an act of faith on the part of the minister and the whole community. The minister must make an intention to celebrate this sacrament in the faith and belief of the church. This is made explicit today when, prior to his ordination as a priest, the deacon makes a formal statement in the presence of a witness (usually the seminary rector) that when he celebrates any sacrament, he will always intend to do what the church requires. Once he is ordained a priest, any sacramental liturgies he performs will always have the desired effect because of his stated intention. For couples being married and men being ordained, the requirement that they "state their intentions" reflects this same teaching. It also assures that they are not being forced into the marriage or orders, which would make the sacraments invalid. In sum, these three things—elements, words, intention—comprise a very important shorthand for what is required for sacraments to occur. And all of these have their roots in the patristic era.

Closely related to these assertions about how sacraments occur is the way St. Augustine uses the word *character* to talk about the sacraments that have a permanent effect and cannot be repeated. Because they imprint a sacred seal, translated into the English word *character*, baptism, chrismation/confirmation, and orders configure one to Christ in a particular way through imprinting a character and cannot be repeated. This teaching is taken up in later theologians, including St. Thomas Aquinas (for Aquinas, see chapter 5).

In addition to the Donatists, St. Augustine found himself faced with another problem related to sacraments in the person of a man named Pelagius. Pelagius taught that moral perfection was attainable in this life through human free will and without the assistance of divine grace. (Catholics teach and believe that we always have free will.) Augustine contradicted this by saying that perfection was impossible without grace because we are born sinners with a sinful heart and will—the result of being sons and daughters of sinful Adam and Eve, our first parents. The Pelagians charged Augustine on the grounds that the doctrine of original sin amounted to Manichaeism—the Manichaeans taught that the flesh was in itself sinful (and they denied that Jesus came in the flesh). This charge would have carried added weight since contemporaries knew that Augustine himself had been a Manichaean layman before his conversion to Christianity. Augustine also taught that a person's salvation comes solely through an irresistible free gift, the efficacious grace of God, but that this was a gift that one had a free choice to accept or refuse.

At least two applications of this controversy and Augustine's assertion of orthodox Catholic belief regarding the liturgy and sacraments are important here. First, St. Augustine's teaching about human flesh reflects Tertullian's statement that "the flesh is the instrument of salvation," meaning that Christ came in human flesh to save us and that we worship God through the use of our human bodies. Second, when we celebrate liturgy and sacraments, we do so by responding to God's gracious invitation (see chapter 17). The phrase often used to describe the community at worship is the *gathered assembly*. This means that we always "gather" at God's gracious invitation and that we receive his grace in and through sacraments. We do not "earn" it. Recall the words of the third Eucharistic Prayer:

> Listen graciously to the prayers of this family,
> whom you have summoned before you…

Thus the phrase *gathered assembly* carries rich and deep theological meanings.

All sacraments somehow pertain to what Augustine regularly calls the great "sacrament mystery," Christ and the church. Note, again, that the term *sacrament* is used of a number of sacred realities, not "just" what we call seven sacraments. In connection with subsequent developments, the following additional aspects of Augustine's teaching are significant: sacraments are sacred signs, they bear a similitude to those things of which they are sacraments, and they are celebrations commemorating an event in such a way that what is signified is received. As applied to sacraments, the term *similitude* refers to a similarity, a likeness, between the element used and what it effects. In baptism, we use water, a primal element (like air) without which we cannot live and that we also use to wash ourselves. In baptism, we are reborn into eternal life. Original sin and other sins are washed away. Thus there is a similitude between the element used (water) and what it effects (a washing away). St. Augustine's use of the term *sign* will influence a number of subsequent theologians (including St. Thomas Aquinas) and official church teaching itself, that is, the magisterium.

A different trend is seen later in the West in Isidore of Seville (d. 636), who stressed the inner working of the sacraments as being concerned with hidden realities alongside the characteristics that Augustine noted, especially those characteristics that speak of the sacraments as signs. Isidore said that "baptism and chrism, the body and the blood are sacraments. And they are for this reason called sacraments, because beneath the covering of bodily things the divine power works secretly the salvation proper to these same sacraments, whence are fruitful when administered in the Church, because the Holy Spirit, abiding in her, works the effects of the sacraments in a hidden manner" (*Etymologiae* 1.6, n.39, PL 82, 255).

ST. CYRIL OF JERUSALEM (313/5–387)

In the East during this period, we have important major sources for the rites of initiation from those we call "the great mystagogues" (from the word *mystagogy*). This period of the church's life is very important because of the reality of the preparation for and the celebration of Christian initiation, in particular because in the revised Order for the Christian Initiation of Adults, the celebration of initiation is followed by the period of "mystagogy." Once the church was able to function in society, in the ongoing celebration of the liturgy and in understanding of what these rites were all about, it became possible for the preparation for baptism-chrismation-Eucharist and its follow-through in church to become more elaborate and public. This means that important places, like the city of Jerusalem, and important bishop-teachers, like St. Cyril of Jerusalem (among others), offered important catecheses on Christian initiation. Originally, these were given orally by bishop-theologians. (Some scholars today argue that what we commonly ascribe to the authorship of St. Cyril was actually delivered by "John the deacon." For our purposes, the confluence of author, place, and text is what matters. Whether it was actually Cyril or John does not change this.)

In preparation for baptism, these mystagogues delivered "catechetical lectures" explaining the Creed, the Lord's Prayer, and so on. After baptism, these catecheses were delivered during the octave (the eight days from the rites of initiation at the Easter Vigil to the following Sunday) and were called "mystagogic catecheses." In the rites for Christian initiation revised and implemented after Vatican II, these periods of communal preparation and mystagogy have been restored and widely implemented. Many of the liturgical rites for this figure prominently in the season of Lent. While other bishop-theologians offered similar catecheses, such as St. John Chrysostom (archbishop of Constantinople) and Theodore of Mopsuestia (bishop of Mopsuestia), we have chosen to focus on the mystagogical catecheses of St. Cyril of Jerusalem because he delivered them in the very place(s) where Jesus suffered and died and then rose from the dead. Such instruction must have left a deep impression on those who were initiated into the church there.

At this period in the church's life, there was usually a three-year period of preparation for initiation. Those who chose to enter this preparation process were (and are) called *catechumens* (from the Greek meaning "one who is under the tutelage of an instructor," often called a *catechist*); they each had a sponsor and became a part of the community that was involved in this preparation. (Today we distinguish those who, like the catechumens in the early church, come from no religious background from those with a background from another Christian church and are called *candidates*.) At the beginning of Lent, usually the First Sunday of Lent, the bishop would become (more) personally involved and celebrate the "rite of election" whereby catechumens are made part of the church, but not yet fully initiated. In the patristic era during Lent, the bishop himself would give catechetical lectures, usually about the Creed, the Lord's Prayer, and the Scriptures. For example, prior to baptism, St. Cyril of Jerusalem delivered eighteen catechetical lectures to the catechumens during Lent as they made final preparation for sacramental initiation at the Easter Vigil. In the Procatechesis, St. Cyril addresses them in its very first words as "those to be enlightened." At the end of the Procatechesis, he addresses them as "those soon to be illuminated." These phrases refer to those who will come into the "light" of faith from the darkness of evil and sin. This also reflects the cosmic elements of the ceremony, conducted in darkness during a vigil that looks forward to the dawn of a new day, with the light of the sun that overcomes the darkness of night as reflective of Christ, who says in the Gospel of John 8:12, "I am the light of the world," and that those who follow him will not walk in darkness but will have the light of life.

The eighteen catecheses were given by St. Cyril, probably in 350, during Lent before the Easter Vigil, in the basilica that the Emperor Constantine had built on Calvary. Throughout them, St. Cyril refers to the fact that up until now, those now preparing for baptism at Easter were not allowed to hear or be instructed on the Creed and the Lord's Prayer because of the discipline called the *disciplina arcani* (the "discipline of the secret") whereby only the initiated (already baptized) knew about these sacred things. The same is true for the celebration of the liturgy of initiation: baptism-chrismation-Eucharist. Catechumens and the enlightened were regularly dismissed from the Sunday celebration of the Eucharist after the homily and were not allowed to be present for the "prayer of the faithful" or "universal prayer" or the rest of the eucharistic celebration. This is one of the reasons why the mystagogic catecheses delivered by St. Cyril—as well as St. Theodore of Mopsuestia, St. John Chrysostom, and to a large extent St. Ambrose in his *De Sacramentis* and *De Mysteriis*—were based on the actual celebration of the sacred mysteries into which the "enlightened" were initiated on the night of the liturgy of initiation.

The five mystagogic catecheses were delivered in the morning during the weekdays of the first week after "the enlightened" had received initiation—what we call "Easter week." The lectures formed a major part of the octave of Easter, meaning the eight days from Easter Sunday to the Second Sunday of Easter (one day more than the seven days of creation, signifying the entry to the new creation of eternal life in God). During these eight days, the newly baptized would wear the white garments they put on following the water bath of the liturgy of baptism, and would take them off and return to wearing ordinary clothes on the Second Sunday of Easter, known as *dominica in albis*, meaning "the Sunday in white garments." (For example, in *Mystagogic Catechesis* 4:8, St. Cyril states that while they should not always wear white garments, it is important that they do so now in order that they can say with Isaiah, "Let my soul rejoice in the Lord; he has clothed me with the garment of salvation.")

We are treating these catecheses very fully because of their importance both historically and for the contemporary rite for the Christian initiation for adults. Each of these five mystagogic catecheses has the same structure. St. Cyril begins with a quotation from Scripture that he then uses to refer to part of the baptismal ceremony, followed by an explanation of what had occurred and what it meant. The following are summaries of St. Cyril's five mystagogic catecheses.

Monday—1 Peter 5:8ff.—refers to being sober and watchful against the devil. The catechesis is about the prebaptismal renunciation of the devil. The cosmic reference to renouncing Satan by facing West is important because that is the location of the setting sun and the onset of darkness each night. St. Cyril then combines this with copious references to events in salvation history recorded in the Bible, both Old and New Testaments. In this first mystagogic catechesis, he refers specifically to "these spiritual and heavenly mysteries" (*mysterion*) and to the need for the newly baptized to turn their minds "from figure (or 'symbol' in other translations) to reality," from events of the Old Testament, that is Moses, to Christ who was "sent into the world by the Father." He recalls that they were to stretch out their hands and to address the devil as though the devil were in front of them, saying "I renounce you." (This phrase or variations on it are still used at baptisms.) Further on, he refers to Satan's "works" and "pomp," meaning things that are futile and yet popularly welcomed through entertainment or inappropriate behaviors. He contrasts invoking the devil with invoking the "sacred and adorable Trinity" over the bread and wine of the Eucharist so that it becomes the body of Christ. (He uses the technical term *epiclesis*, a Greek term meaning "invocation," which is part of the eucharistic prayers we use at Mass that were added to the revised liturgy and that is part of almost all of the prayers in the revised liturgy that are used to bless things, for example, water at baptism.) St. Cyril ends by reminding the newly baptized that these rites for renouncing Satan took place in the "forecourt" outside the basilica where the rest of the ceremonies took place. He refers to entering "the holy of holies at the next stage of our initiation into the mysteries."

Tuesday—Romans 6:3–14—refers to being baptized into the death of Christ Jesus. This Scripture passage is read to this day at the celebration of the Easter Vigil in the Roman Rite. St. Cyril reminds the newly baptized that they stripped off their clothing "since you have taken off the old self with its practices" (Col 3:9 NABRE). He reminds them that they were like Adam who stood naked in paradise and was not ashamed. The first anointing with exorcised oil symbolized their partaking in Christ's riches. The triple immersion in water and profession of faith follows, which recalled Christ's burial in the tomb for three days. Again, the fact that these catecheses were delivered in the very place of Jesus' death and resurrection meant that this reference was likely seared in their imaginations. On the water of baptism, he says, "The water of salvation became both tomb and mother for you," that is, the water bath was simultaneously a death to sin and an event that gave them new life as they received life from their mother's wombs. He asserts that while they did not really "die," were not really "buried," and did not really hang on the cross, nevertheless "whereas imitation is only an image, our salvation is a reality" (he uses the Greek *aletheia*, meaning that our salvation is "true"). He goes on to emphasize how through the rites of baptism, the newly initiated participate in Christ's sufferings and from them, receive the forgiveness of their sins. Recall that this was the very place where Jesus himself suffered and died and then rose again from the dead.

Wednesday—1 John 2:20–28—refers to being anointed by God, which leads St. Cyril to explain what it meant that when they came forth from the water bath, they were anointed with sacred chrism. He states that chrism is not merely an ointment, but after the invocation (like that noted above for the eucharistic bread and wine through the epiclesis), the chrism is "no longer ordinary ointment but Christ's grace, which through the presence of the Holy Spirit instills divinity in us." That they were anointed on the forehead, ears, nostrils, and chest indicates what we saw in the *Apostolic Tradition*, namely a generous use and application of oil. In the *Apostolic Tradition* it was termed the "oil of thanksgiving." Here, in St. Cyril, it is specified as holy "chrism" (in Greek, *myron*). Again, after making a number of references to Old and New Testament texts, St. Cyril asserts that what happened to Aaron and Solomon "by way of figure, but to you not in figure but in truth." He concludes with the exhortation to "preserve this gift without stain," thereby recalling the moral formation that took place as part and parcel of the catechumenate.

Thursday—1 Corinthians 11:23ff.—St. Paul's account of the Last Supper leads St. Cyril to a catechesis on the Eucharist. He describes the reality of partaking in the Eucharist by saying that "the body has been bestowed on you in the form of bread and his blood in the form of wine" (a more precise translation of "form" would be "'in' or 'as' a type" of bread/wine). He then goes on to assert an ecclesiological reference, intrinsic to Eucharistic participation, when he says, "In this way by sharing in Christ's Body and Blood, we become one Body and one Blood with Christ. In this way we become 'bearers of Christ'…and so we become 'sharers in the divine nature'" (2 Pet 1:4). The emphasis here is clearly on participation in the sacred meal of the Eucharist, which is both an ecclesiological event of the church and the means of our becoming more and more like Christ (which is what the term *divinization* means). He ends with a brief reminder of the reality of the change from bread and wine into the body and blood of Christ. While the sense of taste and its appearances would have us believe otherwise, the reality is that it is the body and blood of Christ.

Friday—1 Peter 2:1ff.—Peter's admonition to put aside all filthiness, guile, and slander leads to a penetrating reminder of the virtuous life that the newly baptized should now be living. Interestingly, St. Cyril immediately refers to the washing of the hands of the "priest and elders encircling God's altar" preceding the Eucharistic Prayer and says that "washing the hands is a symbol of the need to be clean of all sins and transgressions." He then comments on the introductory dialogue to the Eucharistic Prayer, which has remained more or less the same even until today, as well as the parts of the Eucharistic Prayer itself. With regard to the epiclesis prayer, he instructs the newly baptized as to its meaning: "We call upon the merciful God to send the Holy Spirit on our offerings, that he may make the bread Christ's body, and the wine Christ's blood, for clearly whatever the Holy Spirit touches is sanctified and transformed." This emphasis on the invocation of the Holy Spirit was a major characteristic of the way theologians and bishop teachers in the Eastern Church approached the issue of change in the elements, whereas often in the West, the words of Jesus at the Last Supper were the words needed for the change in the elements. St. Cyril's instructions about how to receive the eucharistic bread reflect reverence for the species, noting that one extends one's hand like a "throne" to welcome the species as "a king." This emphasis on the reality of the body and blood of Christ in the Eucharist may well seem to contradict his next admonitions, when he encourages them to take the Eucharist and to use it to bless their eyes; this is sometimes understood to reflect the healing that comes from participating in the Eucharist. That no disrespect for the Eucharist is intended is immediately underscored when St. Cyril urges them to be very careful when holding the species and not to drop a particle of it.

DISCUSSION QUESTIONS

1. How does the emphasis on the ecclesial appreciation of sacraments help us to understand how sacraments function in the church today, especially given the emphasis that American culture traditionally places on the individual?

2. There is an underlying theology of creation operative in our celebration and understanding of sacraments: for example, the use of water in initiation and of gestures in the celebration of baptism. How is this evident in our celebration of sacraments today?

3. The Order for the Christian Initiation of Adults calls for the weeks after baptism, chrismation, and the Eucharist as a time of mystagogy. This is based on the patristic evidence and example. How does the patristic data influence or not influence our experience of mystagogy today?

PRIMARY SOURCE: ST. CYRIL OF JERUSALEM, *MYSTAGOGIC CATECHESES*

English translation from F. L. Cross. *St. Cyril of Jerusalem's Lectures on the Christian Sacraments*. Crestwood, NY: St. Vladimir's Press, 1977, reprinted from 1951. Contains both Greek and English texts.

Also see Edwin Yarnold. *The Awe Inspiring Rites of Initiation*. Edinburgh: T and T Clark, 1994, 68–95.

Among Greek texts, see the parallel Greek and Latin in Bernhardus Geyer and Johannes Zellinger. *Florilegium Patristicum tam veteris quam medii aevi auctores complectens*. Cologne: Bonnae Sumptibus Petri Hanstein, 1935.

Among the important issues: references to the cosmos, salvation history, and the church building of the Holy Sepulchre in Jerusalem in relationship to this mystagogical text and other texts and rites of the liturgy.

It is essential to read the Scripture citations in full to appreciate how the Scriptures frame the catecheses, which are filled with these and other scriptural and liturgical allusions.

MYSTAGOGIC CATECHESIS 1—1 PETER 5:8FF.

1. "Concerning these spiritual and heavenly Mysteries…" (the Greek is *mysterion*, recalling the ways in which liturgical rites are called "mysteries" and how they enable those who participate in them to share in the *mystery* of God's salvation)
   "Divine and life-giving Baptism,"
2. "Ye entered into the outer hall of the Baptistery…"
   "And there facing West, ye heard the command to stretch out your hand, and as in the presence of Satan ye renounced him."
   "This figure (*typos*) is found in ancient history" (= the OT).
3. "Now turn from the ancient to the recent, from the figure to the reality (*apo tou typou epi ten aletheian*)" (= from Moses to Christ).
4. "The west is the region of sensible darkness, and he [the devil] being darkness has his dominion also in the darkness."
   "Ye therefore, looking with a symbolical meaning towards the West, renounce that dark and gloomy potentate."

5. "And all thy works (*kai pasi tois ergois sou*)."
6. "And all his pomp (*kai pase te pompe sou*)." The text continues with a full description of the pomps.
7. "Things also hung up at idol festivals, either meat or bread, or other such things which are polluted by the invocation of unclean spirits, are reckoned in the pomp of the devil."

    The important term *epiklesis* ("epiclesis," or here translated "holy invocation") is used when he states that it is by "the holy invocation of the Adorable Trinity," and also, "Such meats belonging to the pomp of Satan, though in their own nature plain and simple, become profane by the invocation of the evil spirit."
8. Other things to avoid.
9. "There is opened to thee the paradise of God, which He planted towards the east, whence for his transgression our first father was exiled; and symbolical of this was thy turning from the west to the east, the place of light."
10. "Then thou wert told to say, 'I believe in the Father, the Son and the Holy Ghost and in one baptism of repentance.'"
11. "All these things were done in the outer chamber..." "When in the succeeding expositions of the Mysteries (*en tais exes mystagogiais*), we have entered the Holy of Holies, we shall then know the symbolical meaning (*symbola*) of what is there accomplished. Now to God the Father with the Son and the Holy Ghost, be glory, and power, and majesty, for ever and ever. Amen."

MYSTAGOGIC CATECHESIS 2—ROMANS 6:3–14

1. "I will lay before you the sequel of yesterday's Lecture, then ye may learn of what those things, which were done by you in the inner chamber, were the emblems."
2. "Ye put off your garment; and this was an image of putting off the old man with his deeds." (see Col 3:9)

    "In this also imitating Christ, who hung naked on the Cross, and by his nakedness spoiled principalities and powers, and openly triumphed over them on the tree." (see Col 2:15)

3. "You were cut off from the wild olive-tree, and grafted into the good one."

"The exorcised oil, therefore was a symbol of the participation of the fatness ["richness"] of Christ (*to oun eporkiston elaion symbolon hen tes koinonias tes piotetos tou Christou*)."

"So this exorcised oil receives such virtue by the invocation of God and by prayer, as not only to burn and cleanse away the traces of sins, but also to chase away all the invisible powers of the evil one."

4. Baptism pool and places of Jesus' passion in the basilica of the Holy Sepulchre:

"And ye made that saving confession, and descended three times into the water, and ascended again; here also covertly pointing by a figure at the three-days burial of Christ." "You also in your first ascent out of the water, represented the first day of Christ in the earth."

"That water of salvation was at once your grave and your mother (*egineto kai meter*)." "Tomb" (*egineto*) is also used by Ambrose; "mother" (*meter*) is also used by Theodore of Mopsuestia.

"Your birth went hand in hand with your death."

5. "Our imitation was but a figure, while our salvation is in reality (*all en eikoni he mimesis, en aletheia de he soteria*)."

6. This baptism is not merely remission of sins:

"It purges our sins, and conveys to us the gift of the Holy Ghost, so also is it the counterpart of Christ's sufferings."

Quotes Romans 6:3–4.

7. "For upon Christ death came in reality, for His soul was truly separated from His body, and His burial was true...and everything happened to Him truly, but in your case only the likeness of His death and sufferings, whereas salvation, not the likeness, but the reality (*epi de umon thanatou men kai pathematon omoioma, soterias de oux omoioma, alla aletheia*)."

MYSTAGOGIC CATECHESIS 3—I JOHN 2:20–28 (PARAPHRASED)

(Where manuscripts give a title, it says,) "On the Holy Chrism (*peri chrismatos*)."

Some translations use "on confirmation," a term that develops only in the early Middle Ages for a separate rite for chrismation.

1. "Being therefore made partakers of Christ, ye are properly called Christs, and of you God said 'touch not my Christs, or anointed. Now ye were made Christs, by receiving the emblem [anointing] of the Holy Ghost; and all things were in a figure wrought in you because ye are figures [note that the Greek term is *antitypon* and not *typos*] of Christ."

   "He also bathed himself in the river Jordan, and having imparted of the fragrance of His Godhead to the waters, He came up from them; and the Holy Ghost in substance lighted on Him, like resting on like."

   "After you had come up from the pool of the sacred streams, was given the Unction (*chrisma*), the emblem of that wherewith Christ was anointed; and this is the Holy Ghost."

2. Theology of anointing specified:

   "Christ was in truth crucified and buried…" "and you in likeness are in Baptism accounted worthy of being crucified, buried and raised together with Him, so is it with the unction also."

3. "But beware of supposing this to be plain ointment (*myron*). For as the Bread of the Eucharist, after the invocation of the Holy Ghost, is mere bread no longer, but the Body of Christ, so also this holy ointment is no more simple ointment (*to agion touto myron*), nor (so to say) common, after the invocation (*epiklesin*), but the gift of Christ; and by the presence of His Godhead, it causes in us the Holy Ghost."

4. Importance of involving senses and parts of the body: forehead, ears, nostrils, chest.

5. "When ye are counted worthy of this Holy Chrism (*chrismatos*), ye are called Christians, verifying also the name by your new birth."

6. "To them [Aaron and Solomon], however, these things happened in a figure, but to you not in a figure, but in truth (*umin de ou tupikos, all alethos*); because ye were truly anointed by the Holy Ghost."

   "First-fruit"

7. "Keep this [anointing] unspotted."

MYSTAGOGIC CATECHESIS 4—1 CORINTHIANS 11:23FF.

1. "Since then He Himself has declared and said of the Bread, 'This is my body,' who shall dare doubt any longer? And since He has affirmed and said 'This is my Blood' who shall ever hesitate, saying it is not His blood?"

3. "Let us partake in the body and blood of Christ; for in the figure [others translate this as "type" since the Greek reads *typon*] of Bread is given to thee His Body, and in the figure of Wine His Blood" (again, the Greek is *typon*).

   "For thus we come to bear Christ in us (*christophori*)."

   "Thus it is that, according to the blessed Peter, we become partakers of the divine nature" (see 2 Pet 1:4).

4. Refers to John 6: "They were offended and went backward, supposing that He was inviting them to eat flesh."

5. "Even under the Old Testament there was showbread; but this as it belonged to the Old Testament came to an end; but in the New Testament there is the Bread of heaven and the Cup of salvation, sanctifying soul and body; for as the Bread has respect to our body, so is the Word appropriate to our soul."

6. "Contemplate, therefore, the Bread and Wine not as bare elements, for they are, according to the Lord's declaration, the Body and Blood of Christ."

   "Judge not the matter from taste, but from faith be fully assured without misgiving, that thou hast been vouchsafed the Body and Blood of Christ."

7. One table with devils, the other with God.

8. Cites Ecclesiastes 9:7–8; white garment.

MYSTAGOGIC CATECHESIS 5—1 PETER 2:1FF., PLUS A PHRASE FROM JAMES 1:2

3. Refers to the kiss of peace. "The kiss is therefore reconciliation, and for this reason holy." Refers to Matthew 5:23 about first being reconciled before offering a gift at the altar. Refers to 1 Peter 5:14 about a kiss of charity.

4. Preface dialogue = the "awful hour" (meaning the awesome moment) of raising minds and hearts at the Eucharistic Prayer (not the words of Jesus only, which come to be called the words of consecration).

6. Preface text, and cites Isaiah 6:2–3.

7. "We call upon the merciful God to send forth His Holy Spirit upon the gifts lying before Him; that He may make the Bread the Body of Christ, and the Blood of Christ; for whatsoever the Holy Ghost has touched, is sanctified and changed."

11–18: commentary on the Lord's Prayer.

19. "Holy things to Holy Men/People." (Invitation to partake in communion). *Ta agia tois agiois.*

20. "You hear the chanter, with a sacred melody inviting you to the communion of the Holy Mysteries (*eis ten koinonian ton agion mysterion kai legontos*) and saying 'O taste and see that the Lord is good'" (Ps 34:9).

21. "Make thy left hand as if a throne for thy right, which is on the eve of receiving the King. And having hollowed thy palm, receive the Body of Christ, saying after it, Amen. Then after thou hast with carefulness hallowed thine eyes by the touch of the Holy Body, partake thereof; giving need lest thou lose any [particle] of it; for what thou losest is a loss to thee as it were from one of thine own members."

22. "And while the moisture is still upon thy lips, touching it with thine hands, hallow both thine eyes and brow and other senses. Then wait for the prayer, and give thanks unto God who hath accounted thee worthy of so great mysteries (*mysterion*)."

4

EARLY MEDIEVAL PERIOD

As with the preceding chapter, we begin by clarifying what we mean by *early medieval period* in order to establish the chronological parameters at issue here. In this chapter, we will sketch out, however briefly, what occurred in the evolution of the church's liturgical experience of the sacraments and its teaching on sacraments from the patristic era (chapter 3) up through the teaching of Peter Lombard (c. 1100–1164). However, many people legitimately regard Lombard as a representative of the "high" Middle Ages. We include Lombard here because his treatise *Liber Sententiarum* includes several assertions and terms—the number (seven) of sacraments, for example—that were original contributions at the time but that would continue to occupy the minds of theologians and influence church teaching from his time to our own day. An appreciation for the way the liturgy was celebrated, the ongoing debates about the reality of the Eucharist, and the fundamental approach to theology taken by different authors help to provide the context for what we learn from this period about the evolution of teaching about theology of sacraments.

LITURGY

In its evolution between the seventh and the twelfth centuries, the liturgical life of the church shifted from the major liturgical centers of Rome, Jerusalem, Constantinople, and the north of Africa to other parts of the world, in particular Europe and the British Isles, as Christianity spread and the forms and prayers of the liturgy were adapted in these new places. Thus we can speak of both *continuity* in the structures of the liturgy and *adaptation* of those liturgical structures to new cultures. (Recall chapter 2: the church would both *adopt* and *adapt* its liturgical rites and prayers to meet ever new circumstances.) For example, the basic structure of the Mass remained the same: the Liturgy of the Word, presentation of gifts, their transformation/consecration during the Eucharistic Prayer, communion, and dismissal. But it also was adapted to meet the challenges offered by new cultural contexts in terms of the style and composition of prayers to be used at Mass, the number and contents of the prayers in the Missals, and the directives on how to celebrate the Mass (originally called *ordines*, now commonly called *the rubrics* from the Latin for "red" because the directions in the liturgical texts were printed in red ink).

Christian initiation experienced a major shift away from adult initiation to condensing that rite to suit the baptism of infants, with chrismation/confirmation normally celebrated later and therefore separately. Some familiar liturgical rites, such as receiving ashes on Ash Wednesday and the rite for the dedication of a church, came from Gaul (present-day France). Here certain dramatic flourishes were added to the comparatively sober and straightforward Roman Rite.

Other liturgical rites, including those rites we associate with Holy Week, originally were observed in Jerusalem, then moved to Gaul and eventually came to Rome. For example, the palm procession, originally observed in Jerusalem on the afternoon of what is now Palm Sunday of the Passion of the Lord, and not originally associated with the Eucharist, was introduced in Rome as part of the Eucharist only in the eleventh century and then as a kind of "introduction" to the Liturgy of the Word.

In this period also, the presumed participation in and comprehension of what was celebrated by the gathered assembly during these early liturgies ceded to a certain passivity on the part of the laity. This was due to a number of factors. The people no longer understood the language in which the liturgy was celebrated (Latin); further, there was an increased physical and psychological distancing of the community from the clergy who led the celebrations and administered the sacraments, and an increased awareness of personal unworthiness that resulted in ever less frequent reception of communion. Within communities of laity and religious, there arose a distinction between the well-educated, who were able to read and sing liturgical texts, and those in religious communities, who were not so educated (sometimes called "lay" brothers or religious). Thus, too, monastic communities and subsequently the mendicants—Franciscans and Dominicans—would celebrate the church's official Liturgy of the Hours (or Divine Office), which was comprised of hymns, psalms, Scripture readings, and prayers, up to seven times a day, while many laity used shorter "books of hours" (not the official Liturgy of the Hours) for their daily prayer.

It is the opinion of some that once the first transition from Greek to Latin had been made, the failure to continue to adapt to the people's language in the liturgies of the West was the greatest force in separating the liturgy from the people and the people from the liturgy. Thus it came to be experienced as more of a priestly and clerical enactment done for and on behalf of the people rather than a rite performed together with them. Language can be both a means of communication and a barrier. When access to the action through language was not possible, the people continued to have access to the visible and tangible aspects of the liturgical celebration. In particular, the devotion to the consecrated and reserved species became the primary eucharistic reality for the populace at large, all the way from kings to peasants. The lack of active participation in the liturgy was one reason why church teachers and theologians started to ask questions about the liturgy and sacraments that differed from what they were asking in the patristic era: theologians and bishops started to focus on what the sacraments *are* and somewhat less about what the sacraments *do*.

EUCHARIST

The shift from emphasizing what sacraments *do* to stressing what they *are* meant that the question of what the eucharistic elements of consecrated bread and wine actually were after their consecration came to the fore. Thus, trying to describe the change from bread and wine into the body and blood of Christ became an important theological consideration. Theologians of the patristic era noted the change in bread and wine but also expounded on what the Eucharist did for the church communities that participated in it. In effect, as we saw regarding St. Cyril of Jerusalem, the patristic descriptions also centered on the church communities that celebrated the Eucharist. In addition, the patristic authors often used such terms as *symbol* (*symbolum*, from Greek *symballein*, meaning "to throw/put together"), *figure* (*figura*), *image* (*imago*), or *type* (*tupos*) to describe the Eucharist. In a Neoplatonic worldview, these terms were meant to distinguish the Eucharist as a "copy" of the "reality" of the exalted Lord Jesus Christ, ascended into heaven and interceding for us at the right hand of the Father. During this period, the word *copy* did not mean a reproduction, which to our way of thinking means something less than real. Rather, it meant that while we are on earth, we yearn to experience the exalted Christ, which will only happen in heaven, but in the meantime, the richest and fullest way to participate in that heavenly reality is through the Eucharist.

The Neoplatonic worldview upholds the value of the Eucharist by the phrase *symbolic reality*. These words are normally not placed in relation to each other in English today, since *symbol* has come to mean something that merely stands for something rather than something really real. But for the Neoplatonists, the phrase *symbolic reality* means that an invisible idea embodies itself in a visible reality in which it is really present and active. The word *symbol* or *symbolic* always contains the meaning of "joining together." Thus, sacraments "join us together" with the saving events of Christ's incarnation, obedient life, suffering, death, resurrection, and ascension.

In addition, this Neoplatonic worldview emphasized that what is celebrated here and now would be fulfilled in eternity. In that sense, the Eucharist was a "promissory reality" of what is yet to be. While many of the fathers in the patristic era were able to argue carefully that the Eucharist was a copy but did not contain the fullness of the exalted Lord, the language they used about "copy" could not be used in later years because word meanings change. The term *copy* could not sustain the distinction between what we experience in and through the liturgy and its completion in heaven without seeming to minimize the reality of Christ's action and presence in the Eucharist. With time, *copy*, *figure*, and *type* came to be thought of as weak in trying to describe the reality of Christ's presence and action in the Eucharist.

Several thinkers from what are now France and Germany contributed to the search for new terminology to describe the Eucharist. During the ninth century, two monks of the same abbey in the north of France, Ratramnus (d. 860) and Paschasius Radbertus (d. 865/8), wrote the first treatises to describe the way we understand the change from bread and wine into the body and blood of Christ. Both were entitled "On the Body and Blood of the Lord" (*De Corpore et Sanguine Domini*). The two monks placed different emphases in their teaching on sacraments. Paschasius stressed the identification of the Eucharist with the historical body of Christ in such a realistic way that his realism eclipsed an understanding of the symbolic nature of this sacrament. Ratramnus, on the other hand, stressed the real but sacramental presence of Christ in the Eucharist, which was not to be identified physically with his historical body. Subsequently, a number of theologians tried to craft appropriate language for the Eucharist that avoided an "empty symbolism" on the one hand and a "fleshly realism" on the other. Rabanus Maurus (d. 856), the archbishop of Mainz, also contributed to this project.

Among the most famous theologians in the following years was Berengar of Tours (d. 1088), whose ideas were judged heretical by Pope Leo IX. In describing the Eucharist, Berengar appealed to what he maintained was authentic Augustinian thought to describe a sacrament as a *sacrum signum* ("a sacred sign"). He compared the water of baptism to the bread and wine of the Eucharist. Just as water symbolizes the cleansing graces of Christ, so the bread and wine symbolize the body and blood of Christ. Unfortunately, by this time the notion of *symbol* had lost its meaning as something real, and the language of *substance* came to replace it as the description of what was real. *Substance* and *symbol* were now irreconcilable. Hence, Berengar was accused of heresy because he did not use the language of substance to affirm the reality of Christ's sacramental presence. Berengar was forced to sign two professions of faith about the Eucharist, each of which contained language that exemplifies the way theologians and bishops at the time struggled with finding adequate terminology to describe the sacrament.

Not long afterward, the Benedictine monk Lanfranc (d. 1089) notably distinguished *accident* from *substance* to describe the Eucharist. He elaborated on this distinction and further distinguished the outward from the inward and appearance from hidden truth. Another French theologian, Alan of Lille (d. 1202), admitted a desire to use appropriate language that avoided "gross realism" on the one hand and "pure symbolism" on the other. Under the influence of Aristotle, he too distinguished accident from substance. He distinguished the already and the not yet, the original from the copy. Thus these scholars set the stage for later theologians from the Scholastic era onward to use the substance and accident distinction to frame the debate and doctrine of the Eucharist.

APPROACHES TO THEOLOGY

One way to help contextualize the debates about sacraments that occurred in the early Scholastic period and have been with us since is to understand the lived contexts within which reflection on the things of God and God's revelation—in effect, what the word *theology* means—took place. Two main approaches emerged during this period—the context of theology done in monasteries and theology done in the cities.

1. *Monastic Theology*. This theology begins in about the sixth century and is found to this day in centers of learning influenced by Western monasticism. St. Benedict of Nursia (d. ca. 543) wrote his *Rule* for monks that spawned the Benedictine order, which is more properly a loosely interconnected number of monasteries. For some monasteries, the motto *ora et labora* ("prayer and work") involves the *labora* of teaching in schools at every level, including universities. This approach to theology largely reflects a patristic method based on the Sacred Scriptures in which one can experience the "giving over" (*paradosis*) of the gospel "tradition" (*traditio*) in the Scriptures by means of the liturgy

and "holy reading" (*lectio divina*). The emphasis in such theology is on an interior experience of deepening conversion and a profession of one's faith before the world by witnessing to one's beliefs in the monastic community and thereby being a "confessor" of the faith. This kind of theology flourished in the twelfth century and coincided with movements toward reform within Benedictinism in places such as Camaldoli (1012), Vallambrosa (1030), and Citeaux (1098).

2. *Scholastic Theology.* Scholastic theology arose in response to the active, pastoral life of the church and the perennial challenge to help explain the faith in new and different ways to suit evolving cultures. The theologian who is regarded as the "father of Scholasticism" is Anselm of Canterbury (1033–1109), author of the famous ontological proofs of the existence of God, who defined theology as "faith seeking understanding"—*fides quaerens intellectum*. Spurred on by the rise of the universities in major cities—such as Paris in the twelfth century—the Scholastics used metaphysics as a major tool in order to establish principles and a logical progression from the universal to the particular. In this they took their cue from Thomas Aquinas, who adapted Aristotelian thought to formulate Christian theology, following the lead of such Islamic scholars as Averroës, who had rediscovered and rehabilitated Aristotle and made his writings available to the Western world. The search for a systematization of theology in this approach reflected the work in other areas of the universities in profane sciences. The followers of St. Dominic (1170–1221) and St. Francis of Assisi (1182–1226) were influential in this university-based theology. To this day, major centers of theological learning are sponsored by Dominicans and Franciscans that reflect this Scholastic approach.

At the same time, it is important not to establish a hard and fast separation between these two approaches to doing theology. For example, while the monastic approach would tend to emphasize reflection on the liturgy celebrated several times a day in the monastery, the mendicants would also celebrate the liturgy in common, and this, in turn, influenced their more systematic approach to theology. St. Thomas Aquinas, for example, admits to a distinction between two approaches to theology, one more contemplative (monastic) and the other more oriented to arguing the reasonableness of the Catholic faith (Scholastic).

Both kinds of theology are based on the Scriptures and the liturgy of the church. The monastic tended toward "rumination" on the texts while the Scholastics tended to want to systematize these ideas using the methodology of philosophy. With regard to language, it can be said that the monastic treatises are more contemplative in tone and the Scholastic, which use increasingly technical language, more inherently logical.

SACRAMENTS IN THE EARLY SCHOLASTIC AUTHORS

The influence of St. Augustine on the developing theology of the sacraments in the early medieval period is clear. The term *sign* is repeatedly used in descriptions about how sacraments operate. Notable, too, is the emergence of terms that theologians and official church documents have used to talk about sacraments—for example, *administer, cause, effects.* The following five authors and their teachings about sacraments specifically are notable. Their discussion of the names for and the number of sacraments should also be noted.

Isidore of Seville (d. 636) speaks of "baptism, chrism and the body and the blood" as sacraments because, underneath the cover of bodily things, God's power works to give salvation. He says that they are fruitful when administered in the church because the Holy Spirit works in a hidden way to effect the sacraments.

Hugh of St. Victor (d. 1141) maintained that the key to interpreting sacraments was God's interventions in history, especially in creation and the incarnation. Within this broad spectrum of what he calls sacramental actions, he uses Augustinian language in asserting that not every *sign* of a sacred thing is a sacrament. For example, paintings and statues would not be sacraments.

He argues that those signs that are sacraments place before the external senses some invisible grace (1) by being similar to the thing represented (water for baptism, food for the Eucharist); (2) by signifying by institution; and (3) by containing some invisible and spiritual grace for sanctification. He then delineates a number of things that contain these three qualities. Among them are the incarnation, the church as the Body of Christ, ecclesiastical orders and ranks, sacred vessels and vestments, the dedication of churches, baptism, Eucharist, marriage, vows, confession, sorrow, and remission of sins, anointing of the sick (the term *extreme unction* emerges later), death and judgment, the death and resurrection of Christ, and the end of the world. Under "lesser sacraments," he includes holy water, blessed ashes, the sign of the cross, and the invocation of the Trinity. He argues that one appropriately uses water in baptism, bread and wine in the Eucharist, and oil for the anointing of the sick because they are similar to that which the sacraments effect (bathing, dining, anointing).

A number of things listed here deserve some comment. When Hugh cites the incarnation, he means that the God and man Jesus Christ revealed God's divinity in human flesh. The reference to the dedication of churches is particularly notable for the importance of the theology reflected in the ritual. In effect, we "baptize" a church as a place where the baptized are the gathered assembly for worship. The fact that the Roman Missal places the prayers for the Dedication of a Church as the first of the "commons" section of the Missal (after the saints' days) indicates the high rank assigned to this liturgy. That Hugo cites "chrism" and not "confirmation" is noteworthy; he thereby reflects the early church tradition (see chapter 3 for the mystagogic catechesis of Cyril of Jerusalem) whereby *chrism* refers both to the kind of oil used in the sacrament (a mixture of olive oil and balsam or another fragrant liquid) and the name for the liturgical ritual. As other early Scholastic theologians reflect on chrismation as taking place separate from water baptism, the term *confirmation* will develop.

The explicit linking of confession, sorrow, doing penance, and remission of sins is significant as these were separated and separable experiences in the earlier evolution of the process of ecclesial reconciliation. After public penance waned as a liturgy (note here a parallel to adult baptism), these elements were combined, and they eventually came to comprise the sacrament of penance.

At this point, the number of sacraments was still not restricted to seven. As already noted, Hugh himself counted such rites as the use of holy water or blessed ashes, the consecration of monks, and burial as "receptacles of grace."

Peter Abelard (d. 1142), in typically Augustinian fashion, states that a sacrament is a sign of invisible grace, that it is the visible image of invisible grace, and that it is a sign of a sacred thing. In discussing those particular rituals that are sacraments, he deals with six, omitting orders from the usual seven we have come to name as sacraments.

Abelard introduces a distinction between "major" and "minor" sacraments, a distinction repeated and adjusted in a number of ways up to the present. Major sacraments, he maintains, are necessary for salvation and minor sacraments are not. For him, the major sacraments are baptism, chrism, Eucharist, penance, and anointing.

Summa Sententiarum (c. 1148) is the first of several twelfth-century documents that attempt to systematize Catholic teaching in general. (The title of the work is used here because the exact authorship is debated.) In speaking about the essence of a sacrament, the author indicates that it is the visible form of invisible grace and that the sacrament *confers* grace. The term *confers* is important because it affirms the instrumentality of sacraments regarding sanctification coming from God and God's grace. Relying on St. Augustine, the author states that a sacrament is a sign of a holy thing and is efficacious (that is, it does something). He then elaborates further on St. Augustine, saying that there are many signs but that a sacrament is a sign that confers that of which it is a sign. In effect, sacraments *do* something for those engaged in them. Not all signs do that. The words used here reflect the by now commonplace early medieval terminology, with *sign* and *efficacy* important in the theological vocabulary of the time.

Regarding what we call specific sacraments, the author deals with baptism, confirmation (not "chrismation"), Eucharist, penance, and extreme unction (not "anointing of the sick"). He omits "orders" (or "ecclesiastical orders and ranks" as Hugh of St. Victor put it) and marriage in this listing, although in other places in this document, the author asserts that orders is a sacrament.

It is not surprising that Peter Lombard (d. 1160) begins the section of his *Liber Sententiarum* (Book of Sentences) by comparing God's institution of the sacraments to the Good Samaritan (Luke 10:30–37) who brought assistance to the wounded man, specifically by bandaging his wounds and applying oil and wine (v. 34). The notion of a sacrament as a remedy for sin was a dominant theme and a determinative way of understanding the economy of the sacraments during the twelfth and thirteenth centuries. (Recall that the technical meaning of *economy* in theology is the way in which God manages our fallen state after original sin and works to restore us to life in God through Christ, with the sacraments as a primary and essential means.) Lombard stands squarely in the Augustinian tradition in the language he uses to describe sacraments. He maintains that every sacrament is a sign but not every sign is a sacrament. A sacrament bears resemblance to the thing of which it is a sign: "A sacrament is properly so called because it is a sign of the grace of God and the expression of invisible grace, so that it bears its image and is its cause" (*Liber* 4, d.1, n.4; PL places this in para. 2). Thus, it is Lombard who introduces the notion of *cause* and *causality* into the definition of a sacrament.

Other twelfth- and thirteenth-century theologians such as Hugh of St. Victor and William of Auxerre (d. 1213) maintained that sacraments "contain" grace (*vasa gratiae*, "vessels of grace"; *vasa spiritualia*, "spiritual vessels"; *vasa medicinalia*, "vessels that heal") in the sense that God himself operates through the sacraments. Lombard specifies causality as essential to an understanding of sacraments by adding that a sacrament is *invisibilis gratiae visibilis forma*, that is "a sacrament is the visible form of an invisible grace," and that a sacrament *efficit quod figurat*, that is a sacrament "produces [the effect] which it represents."

In addition, Lombard determined that there are seven "sacraments of the New Law…baptism, confirmation, the bread of blessing, that is, the Eucharist, penance, extreme unction, orders, marriage" (*Liber* d.2, c.1). This designation of seven sacraments confirms what others had pointed to: that seven was a significant number for completion, totality, and inclusiveness (for example, the seven days of creation in Genesis). Seven is appropriate for the number of sacraments because it is the sum of three, for the three persons in one God, and four, a reference to cosmic perfection (the four directions of north, south, east, and west or of the seasons summer, fall, winter, and spring). Adding three for the divine and four for the earthly yields seven, to mean totality, completion, or perfection.

SACRAMENTAL THEMES THAT EMERGE IN THIS PERIOD

We now move to a description of five aspects of the church's teaching about sacraments. These emerged during this period and find resonance in future centuries as the church continues to elaborate on and refine its teaching about sacraments.

RES ET SACRAMENTUM—MAKING DISTINCTIONS

The debate about how to describe Christ's presence in the Eucharist led, in the twelfth century, to the formulation of the expression *res et sacramentum*. St. Augustine had introduced the term *res* to sacramental language to signify the grace of union with Christ as the ultimate effect of eucharistic participation. Berengar affirmed that the Eucharist was the sign of Christ's body and the efficacious symbol of spiritual nourishment and union with Christ. However, he denied that Christ's true body was present in the sacrament. Berengar held that there were two elements in the sacrament: the external sign or sacrament (*sacramentum*) and the ultimate effect, the grace of spiritual nourishment and charity (*res*). In order to preserve the symbolism of the Eucharist and to safeguard the reality of Christ's presence in the Eucharist, eleventh-century theologians such as Lanfranc of Canterbury and Guitmund of Aversa (d. 1095) searched for a third element to describe the sacramental action. A definitive formulation was established by Hugh of St. Victor and Peter Lombard in the twelfth century and endorsed by Pope Innocent III (d. 1216) at the beginning of the thirteenth century.

These theologians added *sacramentum et res* to the *sacramentum tantum* ("only the sacrament" or external sign) and the *res tantum* ("only the thing/reality effected"). Innocent III stated that the "form" of the Eucharist was bread and wine (a sacrament and not the reality), the truth is of the body and blood (both sacrament and reality), and the power is of unity and charity (reality/thing effected). When Innocent spoke of the *sacramentum tantum,* he meant the permanent sacrament and not the words of consecration. However, in later years, the expression *sacramentum tantum* was applied to the sacramental rite that has for its immediate effect the *res et sacramentum* and for its ultimate effect the *res tantum* or the effect of the sacrament or sacramental grace.

INSTITUTION

During this period, a synthesis emerged about sacraments that integrated the church as the means of salvation into Christology within the scope of a universal salvation history. Here sacraments were regarded as instituted by Christ since they are part of the divine plan of salvation (the Pauline mystery of salvation for all). Sacraments receive their precise determination from the various stages of Christ's life and ministry, and they attain their purpose in the church. Sacraments thus were understood as high points of the saving revelation of God in the church's present experience of Christ's redemption through the operation of the Holy Spirit. Hence they continued to be understood as self-expressions of the church and as part of how the divine economy of salvation was experienced in the present. Former arguments about the institution of where and when during Christ's ministry a specific sacrament was instituted have moved in recent years to discussions about examples of the biblical basis for liturgy and sacraments as derived from the Scriptures (see chapter 1).

This avoids a "proof-texting" approach, which often yielded precarious conclusions upon which to base sacramental institution (see chapter 6 on the Council of Trent).

VALIDITY

Lombard's definitions of sacrament would be subjected to the scrutiny of the prevailing metaphysics of the schools and teachers. The parts that deal with "sign-cause" and the "reality signified and caused" would occupy the attention of Scholastic theologians. Important in these discussions was the influence of Aristotle, who argued that every natural body consists of two things—matter and form. This is often referred to as the theory of hylomorphism. As applied to the sacraments, a hylomorphic interpretation of sacramental sign attributes the function of matter to the sensible things used in the celebration and the function of form to the words that accompany the application of matter to the subject of the sacrament. Here the form specifies the significance of the matter used. This interpretation has its advantages, especially since it points out what is essential for a sacrament to be valid—that is, the assurance that it "works"—and licit—that it works within the contours of church law.

The question of sacramental validity in the twelfth century was essentially a discussion of sacramental objectivity; as such it was the concern of both canonists and theologians. While it was only in the fourteenth century that the terms *valid/invalid* appear in connection with the sacraments, and at first only in connection with marriage, the beginning of this kind of language is evidenced in Lombard.

EX OPERE OPERATO, EX OPERE OPERANTIS

Although the theology of this period does not neglect the importance of faith and other human actions as determinative for sacramental efficaciousness, in practice, their role would be reduced to conditions without which the sacraments do not occur. Even though Lombard raised the question of causality, this notion did not find a completely satisfying or universally accepted explanation at the time, although Aquinas's theory of instrumental causality described in the next chapter is most influential.

What was agreed upon is the fact that Christian sacraments are "efficacious" (they "work") *ex opere operato*. This technical phrase is translated as "by the work done/worked." It is sometimes also rendered by the phrase *opus operatum*. Thus, sacraments accomplish what they are intended to accomplish by means of the sacramental rite itself, not because of the worthiness or holiness of the minister or participant. At the same time, sacraments function *ex opere operantis* ("by the work of the doer") in that the "effectiveness" of the sacraments depends on the moral rectitude of the minister or recipient. When these terms evolved, they did so together. Thus, any kind of understanding that sacraments function automatically or quasi-magically (by emphasizing the *operato* part of the quotient) is not consistent with either the church's sacramental teaching or practice (which emphasize participation or at least attention and the intention to participate). Both *operato* and *operantis* are intrinsically interrelated and necessary to understand how sacraments "work." At the same time, this couplet can be a shorthand way of understanding that sacraments can function with ministers whose lives do not reflect totally or fully the depth of conversion and of spirituality that they should, as we saw with St. Augustine. From the time of Augustine to the church today, the church has relied on the grace of God to work through sacraments and has not relied on the moral perfection of the minister for sacraments to "work." While this does not mean that conversion and deep spirituality do not matter, it does mean that any attempt to judge worthiness or rectitude in the ministers does not impair the functioning of sacraments.

RIGHT INTENTION

With regard to Lombard's assertion about what is signified and effected in sacraments—that is, grace and the experience of salvation —a notable gamut of opinions will evolve. One difficulty with such attempts at codification is that the dynamism of the biblical understanding and liturgical experience of "justification" suffers in the process. Some would say that a certain "reification" (becoming like a "thing") of what is intrinsically a liturgical, active dynamic occurs. Lombard is true to Augustinian thought when he speaks about the involvement of the minister in sacraments. Lombard stresses the importance of the minister's "right intention" when celebrating sacraments. It is from Lombard's works that the formula emerged, "The intention of doing what the church intends and does" in sacraments.

This is another way of assuring that there is no quasi-magical misunderstanding that sacraments are automatic. Rather, they are acts of faith done in faith in the community of the faithful. They must be "intended and intentional."

DISCUSSION QUESTIONS

1. Review the names of the sacraments in this chapter as listed by the five authors cited above. Note the differences among them; for example, some use "chrismation" and others use "confirmation," and where some use "anointing of the sick," others will use "extreme unction." What emphasis does a different name for a sacrament give to understanding the nature of that sacrament?

2. How has the consideration of right "intention" in this chapter helped you to understand why, in the present celebrations of infant baptism and marriage, the minister (bishop, priest, or deacon) asks whether those who present their child for baptism or themselves for marriage understand what they are undertaking?

3. How does an appreciation of the state of the liturgy, debates about the Eucharist, and the two kinds of theology that were operative during the early Scholastic era help you to understand why and how sacraments were described as they were during this period?

PRIMARY SOURCE: PETER LOMBARD—"BOOK OF SENTENCES" (*LIBER SENTENTIARUM*)

Lombard's work introduces a new genre for theological writing. He offers a systematic treatment of Catholic doctrines based on quoting and commenting on the Sacred Scriptures and church fathers (most notably St. Augustine).

The "Book of Sentences" consists of four books with 182 "sentences." Book 1 concerns "The Mystery of the Trinity"; in Book 2 he writes "On Creation" and, in Book 3, "On the Incarnation of the Word"; Book 4 concerns "The Doctrine of Signs," in which he explains that the principal signs and instruments of grace available to Christians as a result of Christ's salvific work are the sacraments.

In the outline that follows, we will be particularly concerned with what Lombard says about "sacrament" in general, baptism because it initiates one into the sacramental life of the Church, and the Eucharist because of the controversies at the time.

Please note that the numbers referred to here are from the Rogers English Language translation. The numbering in the Migne *Patrologia Latina* text (PL) is not the same. The Migne reference is at the end of the sentences below.

Among the more convenient Latin texts is from Migne, *Patrologia Latina* 191: 839–964.

The English translation used here is from Elizabeth Frances Rogers, *Peter Lombard and the Sacramental System* (Merrick, NY: Richwood Publishing Co., 1976, reprinted), 79–246.

DISTINCTION I

1. The treatise begins with a reference to the parable of the Good Samaritan (Luke 10:30ff.). Therefore, it is not surprising that the very first words are "the Samaritan who tended the wounded man applied for his relief the dressings of the sacraments against the wounds of original and actual sin." The notion of sacraments as "remedies" reflects a strong emphasis in the developing sacramental theology of the time about the healing and "medicinal" value of the sacraments.

    Lombard then states that four questions present themselves: "What a sacrament is; why it was instituted; wherein it consists and how it is performed; and what the difference is between the sacraments of the old and new covenants."

2. In "defining" a sacrament, Lombard repeats St. Augustine's assertion that "a sacrament is a sign of a sacred thing (*res*)" and

then cites Berengar's statement that "a sacrament is the visible form of an invisible grace."

4. In discussing how "signs" and "sacraments" differ, he says, "A sacrament is properly so called, because it is a sign of the grace of God and the expression of invisible grace, so that it bears its image and is its cause (*quod ita signum est gratiae Dei, et invisibilis gratiae forma, ut ipsius imaginem gerat et causa existat*)." (PL para. 4)

He says that sacraments are "a means of sanctification (*sed etiam sanctificandi*)" and that "things which were instituted only to signify are signs only, and not sacraments (*Quae enim sanctificandi gratia tantum instituta sunt, solum signa sunt, et non sacramenta*); such as the sacrifices of flesh, and the ceremonial observances of the old law, which could never justify those who offered them."

5. Lombard then states that the sacraments were instituted for a threefold reason: "for *humility*, *instruction*, and *exercise*." The discussion that follows is important because it refers to "worship" and "the use of sensible things." (PL para. 3)

At the end of this section, he relies on both the *Summa Sententiarum* and Hugh of St. Victor in asserting that "there are two parts of which a sacrament consists, namely *words* and *things*: *words* as the invocation of the Trinity; *things* as water, oil, and the like (*Duo autem sunt in quibus sacramentum consistit; scilicet verba et res: verba ut invocatio Trinitatis; res, ut aqua, oleum et hujus modi*)." (PL para. 4)

DISTINCTION 2

1. In delineating sacraments of the new law and why they were instituted Lombard states,

Let us now come to the sacraments of the new covenant; which are baptism, confirmation, the blessing of bread, that is the eucharist, penance, extreme unction, ordination, marriage. Of these some offer a remedy for sin (*Quorum alia remedium contra peccatum praebent*) and confer helping grace as baptism (*et gratiam adjutricem conferuat, ut*

87

baptismus); others are merely a remedy, as marriage (*alia in remedium tantum sunt, ut conjugium*); others strengthen us with grace and virtue, as the eucharist and ordination (*alia gratia et virtute non fulciunt, ut Eucharistia et Ordo*).

As noted above, the words used to name the sacraments are important, for example *confirmation* and *the blessing of bread*.

DISTINCTION 3

1. In delineating "what baptism is," Lombard states, "By baptism we mean an immersion (the Latin is *intinctio*, a term with other connotations in liturgical practice), that is, an exterior cleansing of the body administered under a prescribed form of words (*sub forma verborum praescripta*). For if the cleansing takes place without the word (*sine verbo*) there is no sacrament, but with the addition of the word to the element (*ad elementum*) it becomes a sacrament; not that the *element* itself becomes the sacrament but the *cleansing* performed in the element (*sed ablutio facta in elemento*)." He then cites Augustine when he says, "Baptism is consecrated by the word; take away the word, and what is water, except water? The word is added to the element, and it becomes a sacrament (*Accedit verbum ad elementum, et fit sacramentum*)." (PL reads *sed accedente verbo ad elementum, fit sacramentum*.)

2. In speaking of "the form of baptism (*de forma Baptismi*)," Lombard expands on the theology of the sacrament: "Therefore the invocation of the Trinity is given as the *word*, by which baptism is consecrated (*Invocatio igitur Trinitatis verbum dicitur quo Baptisma consecratur*)." He then goes on to say that "whoever was immersed without the invocation of the Trinity, did not have the sacrament of regeneration (*sine invocatione Trinitatis mersus fuisset, quod sacramentum regenerationis non haberet*)," and that "he is not a complete Christian unless he is baptized in the name of the Father and of the Son and of the holy Spirit (*perfectus Christianus non est, nisi in nomine Patris, et Filii, et Spiritus sancti fuerit baptizatus*)."

The discussion of the institution of baptism and the cleansing properties of water are addressed (dist. 5–6). Lombard reiterates the patristic rationale for immersion (*de immersione*) three times because of Christ's entombment (*etiam triduanae sepulturae sacramentum signamus*). (PL para. 9)

DISTINCTION 4

The title of this section reflects its importance in the evolving discussion of the efficacy of sacraments: "Of those who receive the sacrament and the thing, and the thing and not the sacrament, and the sacrament and not the thing." Significant in this discussion of the efficacy of baptism is that the baptism of infants is noted in the first paragraph and adults, by inference, in the second.

1. "Here we must say that some receive the sacrament and the thing, some the sacrament and not the thing, some the thing and not the sacrament. All infants (*perituri sunt parvulis*) receive the sacrament and the thing at the same time, who are cleansed in baptism from original sin (*ab originali mundantur peccato*)."
2. When discussing "those who receive it without sincerity," Lombard states that "those indeed who receive it without faith or without sincerity, receive the sacrament and not the thing (*sacramentum, non rem, suscipiunt*)."
4. This discussion concerns what is traditionally termed "baptism of/by blood." In terms of the *res* and *sacramentum* discussion above, this is to say that these people receive "the thing" (meaning salvation) through shedding their blood and not by means of the rite of the sacrament.
7. The language of "cause" returns here in a discussion of what "the sacrament of baptism does." "It is, in fact, the sign of everything of which it is the cause (*omnis etenim rei signum est, cujus causa est*)."

DISTINCTION 5

1. In discussing the issue of baptism done by a good or bad minister, Lombard, like so many others before him and since,

relied on Augustine's insights. He quotes Augustine: "For baptism derives its character from him through whose power it is given, not from him through whose ministry it is given (*Baptismus talis est qualis ille in cujus potestate datur, non qualis est ille per cujus ministerium datur*)."

DISTINCTION 6

1. To the question, "Who are permitted to baptize?" Lombard relies on Isidore of Seville in asserting, "It is established that baptism is administered only by priests (*sacerdotibus*), and it is not lawful for deacons (*diaconibus*) to perform the ministry of it without a bishop or priest (*episcopo vel presbytero*), unless they are absent at a distance, extreme necessity requires it, and then it is also allowable for the faithful laity (*laicis fidelibus*) to baptize."

The two Latin terms here for what is translated "priest" are noteworthy. *Sacerdos* carries with it notions of offering sacrifice whereas *presbyter*, especially when used in relation to the word *episcopos* for bishop, carries with it connotations of the relationship between bishop and priest/presbyter, where *presbyter* means "elder" and carries with it connotations of being a coworker with the bishop and a member of a "college" of coworkers.

Terminology about ministers carries over into distinction 7.

DISTINCTION 7

The fact that the title is "Of the Sacrament of Confirmation" (*De Confirmatione*) signals the shift from understanding it as intrinsically connected to water baptism. Now it is a standalone celebration in which notions of "strengthening" and "making more secure" enter the conversation, as opposed to being a sacrament of initiation.

1. Lombard notes that the "form" is clear and stated by "the bishop (*episcopus*) as he signs the baptized with the sacred chrism (*cum baptizatos in frontibus sacro signat chrismate*)."
2. That confirmation is performed only by "high priests" (*summis sacerdotibus*) means that the local diocesan bishop celebrates

the sacrament. That he may be assisted by "presbyters" (*presbyteris*) is cited, but only to touch the baptized on the breast and not to sign them with chrism on the head.

3. In describing what confirmation is, Lombard relies on the important (and in that period, a new and unique) contribution of Rabanus Maurus, namely, that confirmation is the gift of the Holy Spirit "for strength" (*ad robur*). The "high priest" performs the "laying on of hands" through which "the Paraclete is given to the one baptized, that he may be strengthened through the Holy Spirit, to proclaim to others that which he has attained in baptism (*ut roboretur per Spiritum sanctum, ad praedicandum aliis illud*)."

DISTINCTION 8

Given the importance of the contemporary debates about the Eucharist and its importance in the lives of the faithful, with increased emphasis on priests (*sacerdotes*) ministering it to the laity, it is not surprising that distinctions 8–13 concern "the sacrament of the altar and the Eucharist" (as cited in the title to distinction 8).

2. The term *figura* is used twice in this paragraph and is often translated as "type" as well as "figure."
3. In this paragraph, the Latin term *typos* is used and translated as "type."
4. The term *substance* is used, which from this point on will characterize a Catholic understanding of the Eucharist.
5. Notice that accident is parallel to substance in naming the change from bread and wine into the body and blood of the Lord as seen in this paragraph, as is the statement that the "names" for the bread and wine are kept even after their consecration.
6. The description of church unity in this paragraph (and the following references to grains of wheat) is an important reminder that this is a consistent part of the theology of the Eucharist even when the emphasis in some eras is more on the individual. The words *signified* and *contained* (*significata et non contenta*) are equally important as the Western church

continues to develop its sacramental teaching. (The PL text has only four assertions here.)

DISTINCTION 10

1. Lombard's distinguishing sign and substance (*substantiam panis*) is important here, where the substance of these elements are "converted into" the body and blood of the Lord.

Part 1, 2

Lombard states clearly that "the words of Christ change the creature." Then he claims that "by the same Spirit the same body and blood of Christ are consecrated from the substance of bread and wine (*ita per eumdem ex substantia panis et vini idem corpus Christi et sanguinis consecratur*)." (PL para. 4)

DISTINCTION 11

Part 2, 3

Lombard states that "we receive the sacrament in a *likeness*" (note that the Latin here is *in similitudinem*, which some English translations render as "symbol"). (PL para. 4)

DISTINCTION 12

3. That Lombard cites Berengar is not a surprise given the controversy he sparked. Notable is Lombard's assertions about what occurs at the breaking of the bread: "A true fraction and distribution performed not on the substance of the body, but on the sacrament, that is on the species. But do not marvel or taunt if the accidents seem to be broken when they are there without a subject." (PL para. 4)
5. That it is the "priest" (*sacerdos*) who offers and consecrates "a sacrifice and oblation, because it is a memorial and representation of the true sacrifice and of the holy immolation made on the altar of the cross" is an important set of statements and development of language about sacraments, for example *sacrificium et oblationem*, and *quia memoria est et representatio veri sacrificii*. (PL para. 7)

Later on in this paragraph, Lombard cites Ambrose and says that "our sacrifice is a copy (note that the Latin text is *exemplum*) of his; the same and always the same is offered, therefore this is the same sacrifice."

6. Lombard uses important and precise theological terminology when he asserts that the Eucharist was instituted for two reasons: "For the increase of virtue, that is of charity, and as a medicine for daily infirmity (*in medicinam quotidianae infirmitatis*)" This reference recalls the parable of the Good Samaritan that Lombard uses to introduce these *Sentences*. (PL para. 8)

DISTINCTION 13

1. With regard to the priest at the Eucharist, Lombard makes two especially important points: that the priest does not say "I offer" but always "we offer" (*offerimus*) and that he acts "in the person of the Church." Regrettably, some English translations say he acts in the "name" of the church, while the Latin asserts *ex persona Ecclesiae*. This phrase is increasingly paired with *in/ex persona Christi*, "in the name of Christ" and is repeatedly used in the Vatican II documents and subsequently to assert the christological identification of the priest.

5

SCHOLASTIC PERIOD

The thirteenth and fourteenth centuries are generally regarded as the period of "high Scholasticism" (preceded by such prominent names as Peter Abelard, Lanfranc, Anselm of Canterbury, and Peter Lombard among the early Scholastics). While the phrase "the thirteenth, the greatest of centuries" can be overdone and has been legitimately critiqued, nonetheless there is something to be said for the high watermark achieved during this period for the Catholic theological tradition and for the legacy that theologians would now do their work at universities as well as in monasteries.

LITURGICAL AND THEOLOGICAL OVERVIEW OF THE PERIOD

It is important not to generalize about this period when it comes to the way the liturgy of the sacraments was participated in, understood, and taught about. For example, it can be claimed that the theological synthesis achieved by the Scholastics made a lasting contribution to the way theology itself was understood and delineated. But it can also be said that for a great many of the faithful and less well educated, this era was not a high point in their participation in the liturgy or even in their comprehension of what was occurring, since Latin was no longer universally known. Even so, the celebration of sacraments, especially the Mass, was a source of religious and social cohesion. Thus we should make no judgment about what was done and how it was done where the liturgy is concerned. Yet, as noted in the previous chapter, an increasing practical separation was taking place between the church's "official" liturgy and popular devotions, such as the prayer books called "books of hours," the stations of the cross, and the recitation of the rosary. At the same time, it should be presumed that those who populated the universities at the time were aware of what was occurring in and through the liturgy.

With regard to the Eucharist, called the "sacrament of sacraments" by many authors, the celebration was done by the priest on behalf of those in attendance. (The Latin term *sacerdos* reflects this function: it means "offerer of sacrifice.") The laity were largely passive (some would say "mute") so that the kind of participation in and comprehension of the liturgy that was presumed during the patristic era and today did not exist in the Scholastic period. However, in communities of well-educated monks and mendicants, their participation in the liturgy influenced their understanding of God, the incarnation, and the sacraments. These included the Dominican St. Thomas Aquinas (1225–74) and the Franciscan St. Bonaventure (1221–74), who celebrated daily Mass and the Hours in their respective communities. While the daily "conventual" (meaning the Mass of the "convent" or house where monks and mendicants lived) was always a privileged liturgical experience, the so-called private Mass was also celebrated. One purpose of a private Mass was to provide for the needs of pilgrims or visitors to a shrine, such as the birthplace of St. Francis of Assisi; thus a few people would gather and the priest would celebrate the Mass for them at this place of devotion. Other private Masses involved an individual priest who would "say" the Mass for himself or for the intentions of someone else as an important devotion. But those experiences were not the robust communal celebration of the patristic era. This practice and the celebration of infant baptisms would bring about changes in church architecture. For example, in addition to the main altar at the center of the church, side altars were constructed to allow for several private Masses simultaneously. The need for side altars for private Masses has largely been eliminated today in favor of priests, especially in monasteries and religious communities, celebrating Mass together, a practice called "concelebration," a ritual that was revised after Vatican II. (See The Roman Missal, *General Instruction of the Roman Missal* [GIRM] 199–251.) While priests may still celebrate Mass "privately," the GIRM now refers to this rite as "Mass at which only one minister participates." The "one minister" so designated is the server because liturgy by its nature is never a solitary event. The server participates by responding to the prayers and dialogues and, in doing so, represents the whole church, which is not physically present but which is always present spiritually and interceded for at every Mass.

By the Scholastic era, adult initiation was all but unknown and infant baptisms were regularly celebrated. Most of the seven sacraments were administered to one or a few individuals—for example, penance and anointing of the sick, or "extreme unction," as it was then known—and the priest's actions were described by the parallel phrases *in persona Christi* ("in the person of Christ") and *in persona ecclesiae* ("in the person of the church") to reflect the Christ-centeredness and church-centeredness of the sacraments. That sacraments were *experienced* as acts of the priest representing Christ was clear, especially when liturgical communities were increasingly passive recipients rather than actively engaged in the act of liturgy.

What also grew in importance was the "miracle" and "morality play." These were sponsored by the church and enacted in town squares as a way of teaching the faith in the vernacular through dramatization of central events of salvation history. (The "passion play," still performed every ten years in Oberammergau, Germany, is a well-known example.) In addition, street processions with the consecrated host in a special vessel called a monstrance (from the Latin word *monstrare*, meaning "to show") became increasingly common. The phenomenon of eucharistic miracles whereby consecrated hosts would "bleed" onto the liturgical cloths led to processions in which these objects were venerated. What we celebrate today as the Solemnity of the Body and Blood of Christ on the Thursday or Sunday after Holy Trinity Sunday originated during this period. Corpus Christi, as it was originally known in Latin, was first celebrated in Liege in Belgium in 1246. St. Juliana Cornillon, a canoness in Liege, was credited with originating the feast. Juliana had influential supporters in the Dominican Order, and in 1264, Pope Urban IV declared Corpus

Christi a feast of the universal church. St. Thomas Aquinas, a Dominican as well as a prominent theologian, is credited with writing many of the texts in the official liturgy for Corpus Christi at the request of Pope Urban IV, and these texts are used to this day.

It was reported that in 1263, in the city of Bolsena in Italy, a "eucharistic miracle" took place involving a priest who had doubts about Christ's real presence in the sacrament. While this priest was celebrating Mass, he broke the unleavened bread, as we always do during the Lamb of God, and the host bled onto the liturgical cloth known as the corporal (from Latin *corpus*="body"). In later years, this corporal was brought to nearby Orvieto for devotional purposes. (Interestingly, Thomas Aquinas happened to be resident in Orvieto at this time.) To this day, a special Mass is celebrated in the cathedral in Orvieto on the Solemnity of the Body and Blood of Christ, followed by a procession of people in medieval costumes, at the end of which is a kind of monstrance containing the corporal of the miracle.

This elaboration on liturgy and popular expressions of belief is important for a number of reasons, not the least of which is to see how liturgy, theology, Catholicism itself, and the society of the time and even its legal systems were deeply intertwined. Not surprisingly, this Catholic culture spawned theological syntheses that would educate and inspire Catholics for generations, even to our own day.

The rise of the universities located in cities, as opposed to monasteries where theologians also continued to teach and flourish, occasioned an unprecedented opportunity for theologians to develop their syntheses principally based on and in relation to the philosophy of Aristotle. This led to the opportunity to systematize and rethink the beliefs of the Catholic Church as influenced by the revival of Aristotelianism.

The thirteenth century brought the greatest of the Scholastic writers, in St. Thomas Aquinas, disciple of St. Albert the Great, and in a system called "Thomism" after him. Another school of theology, called Scotism after the great Franciscan theologian John Duns Scotus (ca. 1265–1308), developed about the same time from the Old Franciscan School, among whose well-known representatives was

St. Bonaventure. Scotism was thus also known as the Later Franciscan School.

With regard to the Scholastic theological syntheses of this period, it should be noted that within Catholicism, a number of issues were debated and refined, and some were left open-ended. They were called "disputed questions" (*questiones disputatae*), sometimes reflecting distinctions between the way St. Thomas and his Dominican confreres would express Catholic teaching and the way, for example, St. Bonaventure and his Franciscan confreres would. Thus in addition to the Scholastic theology as developed by St. Thomas, several other influential authors were at work at the same time on the same project of integrating faith and reason, revelation and philosophy.

STUDY OF SACRAMENTS

We will follow St. Thomas's exposition about the sacraments from the third part of his *Summa Theologiae*, questions 60–65 (normally cited *ST*, 3a, q. 60–65). It should be noted, however, that Aquinas's treatment of sacraments did not end here but continued in this third part of the *Summa* in q. 66–72 about baptism and confirmation, q. 73–83 about the Eucharist, and q. 84–90 on the sacrament of penance.

Where appropriate, we will indicate nuances, or differences of opinion from other contemporary authors such as Alexander of Hales (1186–1245), St. Bonaventure (1217–74), and St. Albert the Great (1206–80). As we saw in the last chapter, Peter Lombard opened his treatment of the sacraments by referring to the parable of the Good Samaritan, thus emphasizing the way sacraments "heal." This emphasis is continued in Alexander of Hales, who discusses the remedial character of sacraments by comparing them with the cure of Naaman from leprosy (2 Kgs 5:10), stating that Naaman's sevenfold ablution parallels the seven sacraments. Bonaventure speaks about sacraments as cures: they expel a disease, restore health, and conserve the health restored. Albert the Great speaks about sacraments as removing the first roots of sin and punishment for sin, and he speaks about them as medicine against the disease of sin and the sorrows accompanying it.

Aquinas himself addresses sacraments in a general way in three passages in addition to part 3 of the *Summa*. In his commentary on Peter Lombard, *Scriptum Super Libris Magistri Petri Lombardi* (1252–56), and in the *Summa Contra Gentiles* (1259–64), he states that fallen humanity needs the Word incarnate to heal. That will lead to the way he deals with sacraments in the *Summa*, that is, in the section on the incarnation. He introduces the questions on the sacraments by stating, "Now that we have completed our consideration of the mysteries of the Incarnate Word, our next topic is the sacraments of the church: for it is from the Incarnate Word that they derive their efficacy." The other place where Aquinas treats sacraments is in the *Secunda Secundae* of the *Summa*, where he states that they are exterior acts of *latria* ("worship") and are part of the virtue of religion. In part 3 of the *Summa*, q. 60–65, he raises the following six issues germane to his thought and to the evolution of the church's understanding of sacraments at the time.

NATURE OF SACRAMENTS (Q. 60)

While other commentators, and Aquinas himself in his earlier works, had approached the sacraments initially and primarily as efficient causes of grace, Aquinas reverts here to Augustine's approach by regarding them initially and primarily as *signs*. (Recall Augustine: "A sacrament is a sign of a sacred thing in as much as it sanctifies.")

Then he asserts that they are prolongations of the incarnation, the mode that God chose to present his own self to humanity and to redeem humanity.

    a. In this part of the *Summa*, Aquinas speaks of sacraments as signs of sacred realities, as distinguished from other signs (a distinction we saw in the previous two chapters), and they are polyvalent signs. The word *polyvalent* (or *multivalent*), that is, having more than one "meaning," is important in considering sacraments because by their nature, sacramental signs cannot be defined or described as a single reality. Sacramental signs

99

always brim over with copious meanings. (This will be covered in chapters 11 and 12.) For example, the water in baptism means vitality (without it, we cannot live) as well as washing, slaking thirst, cooling, even drowning. The consecrated bread and wine of the Eucharist means food, real and abiding presence, sacrament of the sacrifice of Christ.

b. Sacraments entail some "matter" that can be perceived by the senses and is particular to each sacrament—for example, water for baptism and bread and wine for the Eucharist.

c. Sacraments also use some "form" of words that are required and prescribed for each sacrament (admitting only of minor additions or omissions). In other words, the church's liturgy provides us with what is required for sacrament—material elements and human words.

In the midst of this first question, Aquinas relies on the important notion of liturgical memorial when he asserts that sacraments have a threefold function: they are *commemorative* ("make memory together") of the passion of Christ (an event of the past), they are *demonstrative* of what was accomplished in the past now made present through grace (present), and they are *prognostic* as a foretelling of future glory (for example, "Thy kingdom come"). This is summarized in the antiphon, written by Aquinas himself, for the Canticle of Mary on the feast of Corpus Christi: "How holy this feast in which Christ is our food; his passion is recalled; grace fills our hearts; and we receive a pledge of the glory to come" [Present Breviary trans.].

THE NECESSITY OF THE SACRAMENTS (Q. 61)

Aquinas argues that we need the sacraments because we humans have a supernatural end. We desire and eventually will go to heaven. In the meantime, we need sacraments to grant us God's salvation here and now as we are on the way toward heaven. But we are also physical human beings. As such we need sacraments as outward signs that use physical realities as ways of experiencing all that is of God—divine—in our mortal bodies—humanity. Sacraments are thus very suited to and respectful of our humanity. They are sensible signs of invisible reality.

SACRAMENTS "CAUSE" GRACE (Q. 62)

Many theologians prior to Aquinas (for example, Hugh of St. Victor) use the verb *contain* rather than *cause* when dealing with how sacraments work. That usage is retained in Aquinas but deepened to mean that it is more than a vessel containing grace. Medieval theologians were divided about whether or how to use the term *cause* to describe how sacraments work. Aquinas asserts that sacraments do cause grace, but in doing so, he distinguished the principal cause of grace—God himself—from the instrumental causes of grace, that is, the sacraments. God, as principal cause, gives us a share in his divine life through the sacraments as his instruments. The sacraments were given to us by God for the purpose of causing grace. Aquinas also writes that sacraments are both signs and causes. The Latin phrase *significando causant* is often used to describe the way sacraments work—they cause by signifying. This suggests that they are required for salvation and that God mediates salvation to us through them as physical entities that affect our physical bodies. In other words, they are proper to humans' faculties of sight, sound, smell, taste, and touch—they are not ideas only; they are God's actions among us. St. Thomas speaks of the sacraments as signs of three things: the passion of Christ, grace, and glory (*ST* 3a, q. 60.3). In this teaching, he shows himself to be in accord with the descriptions of the sacraments in Scripture, where they appear as signs of redemption. The clearest instance is Romans 6, in which baptism is described as our burial and resurrection with Christ. In this and the other sacraments, Christ's work of redemption becomes ours sacramentally, that is, through the signs of that salvation; and by reason of this, we are given God's life, grace. Again, since grace is the seed of glory, and the ultimate effect of what Christ does sacramentally is our glorification, each sacrament is a sign of this culmination of the Christian life. St. Thomas's teaching that the sacraments are signs is obviously in keeping with the patristic descriptions, especially from St. Augustine, which speak of them as belonging to this genus. While with the development of Scholastic theology attention was drawn to the fact that these signs are causes of the grace they signify, St. Thomas in his treatment kept the proper balance, seeing them as signs that cause and that do so in accordance with their nature as signs.

During this same period, other theologians will offer different explanations about how sacraments cause grace. St. Bonaventure will argue what is often called a "dispositive" causality, meaning that just as God established a covenant with humanity by his divine initiative to save us, sacraments are the occasions when God continues to act among us in a covenantal way. Sacraments are called "a divine pact." Hence Bonaventure does not ascribe direct causality to the sacraments, but to God himself. Alexander of Hales will assert that sacraments accomplish what they signify, but he does not describe how these work. He speaks about sacraments as "divine medicine" containing grace, but he avoids saying that they themselves "cause" grace. The closest to Aquinas's treatment of causality is Albert the Great, who will argue that sacraments are material causes that contain grace. He uses the example that a vial contains medicine but that a syringe is needed to convey the medicine where needed. God is the physician who heals the soul effectively. Grace is the medicine that heals.

We will deal with what the Council of Trent taught about sacramental causality in chapter 7. But it is important to note here that the council fathers avoided the word *cause* and instead relied on the term *confer*. It simply asserted that sacraments confer grace. The teaching from Trent is not tied to any of the theories we described here or to any other theories. For orthodox Catholic belief, one must believe *that* sacraments confer/cause grace. But one is not bound to any one particular theory to describe *how*.

SACRAMENTAL CHARACTER (Q. 63)

While the term *sacramental character* has been used since Augustine (see chapter 3), varying explanations have been offered for what it means. Aquinas will assert that sacramental character exists and is conferred in the (unrepeatable) sacraments of baptism, confirmation, and holy orders. Character deputes one to participate in divine worship (through the liturgy), it is a spiritual power enabling us to perform spiritual activities, and it imparts in us a participation in Christ's priesthood. These are important dynamic theological assertions about what sacramental character does and means, as opposed to an assertion that one possesses a character alone. That character imprinted is said to be indelible means, in effect, that one cannot be unbaptized, or unconfirmed, or unordained. Baptized and confirmed Christians are enabled to participate in the Eucharist by virtue of the sacramental character imprinted on their souls. The priest is ordained to celebrate the liturgy and sacraments with and on behalf of the Christian community. Their "deputation to worship" configures them to preside at liturgy and sacraments. This is part of the origin for the phrase *once a priest, always a priest.* Through these sacraments, we are so made to be like Christ that this can never be taken away.

Other theologians will offer their own nuances to Thomas's teaching. Alexander of Hales asserts that a character is a "figure." (Note chapter three in which we saw the Eucharist described as a *figure of Christ.*) This character configures the Trinity in the baptized, confirmed, and ordained person. Albert the Great will say that the character is a kind of "habit" for faith and for grace through spiritual light and heat. St. Bonaventure will also use the term *habit* to describe sacramental character. With regard to the character imprinted at "holy orders," there was some debate in the Scholastic period about when this occurred, with most maintaining that it occurred at priestly ordination, not the ordination of a bishop. But other theologians maintained that a character was imprinted with each of what was then called the "minor" and "major" orders: porter, lector, exorcist, acolyte, subdeacon, deacon, and priest. Note that in this listing there is no mention of a bishop because the theology and church practice at this time was that one was ordained a priest and then *consecrated* a bishop. The distinction was that all the "powers" that a bishop would need to perform sacred duties, like ordination, were already given at priesthood ordination but were not made active and viable until one was consecrated. (See chapter 7, where the Council of Trent deals with sacramental character.)

THE CAUSES OF THE SACRAMENTS (Q. 64)

This section complements q. 62 (above) and describes the agents involved in sacramental causality. As above, Aquinas says that the principal agent is God, who institutes the sacraments communicating Christ to us through them. Then because sacraments are actions in which we engage, human ministers are required for them. Hence Aquinas goes on to say that Christ's power is communicated to ministers, that is, the ordained priest or bishop (there were no permanent deacons at the time he wrote).

Ministers must have the right intention to perform the sacrament, so that sacraments are never to be understood as automatic or even "magic." They are also to come to sacraments with correct faith. But because they act through Christ's power—*in persona Christi*—their unworthiness or sinfulness can never diminish that the sacraments function precisely because they are acts of Christ, not of themselves. This assertion takes us back to St. Augustine, whose same teaching on this issue is in his response to the Pelagian heresy.

With regard to those who participate in the sacraments to receive them, there are important nuances about the right "intention" for the different sacraments. For the valid and fruitful reception of baptism in the case of an infant, no personal act is required since such is manifestly impossible. In adults, there can never be a validly received sacrament without a willingness to encounter God (at least a "habitual" intention) and, in all sacraments other than baptism, the previous reception of this initial sacrament. For the sacrament to attain its purpose, the infusion or increase of grace, there must be, in the sacraments of baptism and penance, a true sorrow for sins, and in the other five, the life of grace. It is customary in theological circles to speak of the absence of a requirement in the recipients as an obstacle (*obex*); an obstacle that prevents valid reception is an obstacle to the sacrament, and an obstacle that prevents fruitful reception is an obstacle to grace. In speaking of the sacraments, it is ordinarily presumed that the conditions necessary for the reception of this grace are verified; only then does the sign fulfill its function of granting a share in God's life. Certain factors, however, give rise to exceptional circumstances in which the full effect is frustrated. To understand these, it is necessary to speak of the distinction between valid and fruitful reception, which will be addressed in the final section of this chapter.

NUMBER OF SACRAMENTS (Q. 65)

We saw in the previous chapters that several theologians argued for a number of things to be called sacraments that we do not call sacraments today, and it was only with Peter Lombard that the number was fixed at seven. But it is important to recall what lies behind the number seven. It is regarded, among other things, as the perfect number because the act of creation in the book of Genesis is described as occurring over seven days. In addition, many theologians speculated about combining the three persons in the Trinity with four things of the earth. Contemporary commentators on St. Francis of Assisi's "Canticle of the Sun" will say that God is praised through "brother sun, sister moon, and the stars," which are regarded as three demonstrations of the Divine in creation. Then the Lord is praised in "brothers wind and air" (counted as one), "sister water," "brother fire" and "mother earth," which together total four from the things of this world. Three and four make seven. Or if we take the Trinity of persons in God (three) and combine them with the four directions of the compass (north, south, east, and west) or the four seasons (summer, fall, winter, and spring), we again have three for the divine and four for the earth. Thus we can say that seven is an important symbolic number with much theological meaning contained in and from it. (That the number seven figures prominently at the Council of Trent will be seen in chapter 7.)

Aquinas's teaching on the number seven deals with the way these seven sacraments render us perfect in all that pertains to the worship of God and as remedies to counteract the harmful effects of sin. Like many others before him, he asserts that the Eucharist is the greatest of all the sacraments because Christ is present substantially, that all the other sacraments of the church are ordered to this one as their end (for example, baptism and confirmation as initiation, ordination to perpetuate the sacrifice of the Mass), and that in actual ritual practice, the other sacraments often end with the Eucharist (for example, in today's liturgical practice all the sacraments except penance can be celebrated in the context of the Mass). As for their necessity, Aquinas argues that baptism and penance are necessary for the individual, and ordination for the church's preservation, especially since the ordained celebrate the Eucharist, the sacrament of sacraments. Sacraments that are necessary to make salvation easier to attain for the individual are confirmation and extreme unction ("anointing of the sick"), and for the church, matrimony.

One of the contributions of Scholastic reflection and the systematic presentation of sacramental doctrine during the twelfth and thirteenth centuries was the distinction of three elements in the sacraments. First, the *sacramentum tantum* is the sign that causes and is not itself caused, which is the rite itself. Second, the *res tantum* is the sacramental grace that is signified and caused but does not signify and cause. Third, the *res et sacramentum*, which is the symbolic reality, is the element that is both signified and caused (by the *sacramentum tantum*) and itself signifies and causes the *res tantum* (in conjunction with the *sacramentum tantum*). The precise identification of this last in each individual sacrament need not be introduced here; it is sufficient to mention that it is generally taught that such a "middle term" does exist in each of the seven. For baptism, confirmation, and holy orders, the *res et sacramentum* is the sacramental character. While variously described, sacramental character refers to sacraments that cannot be repeated and to the fact that these sacraments configure one to Christ in a particular way (belonging, ministering).

The distinction among the three elements is helpful in speaking of the difference between a sacrament that is merely validly received and one that actually imparts grace, or is fruitful. Whenever the minimum conditions on the part of the recipient are realized, presuming all else to be present on the part of the minister and the rite itself, the sacrament is truly received; that is, the *res et sacramentum* is verified even if, through lack of disposition, grace is not infused.

There is a line of continuity from the patristic era through the early Scholastics to high Scholasticism. The theologians of high

Scholasticism were able to build upon the data from the patristic era and develop some important distinctions and assertions already made by the early scholastics. In each of these eras, theologians and bishops developed the kind of descriptions about the sacraments that was needed at and for that time and place in church history. But the grand Scholastics set an important framework and confirmed as well as developed important terminology that occupied the attention of the church for centuries.

DISCUSSION QUESTIONS

1. Review the Rite for Baptism of Children and find the four places in which the minister (deacon, priest, or bishop) asks the parents about their "intention" to have their child baptized. Compare this with the previous rite for infant baptism, which contains no such request. Discuss the advantages of the new rite in terms of intention.

2. How do the sacraments of baptism and confirmation use things from creation and human manufacture for their celebration?

3. Research several possible meanings for the word *configure* and discuss why this is such an important term to describe what baptism, confirmation, and ordination do.

PRIMARY SOURCE: ST. THOMAS AQUINAS— *SUMMA THEOLOGIAE*, 3A, Q. 60–65

Critical edition: *Summa theologiae, Tertia Pars.*, q. 60–90 *with the supplement to the Tertia Pars.* Leonine Edition. Vol. 12. Rome, 1906.

English translation: Thomas Aquinas. *Summa Theologiae.* Vol. 56. *The Sacraments* (3a., q. 60–65). Edited by David Bourke. London: Blackfriars/New York: McGraw Hill, 1975.

This is arguably the most conveniently available source, but the translation is not always as rigorous as it might be. Hence in what follows, there are several references to what the translation says and what it might say.

In addition to the overview of the questions above, take note of the following:

Q. 60. *What a sacrament is.*
>   Art. 1: note the terms *signi*, *sacrando*, and *medicando*: "signs," "to make sacred," and "to heal."
>   Art. 3, reply: note the references to the passion of Christ, past, present, and future as well as *causa sanctificante prout est causa sanctificans*.
>   Art. 4: citation of Augustine *accedit verbum ad elementum, et fit sacramentum* and how that influences Aquinas.
>   Art. 5: import of "sensible realities" for signs: *res enim sensibiles requiruntur in sacramentis ad significandum*.
>   Art. 5: meaning of "the materials…such as people generally have in their possession or such as it costs little trouble to obtain."
>   Art. 6, *sed contra*, reply 2: the import for sacramental theology of "therefore from words and things as combined in the sacraments a certain unity is constituted similar to the unity constituted by form and matter," and that "materials" also include actions.
>   Art. 7, *sed contra*, reply 1–3: about words and mispronunciations in light of the use of Latin at the time and the vernacular translations of the liturgy today.
>   Art. 8, reply: about baptism in the Trinity; terminology: *Si quis ita baptizare conetur ut unum de praedictis nominibus praetermittat, scilicet Patris et Filii et Spiritus sine perfectio baptizabit*. This sentence, which led to the trinitarian formula, contains the term *invalid* in English translation, where the Latin is *et ideo non perficitur sacramentum*.
>   Art. 8, reply: about adding the name of the Blessed Virgin Mary and whether the sacrament is "invalid," where the Latin says *non esset baptismus*. And further down about "not be deprived of its full validity," where the Latin states *non tollitur perfectio sacramenti*.

Q. 61. The necessity of sacraments.

Art. 1, *sed contra*: cites Augustine. English uses "some system of symbols" for *nisi aliquot signaculorum vel sacramentorum visibilium consortio colligentur.*

Art. 1, reply 2: meaning of "the grace of God is the sufficient cause of man's salvation. Now God bestows grace upon men in the manner appropriate to them (*secundum modum eis convenientem*) and this is why the sacraments are necessary to men in order that they may obtain grace."

Art. 2, *sed contra*: meaning of "spiritual medicines applied as remedies against the wounds of sin"; Latin: *spirituales medicinae, quae adhibentur contra vulnera peccati.*

Art. 3, reply: meaning of "sacraments are necessary for man's salvation inasmuch as they constitute certain sensible signs of invisible things by which man is sanctified (*Dicendum quod sacramenta necessaria sunt ad humanam salutem inquantum sunt quaedam sensibilia signa invisibilium rerum quibus homo sanctificatur*)."

Q. 62. The chief effect of the sacraments, which is grace.

Art. 1, reply 1: "This is why the sacraments of the New Law are causes and signs at the same time"; Latin: *sacramenta novae legis simul sunt causae et signa.*

Art. 1, reply 1: "They effect what they figuratively express (*efficiunt quod figurant*)."

Art. 3: meaning of "contain grace," *contineant gratiam.*

Art. 5, *sed contra*: meaning of "from the side of Christ asleep on the cross flowed the sacraments which brought salvation to the Church"; Latin: *ex latere Christi...*

Q. 63. The other effect of the sacraments, which is character.

Art. 1, *sed contra* and reply: paragraph about military usage of "character."

Art 1, *sed contra*: import of "Aristotle tells us there are three things in the soul, power, habit and passion."

Art. 2, reply: paragraph about "divine worship consists either in receiving some divine things or in handing them on to others" "deputed to receive or to hand on to others" and "character connotes a certain spiritual power ordered to those things which pertain to divine worship." Latin: *et ideo character importat quandam potentiam spiritualem ordinatam ad ea quae sunt divini cultus.*

Art. 3, *sed contra*: relationship in the reality of "character"; of Trinity and Christ himself.

Art. 5, reply: sacramental character consists in a certain participation in Christ's priesthood present in his faithful." Latin: *participatio sacerdotii Christi...*

Q. 64. *The causes of the sacraments.*

Art. 1, reply: meaning of "priests are said to illumine the holy people not indeed by infusing grace into them, but by conferring the sacraments of grace upon them." Latin: *Similiter etiam sacerdotes illuminare dicuntur sacrum populum, non quidem gratiam infundendo, sed sacramenta gratiae tradendo.*

Art. 1, reply 2: "Prayers which are uttered in the conferring of the sacraments..." Latin: *ad secundum dicendum quod orationes quae dicuntur in sacramentorum collatione...* Also, meaning of "on the part of the Church as a whole..." Latin: *sed ex parte totius Ecclesiae...*

Art. 3, reply: "power of principal minister or the power of excellence..." The four elements that follow: passion of Christ, sacraments consecrated in Christ's name, sacraments derive their power from their institution, and cause does not depend on its effect but vice versa.

Art. 5: about unworthy ministers. How to relate this to other church scandals or issues that could be impacted by this post-Pelagian sacramental theology.

Art. 5, reply 1: "The effect achieved in those who receive the sacraments is not to assimilate them to the ministers, but to bring them into configuration with Christ." Latin: *Et ideo effectus consequitur in suscipientibus sacramenta non secundum similitudinem ministrorum, sed secundum configurationem ad Christum.*

Art. 7: about angels and humans.

Art. 8: intention required.

Art. 8, reply 1: "Intention is required, for it is by this that he subjects himself to the principal agent, namely in such a way as to intend to do what Christ and the Church do"; Latin: *quae se subjiciat principali agenti, ut scilicet intendat facere quod facit Christus et Ecclesia.*

Art. 9: importance of ecclesiology here.

Art. 9, reply: "The minister functions as an instrument, he acts not in his own power as an individual but in the power of Christ"; Latin: *sed in virtute Christi.*

Art. 9, reply 1: "The minister of a sacrament acts in the person of the whole Church..."; Latin: *agit in persona totius Ecclesiae.*

Issue: difference between *virtute* and *persona.*

Q. 65. *The number of sacraments.*

Art. 1, reply: two effects: " to render man perfect in all that pertains to the worship of God as expressed in the religion of Christian living and also as a remedy to counteract the harmful effects of sin"; Latin: *ad cultum Dei...*

Art. 2: the "hierarchy" of sacraments starting with baptism "as a spiritual regeneration"; Latin: *est spiritualis regeneratio.*

Art 3: why the Eucharist is the "sacrament of sacraments."

Relation between those sacraments that imprint a character and those that do not: "sacramental character constitutes a special kind of participation in the priesthood of Christ (*quaedam participatio est sacerdotii Christi*). Hence the sacrament which unites Christ himself to man is more sublime than one which imprints the character of Christ upon him" (reply 3).

6

REFORMATION AND THE COUNCIL OF TRENT

The purpose of this chapter is (1) to present an overview of the Reformation controversies as they reflect differences in the understanding and practice of the sacraments, especially the Eucharist; (2) to illustrate this by exploring the writings of Martin Luther on the Mass; and (3) to delineate the precise definitions from the Council of Trent that dealt with the issues of the Reformation about sacraments in general.

THE PROTESTANT REFORMATION

What is often termed the Protestant Reformation in the sixteenth century was less a systematic program for church reform than processes spearheaded by a number of individuals, largely through preaching, teaching, and writing. The calls for reform of many of the practices of the Catholic Church led to hard and long-lasting separations in what had been a united Western Catholicism.

The Reformation controversies of the sixteenth century were about both practice and doctrine, as these are essentially interconnected. As for practice, the Reformers objected to the concentration on the priestly acts of consecration and sacrifice and to the fact that the actual reception of communion had largely been replaced by the veneration of the species at the consecration. They also wanted the Lord's Supper to be made available once again in both kinds to all the faithful. Furthermore, they did not accept the language of sacrifice when associated with propitiation. For them, the once and for all sacrifice was that of Christ on the cross, and the purpose of the sacrament was to make its mercy and forgiveness available to the communicants. Hence, they expunged the Mass of all language of sacrifice other than that of thanksgiving and self-offering. This change, however, was not a retrieval of the early Christian understanding of sacrifice, since the Reformers saw this metaphorical sacrifice not as essential, but as an accessory to the Lord's Supper. Its only essence was the offering of the sacrament to the faithful. For defenders of the Catholic faith, this change in theology denied the essential doctrines of real presence, transubstantiation, and propitiatory sacrifice offered by the priest for the living and the dead. It would take many volumes to discuss the exact doctrinal and theological positions of both Catholic apologists and Reformers. Nonetheless, the situation was one of impasse and led to the defensive definitions of the Council of Trent that were concerned with both the faith and practice of the Catholic Church. It established the medieval Eucharist as the core Catholic practice for four more centuries, even though the postconciliar reforms did purge it of many of its more impious and superstitious abuses.

Interestingly, some of the Reformers had been ardent defenders of the Catholic faith who then turned on the institutional church and its practices. Martin Luther, for example, was an Augustinian monk and an outstanding preacher and teacher of the Catholic faith. Initially, he did not intend to break from the Catholic Church but to *reform* what were obvious abuses, especially those concerning the sale of indulgences. More openness to communication on both sides may have avoided escalating misunderstandings, but instead, in 1520, three years after Luther posted his famous Ninety-Five Theses, he was excommunicated by Pope Leo X. Eventually, he married and issued several documents that were increasingly polemical and critical of the Catholic Church. It has been wisely asserted that what Thomas Aquinas means to the medieval church in terms of his teaching on the sacraments, especially the Eucharist, so Martin Luther meant in his teaching on the sacrament of the altar to the Reformers and their followers.

In 1521, Henry VIII of England, in reaction to Luther's attack on the seven sacraments and the papal system, published *The Defense of the Seven Sacraments*, which also upheld papal primacy. *The Defense* was dedicated to Pope Leo X, who, in turn, rewarded Henry with the title "defender of the faith" (*Fidei defensor*). This title was later revoked following King Henry's break with the Catholic Church, which occurred in reaction to the pope's refusal to annul his marriage to Catherine of Aragon, who failed to produce a male heir for the throne. As a result, Henry broke from the Roman Catholic Church, refusing to acknowledge the authority of the pope, and made himself the head of the Church of England. Consequently, the Catholic Church was persecuted in England and countless martyrs, including Thomas More, lost their lives for the Catholic faith.

LUTHER'S CRITIQUES OF CATHOLIC THEOLOGY AND PRACTICE

Commentators have observed that to understand Luther, one must recognize a series of "either...or" rhetorical and methodological assertions that dominate his writings. Among them is the underlying assumption that the Eucharist is a *beneficium* ("gracious benefit") to us rather than a *sacrificium* ("the sacrifice we offer to God"). Another is that the Eucharist is a gift from God *to* us, not *from* us to God. In addition, many of Luther's critiques are based on his famous *solus Christus* (Christ alone, not the saints as intercessors), *sola scriptura* (Scripture alone, not tradition or the magisterium), and *sola gratia*, (grace alone, not good works). Catholic theologians would counter with a "both... and" rhetoric, seeing the Eucharist as an act both of Christ and of the whole church, as both a sacrifice and a benefit, as both from God to us and from us to God, and as both grace and good works.

The following treatises by Luther touch on the sacraments in general and on the Eucharist in particular.

THE BLESSED SACRAMENT OF THE HOLY AND TRUE BODY OF CHRIST, AND THE BROTHERHOODS (1519)

In many ways, Luther wrote from the same (late) medieval context to which Aquinas contributed so fully. The theological assertions by

Aquinas about sacraments dominated theological writing, though authors differed on how they elaborated on them. Luther was no exception in that he, like Aquinas, was heavily influenced by St. Augustine, in particular his emphasis on sacraments as *signs* and the supreme importance of fostering church belonging by their celebration. Unlike Aquinas's highly systematic treatment of sacraments in the *Summa,* Luther's teachings are rhetorically highly charged and often polemical because he wrote them in response to issues that arose and not as planned systematic treatises.

Luther states that the Eucharist has three parts: (1) the sacrament or external *sign,* (2) the fellowship of all the saints, and (3) the faith that is required with both the sign and significance of the sacrament.

1. When speaking about the sign of the Eucharist, he states that its form or appearance is bread and wine. Then he repeatedly recommends that "in a general council that all persons be given both kinds, like the priests." Recognizing water as the sign of baptism, he maintains that it would be more fitting to immerse in water rather than to pour it, "for the sake of completeness and perfection of the sign."
2. His assertions about "fellowship" use the Greek term *synaxis* and the Latin *communio.* In his fulsome description of "fellowship" and "communion of love," he chastises preachers for not preaching sufficiently about these concepts.
3. His claims about the importance of *faith* in the sacraments run counter to the prevailing distinction between *opus operatum* and *opus operantis.* He emphasizes that the sacraments must be used in faith (for him, this is *opus operantis*).

Toward the end of the treatise, he says that there are two principal sacraments in the church, "baptism and the Bread." "Baptism leads us into a new life on earth; the bread guides us through death into eternal life."

His treatment of "the brotherhoods" concerns smaller groups within the church dedicated, for example, to a patron saint. He criticizes them for inappropriate behavior, such as gluttony and drunkenness. He also writes that there is one baptism, one Christ, one sacrament, one food, one gospel, one faith, one Spirit, and one spiritual body (from Eph 4:4–5) and that each person is a member of the other (Rom 12:1). No other brotherhood is so close as this biblical teaching.

THE BABYLONIAN CAPTIVITY OF THE CHURCH (1520)

This major treatise deals largely with indulgences and, more specifically, scandalous practices that grew up around them. Phrases such as *the tyranny of Rome* are found throughout the work. Initially, Luther denied the divine authority of the papacy, but he did admit to its human authority. Then he says, "The papacy is the kingdom of Babylon."

Luther then expounds fully about the value of communicating under two species (citing, for example, John 6:55). He calls those who do not offer communion under two species "wicked men." He acknowledges three sacraments: baptism, penance, and the bread. However, then he says that if he were to speak in accord with the Scriptures, there would be only one sacrament—Christ himself (from 1 Tim 3:16). A bit later on, he asserts that the blood in the Eucharist is poured out "for you and for many for the forgiveness of sins."

Luther uses the "Babylonian captivity" metaphor when he asserts that the sacraments have come under the tyranny of Rome. The second "captivity" involves the opinions of the Thomists about sacraments, because they are too philosophical—for example, in using the term *transubstantiation* to describe the change in bread and wine (used by Aquinas in the *Summa* and also in the church's magisterium at the Fourth Lateran Council in 1215 under Pope Innocent III). The third "captivity" is that the Mass has been turned into a good work and a sacrifice. He regards the Eucharist as a last testament of Christ to the church to be received, not offered. He also wants to put aside whatever has been added to the Last Supper by way of vesture, ornaments, chants, prayers, organs, and "the whole pageantry of outward things."

He laments that no layperson can hear the words of Christ spoken during the (Roman) Canon, "as if they were too sacred to be delivered to the common people."

Luther returns to the issue of church income when he poignantly says, "The Mass is the foundation of their anniversaries, brotherhoods, applications, communications, etc., that is to say, their fat income." While he objects to the notion of offering the Mass, he admits that prayers should be offered to God. Toward the end, he states that we can offer "prayers" but not the Mass and that the Mass is a sacrament, not a work, a testament and not a sacrifice.

THE SACRAMENT OF THE BODY AND BLOOD—AGAINST THE FANATICS (1526)

Luther devotes the first part of this treatise to reiterating his call for the Eucharist to be made available to the faithful under two species and to expressing his abhorrence of sacrificial language attached to the Mass.

In the second part, "Concerning Confession," Luther asserts that there are three kinds of confession: (1) *Before God.* Among the scriptural references is John 3:3, "Unless one is born anew, one cannot see the kingdom of God." This statement leads to the claim that we are all born sinners. (2) *To one's neighbor.* Here he uses Matthew 5:23–25 and 6:14–15, as well as the Letter of James 5:16, "Confess your sins to one another." (3) He argues that "private confession" to a priest developed from public confession is "a sacrament." He decries the practice of delineating and classifying kinds of sins and the teaching from the Fourth Lateran Council requiring confession of sins once a year. At the same time, he writes that private confession can have a good purpose "for the simple, childlike people." That he would number himself among them is attested by the fact that he frequently availed himself of confession—so deep was his sense of personal unworthiness.

LUTHER'S LITURGICAL INNOVATIONS

Initially, Luther was resistant to making changes in the Roman liturgy. He preferred to keep it as it was while insisting that preaching should occur at every Mass (see *Concerning the Order for Pubic Worship*, 1523).

FORMULA MISSAE (1523)

Here, Luther directed that the Latin language was to be retained in the liturgy but that preaching was to be in the vernacular. He emphasized the importance of the Liturgy of the Word and insisted on preaching at Mass (*sola scriptura*). He removed the prayers prior to the Eucharistic Prayer, called the "offertory," because they and the accompanying gestures of holding up the bread and wine smacked of the very thing he abhorred—sacrifice. Luther also abbreviated the texts of the Roman liturgy, taking out words and phrases that were not directly from the Bible (again, *sola scriptura*). The Eucharistic Prayer (also called the Canon of the Mass) now consisted only of the words of Jesus at the Last Supper ("words of consecration"). After these words, the people were to sing the *Sanctus* and *Benedictus*, texts that were from the Scriptures and therefore, in his estimation, allowable. The elevation of the elements of consecrated bread and wine followed, to be, as he said, a visual or pictorial "act of memory." The elevation was followed by the Lord's Prayer, the sign of peace, and communion.

DEUTSCHE MESSE (1526)

This very title indicated the shift from Latin to the vernacular for the liturgy. Luther's instructions begin with the now familiar assertion that the aim of the liturgy was to preach and teach God's word. Instead of the (Latin) "introit" (now called the "entrance antiphon") that was sung to (mostly Gregorian) chant, Luther composed a number of vernacular hymns for singing. He also replaced the verses of the psalm that were sung between the readings (now called the "responsorial psalm") with another vernacular hymn. This hymn was followed by a sermon (hence this is sometimes called "the sermon hymn"). The sermon was then followed by a paraphrase of the Lord's Prayer (also composed by Luther himself), which led immediately to the consecration of the bread. Then, following the consecration was the *Sanctus*, sung in German, or another hymn that he composed. This hymn was accompanied by the elevation of the bread. The consecration of the wine followed, and the remainder of the *Sanctus* or hymn was sung with the elevation of the chalice.

OBSERVATIONS

Clearly the preaching and teaching of the word of God was uppermost in Luther's theology and his liturgies. He also insisted on the regular reception of communion under both species, which was not the custom in the Catholic Church at the time. (That this was not wholly successful is attested by the fact that in many Lutheran churches, "communion" was celebrated four times a year.) There was a collective celebration fostered by singing hymns in German. Some scholars doubt whether these liturgies were truly communal in the sense of what was presumed in the patristic church. The subjectivist and individualistic notions about liturgy in the Catholic Church at the time also prevailed in the growing Lutheran movement. Luther's emphasis on the localized real presence of Christ in the Eucharist mirrored the Catholic teaching, though he did not use the term *transubstantiation*. In the liturgy, the minister said and did almost everything. Again, this mirrored contemporary Catholic practice.

COUNCIL OF TRENT (1545–63)

In their responses to the Reformers' criticisms, the council fathers did not intend to formulate a systematic doctrinal summary on sacraments but, rather, dealt with individual areas of concern expressed by the Reformers. Hence, the statements of Trent cannot be said to comprise a systematic treatment of sacraments in the manner of Thomas Aquinas in his *Summa*. They clarified some overall sacramental questions in the seventh session (1547), and gave doctrinal statements on the Eucharist in the thirteenth (1551). They also debated eucharistic doctrine and practice in the twenty-first session (1562). In the twenty-second session (1562), they made their clearest assertions about the sacrifice of the Mass. Finally, they discussed orders at the twenty-third session (1563) and reformed marriage legislation at the twenty-fourth session (1563).

HOW TO READ TRENT'S TEACHING

Because of their historical context, it is no surprise that the statements from the Council of Trent are duly regarded as a watershed in terms of church teaching about a number of matters, including the sacraments. As such, they are best regarded as having four properties:

1. They are *laconic* in that they are not elaborate expositions. Especially when compared to the documents of Vatican II (see chapter 7), these are far more modest in size.
2. They are *specific* in that they deal with specific issues. For example, they discuss the number of sacraments specifically, and not with underlying concepts about sacraments.
3. They are *reactive to errors*. Catholicism had to revisit and articulate what it stood for in the face of contrary religious assertions and practices by the Reformers and their followers.
4. They are also *open-ended*. There was no intention to limit either rhetoric or debate about sacraments. In effect, this principle is a function of the first three properties and opened the way for catechisms based on the Council of Trent as well as for subsequent theologians to elaborate on assertions in a catechetical and probative way.

In addition, it is important to evaluate what kind of teachings Trent asserted and where. The "canons" from the Council contain what Catholics must believe about church teachings. The "decrees" are accompanying explanations, albeit brief and reactive as well.

The canons of Trent are worded negatively. The fathers judged the clarification of doctrine to be so crucial and allegiance needed to be so firm that the statements are very pointed. They begin with the phrase, "If anyone says…" followed by a statement that is wrong (that is, heresy), ending up with the phrase, "Let them be anathema" or "damned." If this rhetoric sounds harsh, it is meant to be. The survival of the Catholic Church was at stake.

The seventh session of the Council of Trent lasted for three months (January 15 to March 9, 1547). Pope Paul III remained in Rome. He assigned two cardinals to preside in his absence, Cardinal Giovanni Maria del Monte (who later became Pope Julius III) and Cardinal Marcello Cervini (who later became Pope Marcellus II). In all, there were seventy-one prelates (not just bishops) in attendance. Voting members at these deliberations included the (superior) generals of the Dominicans, the Conventual Franciscans, the Hermits of St. Augustine, the Carmelites, and the Servites. In addition to these (voting) members, there were officially appointed theologians: Dominicans, Franciscans, Conventual Franciscans, Augustinians, Carmelites, Servites, and diocesan clergy. Some representatives of European nobility and other lay leaders also attended. At times, the debates involved disagreements among different Catholic theologians, most prominently the differences of opinion between the Dominicans and Franciscans. It was necessary for the pope's legates to remind the council fathers that their concerns were with defending the faith to the outside public who were largely influenced by the Reformers. It was not to settle (legitimate) theological disputes among Catholic theologians.

OFFICIAL CHURCH TEACHING ON SACRAMENTS FROM CANONS OF THE COUNCIL OF TRENT

Canon One

"If anyone says that the sacraments of the New Law were not all instituted by our lord Jesus Christ; or that there are more or fewer than seven: namely, baptism, confirmation, eucharist, penance, last anointing, order, and matrimony; or that one or other of these is not truly and in the full sense a sacrament: let him be anathema."

The issue here concerns the Reformers' insistence that only sacred ceremonies that could be found directly in the Scriptures were sacraments. Moreover, as we saw above, Luther counted different numbers of sacraments in different places: two or three. In addition, his concern for competency in preaching and leading the liturgy caused him in some places to regard "the ministry" as "sacramental." This canon states *that* there are seven sacraments, but not *where* or *how* they were so instituted.

Canon Two

"If anyone says that those same sacraments of the new law are no different from the sacraments of the old law, except by reason of a difference in ceremonies and in external rites: let him be anathema."

This canon reacts to Luther's assertions about ceremonies and words that the church came to use to celebrate the sacraments, which he rejected unless they were evident in the Scriptures.

Canon Three

"If anyone says that these seven sacraments are so equal to each other that on no ground is one of greater dignity than another: let him be anathema."

This canon concerns the teaching of Thomas Aquinas, among others, that some sacraments are more important than others. For example, baptism, as necessary for salvation, is more important than marriage and orders, which one need not receive.

Canon Four

"If anyone says that the sacraments of the new law are not necessary for salvation but are superfluous, and that people obtain the grace of justification from God without them or a desire for them, by faith alone, though all are not necessary for each individual: let him be anathema."

This canon helps to explain the previous canon and reacts to the more "spiritualist" strain among the Reformers who deny the necessity of the sacraments outright (despite the biblical warrant about being "born again" in John 3).

Canon Five

"If anyone says that these sacraments have been instituted only to nourish faith: let him be anathema."

Again, the necessity of sacraments for salvation is at issue here.

Canon Six

"If anyone says that the sacraments of the new law do not contain the grace which they signify; or do not confer that grace on those who place no obstacle in the way, as if they were only external signs of the grace or justice received by faith, and some kind of mark of the christian profession by which believers are distinguished from unbelievers in the eyes of people: let him be anathema."

The issues here concern sacramental causality. However, note that Trent does not use the word *cause*, but rather the word *confer* (Latin *conferat*). This distinction allows for several possible interpretations for sacramental "causality." The use of *confer* lessens any kind of rhetoric that would make the sacraments "automatic." The use of *do not place any obstacle* means that the teaching implies that the emphasis is always on God's graciousness being overwhelming. Sacraments function unless a person places an obstacle in the way, such as admitting lack of faith in Christ or in the functioning of the sacrament. Behind this canon is the delicate balance between *ex opere operato* and *ex opere operantis*. The presumption is that they are two sides of one coin and that the sacraments are not so automatic as to constitute magic.

Canon Seven

"If anyone says that grace is not given by the sacraments of this kind always and to all, as far as depends on God, even if they duly receive them, but only sometimes and to some: let him be anathema."

God's initiative and the giving of grace in and through sacraments are at issue here. We do not "earn" grace from sacraments, we receive it.

Canon Eight

"If anyone says that grace is not conferred by the sacraments of the new law through the sacramental action itself [*ex opere operato*], but that faith in the divine promises is by itself sufficient for obtaining the grace: let him be anathema."

The issue here is that God is always present and active in and through the sacraments. This canon reminds us of God's covenant relationship with the chosen people in the Scriptures, despite their infidelity and sin.

Canon Nine

"If anyone says that in three sacraments, namely, baptism, confirmation and order, a character, namely a spiritual and indelible mark, is not imprinted on the soul because of which they cannot be repeated: let him be anathema."

This teaching goes as far back as St. Augustine, with "irrepeatability" a key element in describing the sacramental character. This is drawn out by Aquinas to concern deputation to worship God through the liturgy. Recalling the medieval debates about the nature of sacramental character from ordination, it is notable that Trent simply asserts "orders" and makes no other specification about which order.

Canon Ten

"If anyone says that all Christians have the power to exercise the ministry of the word and of all the sacraments: let him be anathema."

Among the issues that lie behind this canon is the nature of ordination, conferring a sacramental power to administer sacraments. A far more egalitarian notion of church belonging and ministry is evident in many statements of some Reformers. However, one nuance in Lutheran practice is that one needed to be credentialed to preach and have the requisite background in Scripture.

Canon Eleven

"If anyone says that, when ministers effect or confer the sacraments, they do not need the intention at least of doing what the church does: let him be anathema."

Again, two of the issues here concern having the right "intention" so that sacraments are not regarded as (quasi-)magical or automatic. The other issue is the use of the word *confer* to describe that ministers of the sacraments are precisely that, ministers. Also, the word *effect* suggests that God "confers" the grace through human instrumentality.

Canon Twelve

"If anyone says that a minister in a state of mortal sin, even if he observes all the essentials which belong to the effecting or administering of a sacrament, does not effect or administer it: let him be anathema."

This assertion has its origin in the Donatist controversy. While a minister's lack of virtue should never be countenanced, the personal unworthiness of the minister cannot be a barrier to receiving grace in the sacraments. Put differently, who would decide, on what basis and how could one tell? In the end, it is the overarching graciousness of God that is always at stake in sacraments.

Canon Thirteen

"If anyone says that the received and approved rites of the Catholic Church in customary use in the solemn administration of the sacraments may, without sin, be neglected or omitted at choice by the ministers, or can be changed to order new ones by any pastor whatever: let him be anathema."

Liturgical rites matter. In the sacraments, "matter" and "form" need to be respected and kept intact in celebration.

SUMMARY

In a very circumspect way, the Council of Trent states that sacraments do not confer grace simply because of "human faith" (canon 5). Sacraments indeed do confer the grace they signify (canon 6). Indeed, the council fathers state clearly the reason for such conferral of grace: God has ordered this (canon 7) *quantum est ex parte Dei,* on God's part. The Council emphasizes this free action of God in its use of the term *ex opere operato* in contrast to the human good work, the human side of faith (canon 8).

About causality, the council fathers simply teach that God acts through the sacraments to give his grace; humans can set obstacles (that is, sin). The sacraments confer the grace they signify (based on Augustine's approach to visible grace). How these three areas are put together in detail is left to theologians and theological opinions. This recalls the debate about sacramental causality in the previous chapter.

TRIDENTINE LITURGY

Up through the Council of Trent there was much episcopal independence about overseeing how the liturgy was celebrated. However, from the time of Pope Gregory VII in the late eleventh century, certain parameters were set forth and followed. It was only at the Council of Trent, however, that the papal jurisdiction over the reform of the liturgy was granted and used for many of the rites. After Trent, a Roman Breviary (Liturgy of the Hours) was published in 1568, and the Roman Missal was published in 1570. Even then, however, certain precedents were allowed to continue, such as the Divine Office specific to individual religious orders (for example, Dominicans and Franciscans). The 1570 Roman Missal was required except where some localities (in and around Milan) or some religious communities (such as Dominicans and Carthusians) had celebrated from a Missal for two hundred years or more. They were allowed to retain their practice. Until the Vatican II liturgical reform, Dominicans could celebrate the liturgy in the way in which they had been accustomed. This practice included an abbreviated introductory rite with brief "prayers at the foot of the altar" and none of the prayers that would be included in the Tridentine Missal at the "offertory."

These specific liturgies were replaced by the reformed liturgies as promulgated by the Constitution on the Liturgy after Vatican II and by the decrees of Pope Paul VI. That the "Tridentine Mass," now called the extraordinary form of the Mass, may be celebrated in certain circumstances under the authority of the diocesan bishop is the result of decisions taken by Pope John Paul II and Pope Emeritus Benedict XVI initially in order to reconcile followers of the dissident group led by Archbishop Marcel Lefevbre and other dissenters who held the post–Vatican II liturgies to be "defective" or even "heretical." Pope Benedict's statements in 2007 (in the document *Summmmorum*

Pontificum and its accompanying letter to bishops) widen this permission for the sake of those who prefer to celebrate with this Missal.

DISCUSSION QUESTIONS

1. Clearly, many of the practices in the liturgy influenced Luther and others to criticize the Catholic Church. Two criticisms were the lack of preaching of the word of God and the lack of communion under both species. Now that these practices have been restored to Catholic liturgy, evaluate your experience of them.

2. It was argued in this chapter that Luther's rhetoric of "either…or" separated realities that should not have been separated, in particular the notion of Eucharist as a *beneficium* and the notion of the Eucharist as a *sacrificium*. Discuss how a rhetoric of inclusion, "both…and," could help to bring together these two central ideas about the Eucharist.

3. The decrees of the Council of Trent on sacraments were written at a very different time and place in the church's life from our own. What do you regard as still relevant to the church's liturgical practices today?

TRENT TO TWENTIETH CENTURY

SIXTEENTH TO NINETEENTH CENTURIES

While much post-Tridentine theology and catechesis followed the Council's teaching through commentaries and catechisms, some works of the period dealt with issues raised by the Reformers. For example, *De Sacramentis* of Melchior Cano (d. 1560) dealt with the faith-sacrament question debated at the Council and evident in its decrees. He affirmed that the sacraments are undoubtedly necessary but in the same measure in which an explicit faith, expressed in sensible signs, is necessary for a person to be saved. The famous Jesuit theologian and teacher Robert Bellarmine (d. 1621) addressed the same issue in *De Controversiis Christianae Fidei* and spoke of the necessity of faith for the efficaciousness of the sacraments. Suarez's work *Commentaria ac Disputationes in III partem D. Thomas* (commentary on Thomas's third part of the *Summa*) represented a kind of manual that noted the Reformers' objections and then listed his analysis based on the Scholastics. Such works influenced manuals of theology that dealt with issues raised by the Reformers and explicitly corrected them in an apologetic way. These manuals clarified issues about the sacraments: the number of sacraments, their efficaciousness, *opus operatum*, institution by Christ, their matter and form, and the role of the ordained minister. Clearly, these are the same issues that were addressed by Scholastic theologians like Aquinas, debated and critiqued by the Reformers, and clarified at Trent.

On a more popular level, catechisms were published that summarized the teachings of Trent. Different catechisms for different countries sponsored by bishops in different localities meant that there were different emphases from catechism to catechism. Almost all of the initial catechisms had an index at the end to guide preachers about what parts of the catechism they should use for their Sunday homily. This list would be in accordance with the liturgical year and the readings of the Sunday. For example, for the First Sunday of Advent, the suggested part of the catechism concerned eschatology (i.e., the end of the world, death, judgment, and salvation), a theme based on the Scripture readings for that Sunday, which included Luke 21:25–33. The Sunday sermon was a primary way for the faithful to receive the teachings from the Council of Trent.

In the nineteenth century, the American bishops repeatedly discussed an arrangement whereby a uniform textbook of Catholic doctrine might be used by all Catholics. Initial discussions in 1852 and 1866 led to proposals for a way to proceed but were not successful. At the Third Plenary Council (1884), many bishops favored a catechism for the nation based on the original by Archbishop Butler of Ireland (1775). A committee of six bishops worked on the project, and in 1885, the bishops published "A Catechism of Christian Doctrine, Prepared and Enjoined by the Order of the Third Council of Baltimore." Some bishops decided to add explanatory notes, clarifications, and additions to this text, making "the Baltimore Catechism" more of a model than one uniform text. "The Baltimore Catechism" consisted of four volumes. "Number One" had thirty-three lessons in question and answer form suitable for first communicants through fifth graders. "Number Two" contained thirty-seven lessons suitable for sixth through ninth graders and those preparing for confirmation. "Number Three," which is based on "Number Two," is intended for those who have been confirmed and includes additional questions, definitions, examples, and applications. "Number Four" was more of an advanced reference work for teachers or for use as an advanced textbook. What is notable is the requirement that those preparing for first communion and confirmation would need to have studied and been responsible for requisite knowledge of the faith suited to what sacrament they were preparing to receive.

At the same time, works on sacraments began to appear that reflected a revival of interest in Scripture, patristics, and the history of theology. Alongside the apologetic style of "manual theology" derived from the teaching of Trent backed up by (largely Scholastic) theologians, other kinds of research were underway to uncover other monuments of the evolution of Catholicism that were not medieval. The book *Symbolik* by Johann Adam Möhler (d. 1838) helped the revival of theology at Tübingen in Germany. Matthias Scheeben (d. 1888), in his classic *Die Mysterien des Christentums*, proposed a theory of sacraments based on sacramental character, arguing that an ecclesial consciousness was essential to understanding the medieval term *res et sacramentum*. This methodology led him to overcome some of the individualism associated with the celebration of the sacraments on a pastoral level and some explanations of them that ignored the intrinsic ecclesial aspect of sacraments since the Middle Ages. It should be recalled that Thomas Aquinas's theology of sacramental character was essentially ecclesial, given his emphasis that all the sacraments that imprinted a character deputed one for worship.

TWENTIETH CENTURY

The twentieth-century liturgical movement was undoubtedly the main stimulus within the church for the contemporary renewal of sacramental practice and a revived understanding of the dynamism of the sacramental action. The work of liturgical scholars in the late nineteenth and early twentieth centuries was responsible for a reawakening of the importance and centrality of liturgy as public worship that, by its nature, required the active participation of all participants. This work was a move toward reemphasizing the universal priesthood of all believers that was not always experienced in pastoral practice, although it was never absent from the theology of liturgy and the church. Official papal endorsement of the movement came in the very early 1900s with the writings of Pope Pius X, such as his *motu proprio, Tra le Sollecitudini*, which affirmed the value of everyone's active participation in the act of liturgy. These included the revival of Gregorian chant, which provided relatively simple melodies for musical participation in the liturgy that required little training.

The contribution of Benedictine monasticism to the liturgical revival is exemplified in the publication of important works on sacramental teaching and in the celebration of the liturgy. Lambert Beauduin's *La Pieté de l'Eglise* (Belgium, 1914; published in English as *Liturgy: The Life of the Church*, 3rd ed. [SAP: St. Michael's Abbey, 2002]) and Ildefons Herwegen's journal entitled *Ecclesia Orans* (Germany, 1918) demonstrate the relationship between liturgy and sacramental doctrine. Herwegen was instrumental in fostering the serious scholarship reflected in the periodical *Jahrbuch für Liturgiewissenschaft,* which contained probing and insightful articles by Dom Odo Casel. Casel's work (part of which was translated into English in 1962 as *The Mystery of Christian Worship*) centered on the mystery of God present and active in the liturgy. He rediscovered the notion of liturgical memorial that is central to understanding Jewish liturgy, part of which was noted in the writings of Thomas Aquinas. Casel revived much of the patristic teaching about the cultic/liturgical dimension of the sacraments and was influenced by the patristic inter-pretation of sacraments based on liturgical rites. This approach was groundbreaking compared with the tradition of the theological text-books that preceded him. They were called "manuals of theology" because they were structured so as to summarize Catholic teachings over against teachings of the Reformers. For Casel, the liturgy makes present and active the mystery of Christ, realized historically in the past, sacramentally represented in the present, and in anticipation of its fulfillment in the kingdom of heaven. The liturgy manifests these mys-teries as the church makes contact with them, resulting in salvation. The essential point Casel reiterated was that Christians experience the mysteries of Christ anew again and again in the liturgy and the sacra-ments. They do not simply gain graces from Christ—they share in the mystery of faith itself at every liturgy. Casel is more concerned with an inner attitude toward liturgical participation than external demonstra-tions of involvement, although the latter was not ignored. Casel's work did not pass without criticism and correction, specifically concerning his overemphasis on parallels between Greek mystery religions and Christian cult, the lack of a stronger ecclesial sense in liturgical com-memoration, and such a high emphasis on Christ to the diminishment of a theology of the Trinity active in the liturgy; nevertheless, his work was seminal and remains highly influential.

Although he was independent of the liturgical movement in Europe, another Benedictine, Anscar Vonier of Buckfast Abbey in Ireland, wrote A *Key to the Doctrine of the Eucharist* (1925) in an effort to illuminate the most central aspects of Aquinas's thought on the Eucharist, principally that which involved the liturgical dimension of the sacraments. The first chapters of the work deal with faith, sacramental signification, and the liturgical setting of Eucharist. Catholic writing had largely ignored these topics since Trent. The central portion of the book deals with the Scholastic teaching about sacraments as emphasized and taught at Trent. However, Vonier's real contribution was to present and interpret the teaching of Aquinas himself, not that of his interpreters. The final section of the book deals with the eucharistic liturgy and banquet, topics that were unfamiliar in eucharistic theology at the time. Thus, Vonier restored to eucharistic doctrine some of the richness not reflected in post-Tridentine theology.

What surfaced in this period was a strong ecclesial foundation for liturgy and sacraments. The patristic adage, "In the sacraments the church generates its children, but is also itself generated" was restored to its rightful position after centuries in which teaching on sacraments was codified theologically, juridically (that is, canon law), and rubrically (following the directions in the liturgical books written in red). Analyzing sacraments from the liturgical perspective led to an increased awareness of their christological and trinitarian foundation. The grace of God comes through, with and in Christ. The self-offering of the church is in union with the unique offering of Christ to the Father, which happened "once and for all" but which is realized and experienced in every liturgy. The sanctifying action of God is realized in sacraments through Christ, who, in turn, gives the participants his Holy Spirit. This emphasis on mediation through Christ in the church characterizes the highly influential writing in mid-century from Edward Schillebeeckx and Karl Rahner.

EDWARD SCHILLEBEECKX (D. 2009)

The christological approach to sacraments characterizes Schillebeeckx's classic book *De sacramentele Heilseconomie* (1952). (This is not to be confused with the shorter popularized version *Christ the Sacrament of the Encounter with God*. The complete volume is replete with copious scriptural, patristic, and medieval authors leading to his conclusions about "encounter," which is then summarized in the shorter text.) Schillebeeckx presents an understanding of sacraments that combines traditional approaches with insights from contemporary anthropology and phenomenology. For him, salvation is a personal act of encounter between the human person and God. Grace is a personal encounter with God. Schillebeeckx roots this theology in his understanding of Christ, whose paschal mystery is "metahistorical" and "transtemporal." These terms mean that the mystery experienced in the liturgy and sacraments is the paschal mystery, which occurred in historical time and space but is not confined to historical time and space. He asserts the unique and once-for-all character of Christ's act of redemption and complements it by stating that this mystery is always offered through sacraments to the church. Christ is thus understood to be the central sacrament, manifesting God's love to the world. (Commentators who borrow from Schillebeeckx will often use the phrases *foundational sacrament* or *ground sacrament* to describe Christ.) The seven sacraments and the entire liturgy are specifications of Christ, the original sacrament. The phenomenon of encounter becomes operative in this approach since the church encounters God through Christ. Individual sacraments are occasions for this encounter to take place. Schillebeeckx emphasizes the role of active faith in sacraments without which they cannot be fruitful. He parallels his christological treatment with an ecclesial understanding that emphasizes that a sacrament is valid only when it is ecclesial.

KARL RAHNER (D. 1984)

The ecclesial foundation of sacraments is emphasized in Karl Rahner's book *Kirche und Sakramente* (1961) (English translation:

The Church and the Sacraments). Like Schillebeeckx before him, Rahner approaches sacramental categories from a fresh perspective. He argues that the church is the fundamental sacrament and that it is in and through the church that one participates in Christ's redemption. He argues that one can adequately understand the sacramental nature of individual sacraments only on the basis of understanding the church itself as sacramental. Rahner held that contemporary exegesis of the Scriptures, specifically the New Testament, makes it impossible to say that Jesus instituted seven specific sacraments since such an approach made the New Testament a source for "proof texting" by taking passages out of context and reading into them. The church recognizes that Christ instituted sacraments in the sense that over several generations, the church reflected on its practice and determined seven rites as uniquely sacraments.

EARLY-TWENTIETH-CENTURY TREATMENTS OF SACRAMENTS

While manuals for theological study still claimed the curriculum for seminaries and many Catholic universities through the 1960s, the early twentieth century saw the publication of "bridge-like" books on sacraments. These books combined the "classical" treatises on sacraments since Trent with information about sacraments resulting from the nineteenth-century research into Scripture and patristic sources. Two examples of such approaches follow.

PIERRE POURRAT (1871–1957)

Theology of the Sacraments by Pourrat, rector of the seminary in Lyons, France, was published in 1910. The subtitle of this text, *A Study in Positive Theology*, aptly summarizes what it contained. Its seven chapters deal with what are familiar concepts about sacraments as defined and described at the Council of Trent. What was unique at the time was the way the author relied heavily on the data from earlier, largely patristic sources to elaborate on these concepts. The chapters deal with "a sacrament defined," "the composition of sacramental rites," "the efficacy of sacraments," "the sacramental character," "the number of sacraments," "the divine institution of sacraments," and "the intention of the minister and recipient." An example of the way Pourrat fleshes out the discussion about and experience of sacraments prior to Trent is "the efficacy of the sacraments." In this chapter, the author begins with the definition from Trent (recall especially canon 6). Then Pourrat takes a veritable historical tour from Tertullian through St. Augustine and the Donatist controversy, to efficacy as described in early medieval and medieval authors to Trent. Toward the end of this chapter, he describes the evolution and meaning of the phrase *ex opere operato*, as well as several theories about sacramental causality (specifically what he calls "moral" and "physical" causality) and the grace produced in sacraments.

BERNARD J. LEEMING (1893–1971)

The book *Principles of Sacramental Theology* by Leeming, the former faculty member of Heythrop College in London, is among the most complete expositions of the sacraments prior to Vatican II. The author states that the general plan for each chapter is to give something of the history of the question at hand, for example, causality, matter, form, intention of the minister, and the different views held (recall the example in chapter 6 about sacramental causality). Then he asserts the church's official position, explains reasons for it, and indicates what might cause some confusion. He summarizes and wisely uses historical data combined with the official magisterium.

Leeming's outline expands on that of Pourrat but still holds to what would be presumed in pre–Vatican II treatments of sacraments.

1. The sacraments and grace. He examines objective efficacy of sacraments, *ex opere operato*, using infant baptism as an example of the efficacy of sacraments. The author then describes how "sacramental" grace is something in the soul that results from receiving a particular sacrament.

2. The sacraments and character. He asserts that the purpose of sacraments is not merely to give the holiness of grace, but also to give in baptism, confirmation, and orders a distinctive and irrevocable mark so that they are not repeated.

3. Sacramental causality. Here, the author argues against the "moral causality" view that sacraments are "occasions" for grace, but rather that sacraments themselves cause grace by being God's instruments. He relies on the terminology of *res et sacramentum*. In asserting the ecclesiological nature of sacramental causality, Leeming reflects on the beginning of the influence of the classical descriptions of sacramental liturgy from the patristic era through the Scholastics. This book also shows the influence of Pope Pius XII's teaching on liturgy and the church (below).

4. The institution of the sacraments. Leeming is very nuanced here in asserting that institution by Christ does not necessarily mean that Christ determined the exact matter and form of the rite of the sacraments.

5. The requirements of the minister. The author deals with the intention to do what the church does, that the minister is presumed to be doing what the church intends and that the validity of sacraments does not depend on the moral goodness of the minister.

6. The sacramental economy (where "economy" means the giving over of the fruits of Christ's paschal mystery to believers). Here, he treats the seven sacraments, the definition of "sacrament," and the interface of sacraments and human nature.

As these (and other) theologians made progress toward reviving theology based on a return to the Bible and patristic sources, the popes in the twentieth century took important initiatives on sacramental practices leading up to the Constitution on the Sacred Liturgy (1963) of Vatican II.

PAPAL TEACHING AND LEADERSHIP ON THE LITURGY

First, Pope Benedict XIV (1675–1758) should be mentioned for his significance in anticipating the trend of thought that would develop beginning with Pope Pius X in the early twentieth century. When it comes to delineating the theology of sacraments in general or the theology of specific sacraments, there is always a dialectic to be kept in balance—theory and practice. In addition to the theological developments made during this period, which broke through a post-Tridentine and highly Scholastic mindset, changes started to be made in the liturgy as codified after Trent, all with important theological consequences. For example, in the years following the Council of Trent, the church's theology of the Eucharist emphasized two things: real presence and sacrifice. These were a condensed version of the principal themes taught in the documents of the Council of Trent and came to be the emphasis in catechizing the faithful. It was clear that frequent reception of communion by the lay faithful was still far from the normal practice. In addition, while priests customarily received communion under both the species of bread and wine consecrated at the Mass they were celebrating, when the laity received communion it was customary for them to receive from consecrated hosts (and not wine) reserved in the tabernacle. In 1742, Pope Benedict XIV decreed that the laity should be encouraged to receive communion frequently, a theme that is taken up forcefully in the early twentieth century (at least in theory) by Pope Pius X. He also decreed that when the laity received communion, they should do so from hosts consecrated at the same Mass at which they participated and not from those reserved in the tabernacle. He judged that the practice of the priest celebrating the Mass and receiving from that Mass while the laity received from the tabernacle was to separate what was inseparable. In other words, the Mass as the unbloody *sacrifice* of Calvary, celebrated by a priest, would be seen to be separate from the reception of communion, the real *presence* of

Christ in the tabernacle. He taught that the "one and the same sacrifice is shared" in the Mass and that all should receive communion from that Mass. Thus, liturgical practices affect how we understand the theology of sacraments. This principle will become apparent as papal thought unfolds in the twentieth century.

Pope Pius X (1835–1914) made several important contributions to the celebration of the liturgy and toward explaining its meaning. In his 1903 *motu proprio* on sacred music, *Tra le sollecitunidi*, the pope asserted that the liturgy was the "true and indispensable source for the Christian life," and he called for "active participation in the sacred mysteries." These phrases soon became benchmarks for the twentieth-century liturgical movement and undergirded changes in the liturgy that were aimed toward making this "true and indispensable source for the Christian life" more readily accessible to all. "Active participation in the sacred mysteries" should be understood as an important experience of Christ's paschal mystery by everyone.

Pope Pius XII (1876–1958) issued three encyclicals that were important milestones in the church's evolution in the mid-twentieth century toward realizing the liturgical reforms of Vatican II. In 1943, the pope issued *Mystici Corporis* ("On the Mystical Body of Christ"), which endorsed the kind of theological scholarship that developed in the late nineteenth century. This encyclical emphasized that every person—ordained and lay—was a member of the Body of Christ and that one of the most important tenets of Catholicism is this sense of belonging to Christ in the church. This secured and solidified the intrinsic relationship of liturgy and ecclesiology.

Also in 1943, Pope Pius XII issued *Divino Afflanto Spiritu*, part of whose subtitle was "on promoting biblical studies." In this encyclical, he gave due credit to Pope Pius X, who fostered biblical scholarship and founded the Pontifical Biblical Institute, and he endorsed and supported efforts being undertaken on the pastoral level toward Bible study as sponsored by many of the leaders of the liturgical movement.

In 1947, the encyclical *Mediator Dei* ("Mediator between God and Man") affirmed the intimate connection between Christology and the liturgy. The true *mediator* between God and the human race is Christ. The way we experience Christ is in the communion of the church celebrated in and through the sacred liturgy. One of the emphases in this document was on the importance of active participation.

By issuing these three encyclicals, Pius XII put in place the three elements that had characterized the twentieth-century liturgical movement: ecclesiology, Scripture, and liturgy. These elements would lead to the kind of theological exposition about liturgy and sacraments embodied in *Sacrosanctum Concilium* at Vatican II.

As early as 1942, Pius XII was considering a complete reform of the liturgy, including sacramental practice. In 1946, he decreed that there should be "a special commission of experts…to reflect on the general reform of the liturgy and offer concrete proposals." Formed in 1948 and named the Pian Commission, this group worked under the Congregation of Rites for twelve years until 1960—two years after Pius XII died and one year after his successor, Pope John XXIII, announced the convening of the Second Vatican Council.

Part of the work of the Pian Commission concerned Holy Week. Over centuries and for a variety of reasons, the celebration of the Easter Vigil at night, common in patristic times and customary now, had evolved to a morning Mass on Holy Saturday at which few people participated. The Lenten fast, which was far more rigorous then than now, ended at noon on Holy Saturday. The revision of the Easter Vigil in 1951 restored it to an evening service, the end of which marked the end of the Lenten fast. Then, in 1955, the whole Easter Triduum—the "three days" from Holy Thursday Evening Mass through Good Friday to the Easter Vigil—was restored and came to be reemphasized as the church's most important "high holy days."

TWO EXAMPLES

The Roman Breviary was published in 1568 and the Roman Missal in 1570. However, each underwent some changes up to 1962, among which were additions of feasts for saints and changes to the calendar of the saints. These Tridentine books were replaced by the liturgies revised after Vatican II and the implementation of the reformed liturgies after Vatican II.

With regard to the Breviary, both Pius X and Pius XII effected the rearrangement of some (parts) of the Psalms and the reduction of psalms that had been used more than once during a week at a time when the Office operated on a weekly instead of monthly cycle (as revised by Vatican II). Their efforts, in effect, aimed at a reduction of duplications and thereby shortened parts of the Breviary. One of the reasons was to insure that parish priests who recited the Breviary on their own would not feel overburdened with this prayer given their pastoral responsibilities. The Latin Vulgate Psalter, mandated for use in the post-Tridentine Roman Breviary, was then revised for liturgical use as the revised Latin Vulgate Psalter.

As already seen, the reforms of the Easter Triduum comprised significant changes in the Roman Missal. Other reforms included the addition of the name of St. Joseph, foster father of Jesus, to the Roman Canon, as mandated by Pope John XXIII. (Some argue that this was done during the debates about the sacred liturgy at Vatican II to illustrate the point that the liturgies could, in fact, be changed. Such was the fierce loyalty to the reformed liturgies after Trent.) Other changes in the Missal and Breviary included the addition of saints' feast days. Today the Mass revised and celebrated after the Council of Trent is called the extraordinary form of the Roman Mass. Yet, the edition that is required to be used is that published in 1962 (not 1570), which itself is an attestation that what is often argued to have been a rigidly fixed liturgy from Trent was, in effect, a liturgy that itself underwent changes. For example, some of the saints were added to the calendar because they were canonized after Trent. The Feasts of the Immaculate Conception and the Assumption had to be added after these dogmas were affirmed in 1854 and 1950, respectively.

DISCUSSION QUESTIONS

1. In the rite for infant baptism celebrated prior to Vatican II, the parents of the children are never addressed, but their

godparents are. What does this mean and how does this influence the revised rite for the baptism of children used today?

2. We have used the phrase *adopt and adapt* to describe how the liturgy of the sacraments evolved from one period to another. Discuss how this same phrase could be used to describe the evolution of theology and liturgy in the nineteenth and twentieth centuries.

3. The liturgies of the Easter triduum are the Evening Mass of the Lord's Supper on Holy Thursday, the Celebration of the Passion of the Lord on Good Friday, and the Easter Vigil on Holy Saturday night. Have you ever participated in them? What made the strongest impression on you and why?

8

VATICAN II

The purpose of this chapter is to summarize the teaching from the
Constitution on the Sacred Liturgy of Vatican II on the theology of the
liturgy and the sacraments, its instruction that all the liturgical rites of
the church should be revised, the indications the council fathers gave
as to the nature of the reforms, and then the process that led to the
revisions. The present rites for the liturgy in the Catholic Church in
use today were revised as a result of this Constitution. The last section
of this chapter summarizes a number of valuable approaches to sacramental theology that have emerged during and in light of Vatican II.

VATICAN II

No church council comes out of a vacuum. As we saw in chapter 6, the teachings of the Council of Trent need to be read in light of
the critiques and polemics that preceded them in the Reformation.
The historical and theological context of Vatican II was very different.
St. John XXIII called the Council so that the church could deal more
effectively with the challenges and opportunities of "the church in the
modern world" (which is a subtitle for one of its four constitutions,
Gaudium et Spes). Among the reasons Pope John XXIII gave for summoning the Council was that the church needed to read "the signs of
the times." Thus, the way the church presented the faith to his and
every generation has need of evaluation. The content and the deposit
of faith are to be preserved, but the idioms and the way it is presented
should always be new and fresh.

We noted in chapter 6 on the magisterial teachings of Trent that
one needs to distinguish between the *canons* of the Council of Trent and

the *decrees* of the Council. With regard to Vatican II, the council fathers issued sixteen documents, but not all of the same theological "weight." The four *constitutions* carry the greatest theological weight; then there were nine *decrees* and three *declarations*. The fact that the document on the liturgy is a constitution (entitled *Sacrosanctum Concilium*, meaning "this sacred council") indicated that the liturgy was of the highest importance in the life of the church. The constitution's declaration that "the liturgy is the summit toward which the activity of the Church is directed; at the same time it is the font from which all her power flows" (no. 10) reflects the centrality of the liturgy in the life of the church. (At times, this is summarized by the phrase "apex and font" or "summit and source.")

In addition to the Constitution on the Sacred Liturgy specifically, the other constitutions from the Council form what might be called the four pillars of the Council's teaching, and what each of them says about the liturgy and sacraments is very important. The other constitutions are the Dogmatic Constitution on the Church (*Lumen Gentium*), the Dogmatic Constitution on Divine Revelation (*Dei Verbum*), and the Pastoral Constitution on the Church in the Modern World (*Gaudium et Spes*). In fact, the Constitution on the Sacred Liturgy and the Dogmatic Constitution on the Church are often very closely linked because of the intrinsic interrelationship between church and liturgy. The Dogmatic Constitution on Divine Revelation is crucially important because it signaled a major reemphasis on the word of God in the life of the Catholic Church (especially as proclaimed in all the revised liturgies). The Pastoral Constitution on the Church in the Modern World provides the church's assessment of the context in which all liturgy takes place, in the daily lives of believers whose mission is to live in life what they celebrate in faith. (This will be delineated in future chapters.)

One example of the interrelationship of the liturgy and the church is in *Lumen Gentium*'s summary about the sacraments. It first distinguishes between the ordained priesthood and the priesthood of the faithful: "Though they differ from one another in essence and not only in degree, the common priesthood of the faithful and the ministerial or hierarchical priesthood are nonetheless interrelated: each of them in its own special way is a participation in the one priesthood of Christ" (no. 10). It then continues,

It is through the sacraments and the exercise of the virtues that the sacred nature and organic structure of the priestly community is brought into operation. Incorporated in the Church through baptism, the faithful are destined by the baptismal character for the worship of the Christian religion; reborn as sons of God they must confess before men the faith which they have received from God through the Church. They are more perfectly bound to the Church by the sacrament of Confirmation, and the Holy Spirit endows them with special strength so that they are more strictly obliged to spread and defend the faith, both by word and by deed, as true witnesses of Christ. Taking part in the Eucharistic sacrifice, which is the fount and apex of the whole Christian life, they offer the Divine Victim to God, and offer themselves along with It. Thus both by reason of the offering and through Holy Communion all take part in this liturgical service, not indeed, all in the same way but each in that way which is proper to himself. Strengthened in Holy Communion by the Body of Christ, they then manifest in a concrete way that unity of the people of God which is suitably signified and wondrously brought about by this most august sacrament.

Those who approach the sacrament of Penance obtain pardon from the mercy of God for the offense committed against Him and are at the same time reconciled with the Church, which they have wounded by their sins, and which by charity, example, and prayer seeks their conversion. By the sacred anointing of the sick and the prayer of her priests the whole Church commends the sick to the suffering and glorified Lord, asking that He may lighten their suffering and save them; she exhorts them, moreover, to contribute to the welfare of the whole people of God by associating themselves freely with the passion and death of Christ. Those of the faithful who are consecrated by Holy

Orders are appointed to feed the Church in Christ's name with the word and the grace of God. Finally, Christian spouses, in virtue of the sacrament of Matrimony, whereby they signify and partake of the mystery of that unity and fruitful love which exists between Christ and His Church, help each other to attain to holiness in their married life and in the rearing and education of their children. By reason of their state and rank in life they have their own special gift among the people of God. From the wedlock of Christians there comes the family, in which new citizens of human society are born, who by the grace of the Holy Spirit received in baptism are made children of God, thus perpetuating the people of God through the centuries. The family is, so to speak, the domestic church. In it parents should, by their word and example, be the first preachers of the faith to their children; they should encourage them in the vocation which is proper to each of them, fostering with special care vocation to a sacred state. (no. 11)

CONSTITUTION ON THE SACRED LITURGY

The Constitution on the Sacred Liturgy ushered in a new era for the church's celebration of the liturgy and sacraments. Its first chapter offers both a synthesis of what the liturgy is and does (nos. 1–20) and general principles for the reform of the liturgy (nos. 21–46). Chapters 2 to 7 specify the areas requiring liturgical reform and offer general principles for this task. Clearly this Constitution, the other decrees from Vatican II, and the theological preparations for the Council mark a watershed in the church's self-understanding in general and for liturgical-sacramental practice and theology in particular.

That this was the first document to be issued from the Second Vatican Council is reflected in its opening paragraph, which capsulizes the self-described aims of the Council and the role of the sacred liturgy in them. Notable here is the wide church and ecumenical context in which the fathers place the liturgy:

This sacred Council has several aims in view: it desires to impart an ever increasing vigor to the Christian life of the faithful; to adapt more suitably to the needs of our own times those institutions which are subject to change; to foster whatever can promote union among all who believe in Christ; to strengthen whatever can help to call the whole of mankind into the household of the Church. The Council therefore sees particularly cogent reasons for undertaking the reform and promotion of the liturgy. (*Sacrosanctum Concilium* 1)

This leads to a brief but very important set of assertions about the theology of the liturgy through which "the work of our redemption is accomplished" (no. 2)—an expression that offers a simple yet profound assertion about the importance of the liturgy. (Compare the prayer over the offerings for the Evening Mass of the Lord's Supper and the prayer over the offerings of the Christmas Vigil Mass, "the beginning of our redemption.")

The statements embedded in no. 2 can be understood to be truly sacramental by the way they reflect about things human and divine, visible and invisible. Sacraments reveal but also lead to the fullness of revelation in the kingdom of heaven.

Chapter 1 of the Constitution, "General Principles for the Restoration and Promotion of the Sacred Liturgy" (nos. 5–46), contains very important information that grounds the reform of the liturgy. This section should be read and studied as the foundation for the instructions on the revision of the sacramental rites. Published in 1963, the Constitution on the Sacred Liturgy led to several subsequent documents reforming the liturgy and commenting about it. As will become clear in what follows, several other documents need to be consulted when studying the reformed liturgies from Vatican II.

MANIFOLD PRESENCE

Among the more notable statements of the Constitution are those about the manifold presence of Christ in the liturgy (no. 7), especially the way the text as worded shows respect for and reliance on the teachings from Trent but then builds on them. Christ is present in the priest ("minister") and the eucharistic species (from Trent), as well as in the proclamation of the word and in the church itself. This is certainly a watershed set of statements, especially when compared with Trent, and it is later expanded upon in no. 35. That our sanctification is accomplished by "signs perceptible to the senses" reflects the constant teaching of the church, as well as a reminder that liturgy is an action that involves all our senses and our intellect. This is also fleshed out more fully in no. 30, which concerns "actions, gestures, bodily attitudes."

ESCHATOLOGY

Paragraph 8 carefully points out that the liturgy is always the threshold of heaven. In reference to the sacraments, this means that there is an "already" and "here and now" aspect to the sacraments, as well as a "not yet" and a "future glory" aspect to them. This parallels no. 2 about human and divine, visible and invisible. (More on this in chapter 18.)

LITURGY, LIFE, AND OTHER PRAYER

Paragraphs 9 and 11, which surround the reference to "summit and source" in no. 10, state that the Christian life involves liturgy *and* concern for others *and* other kinds of prayer. This reflects the presumed life context for the liturgy, the challenge that liturgy always requires living the sacrificial Christian life, and the challenge that liturgy needs to be supported by other kinds of prayer. That these can include devotions is stated in no. 13; however, the paragraph offers the caution that devotions should be harmonized with the liturgy and not take its place. Again, the liturgy takes priority.

PARTICIPATION

The following paragraphs about the supreme importance of active participation in the liturgy demanded by the nature of the liturgy itself (no. 14), as well as the instruction of the faithful about the liturgy (nos. 15–19), are central to the post–Vatican II reform of the liturgy. While the emphasis in nos. 15–19 is primarily on pastors and the training of clerics, this can and should be applied to all the baptized, especially those who serve in liturgical ministries, as pointed out in no. 19.

ALL LITURGIES REVISED

In no. 21, the council fathers make the following statement, brief but with significant impact on the church: "In order that the Christian people may more certainly derive an abundance of graces from the sacred liturgy, holy Mother Church desires to undertake with great care a general restoration of the liturgy itself." This is further amplified: "The liturgical books are to be revised as soon as possible; experts are to be employed on the task, and bishops are to be consulted, from various parts of the world" (no. 25).

Vatican II was the first event in the church's life that undertook to revise all of its liturgies at the same time. The process was nothing less than herculean, the implementation is ongoing, and the consequences will be felt by generations of Catholics yet to come.

The council fathers assert the following as a major principle for this reform:

> For the liturgy is made up of immutable elements divinely instituted, and of elements subject to change. These not only may but ought to be changed with the passage of time if they have suffered from the intrusion of anything out of harmony with the inner nature of the liturgy or have become unsuited to it.
>
> In this restoration, both texts and rites should be drawn up so that they express more clearly the holy things which they signify; the Christian people, so far as possible, should be enabled to understand them with ease and to take part in them fully, actively, and as befits a community. (no. 21)

Each of these statements deserves to be reflected upon because they all required (and require) that the procedure of the reform be based on historical data and on value judgments based on that data and on pastoral concerns. Hence, the liturgy is tradition-based but not a museum piece. The revised rites are largely from traditional sources, and yet they were also revised to suit contemporary needs. This is deepened in no. 23:

> That sound tradition may be retained, and yet the way remain open to legitimate progress careful investigation is always to be made into each part of the liturgy which is to be revised. This investigation should be theological, historical, and pastoral. Also the general laws governing the structure and meaning of the liturgy must be studied in conjunction with the experience derived from recent liturgical reforms and from the indults conceded to various places. Finally, there must be no innovations unless the good of the Church genuinely and certainly requires them; and care must be taken that any new forms adopted should in some way grow organically from forms already existing.

LITURGY AND ECCLESIOLOGY

In nos. 26–29, the council fathers profess the essentially ecclesial nature of all liturgy. Paragraph 27 still offers food for thought and motivation for action: "It is to be stressed that whenever rites, according to their specific nature, make provision for communal celebration involving the presence and active participation of the faithful, this way of celebrating them is to be preferred, so far as possible, to a celebration that is individual and quasi-private." (More on this in chapter 17.)

"NOBLE" SIMPLICITY

Unlike some other liturgical families (for example, some Eastern rites and some non-Roman Western rites such as the Mozarabic in Spain), the Roman rite has been characterized by being fairly direct and straightforward. The council fathers put it this way: "The rites should be distinguished by a noble simplicity; they should be short, clear, and unencumbered by useless repetitions; they should be within the people's powers of comprehension, and normally should not require much explanation" (no. 34).

LATIN AND THE VERNACULAR

Paragraph 36 begins by asserting that "particular law remaining in force, the use of the Latin language is to be preserved in the Latin rites." It then indicates that the vernacular may be used given the judgment of bishops' conferences with the approval of the Apostolic See (the Vatican). Prior to Vatican II, several liturgies were regularly celebrated in the vernacular, among them baptism and marriage. While the Mass and the Divine Office were celebrated in Latin, vernacular hymns were regularly used at Mass, and some places took advantage of a 1958 decree from the Congregation for Rites that permitted parts of the Mass to be said in "dialogue," with the priest praying in the vernacular. However, shortly after the Constitution on the Sacred Liturgy was promulgated, bishops started receiving requests from the lay faithful for increased use of the vernacular in the liturgy, and the Roman authorities regularly gave approval. This is a clear example of where pronouncements in a Vatican II constitution have been amplified by further decisions made with church approval. Further on (in nos. 53–54), the use of the vernacular for the readings at Mass is endorsed.

UNITY, NOT "UNIFORMITY"

There is clearly one Roman rite with a normative Latin edition, or *editio typica,* for each rite published in accord with the directives of the Constitution on the Sacred Liturgy. However, the Constitution itself asserts that this does not mean rigid uniformity (no. 36), but that various cultures and places will adapt (or *inculturate,* to use the more precise term) the liturgy for particular locations. This process continues to occur with the church's authoritative approval. Thus, for example, translations into the vernacular languages themselves are affected, as are music, art, and architecture. The issue raised in no. 40 about "more radical adaptation" is very much a work in progress. In addition, the issue of "competent ecclesiastical authority" (which in the American context means the United States Conference of Catholic Bishops) in relation to the permission granted for such by "the Apostolic See" is also a work in progress. One example regarding a territorial adjustment to the Mass is the Vatican-approved Mass of the Roman Rite for the Dioceses of Zaire (1988). Another is the approval in the *Statutes* for the Neo-Catechumenal Way (2008, renewed 2013) for adjustments to the Roman Rite of the Mass, including the exchange of the sign of peace at the presentation of the gifts, that all stand for the Eucharistic Prayer, that all receive communion simultaneously in the hand, and so forth.

ONGOING REFORM

The reform of the liturgy was understood to be an ongoing process and not a one-time event; this is clear from the request that the bishop is to create a liturgical commission, a music commission, and a commission on sacred art. In effect, most dioceses in the United States have at least a liturgical commission, if not all three as decreed. This has also meant that the United States Conference of Catholic Bishops has a standing Committee on Divine Worship that has, to date, published guidelines on music in the liturgy (*Music in Catholic Worship, Liturgical Music Today,* and *Sing to the Lord*) and on art and architecture (*Environment and Art in Catholic Worship* and *Built of Living Stones*). That these base texts are very often supplemented by guidelines for a particular (arch)diocese shows the involvement of the local bishop and the commission(s) in his diocese carrying forward the ongoing reform of the liturgy.

LITURGY CONSTITUTION ON INDIVIDUAL SACRAMENTS

It would be very important to read each of the following chapters of the Constitution on the Sacred Liturgy to discover the salient points of what should be reformed in the church's sacramental rites along with the important theological teachings that guide them. Also, access to *The Rites of the Catholic Church as Revised by the Second Vatican Council* (or any other primary source for these rites) would be very helpful. Many of the rites for celebrating the sacraments have undergone a second revision that adjusted or amplified what was done in the first revision—for example, the celebration of the Eucharist as seen in the Roman Missal, rites of ordination, and so forth. Hence, it would be important to secure the latest version of the revised sacramental rites. The following are salient issues outlined in the Constitution about the revision of the sacramental rites:

1. The Eucharist (chapter 2, nos. 47–58)
   a. Theology of the Eucharist
   Paragraphs 47 and 48 set the theological tone for what the Eucharist is and the way the Mass should be revised. (Since these are particularly dense theologically, the text is broken down and comments made on individual phrases. Italics added.)
   No. 47: Christ instituted the Eucharist "in order to *perpetuate*…"
   meaning that it is not repeated, reenacted, or redone, but that it is the very same sacrifice perpetuated over the centuries in the Mass
   "the sacrifice of the Cross throughout the centuries *until He should come again*…"
   eschatology, the "not yet-ness" of all sacraments, always in joyful hope for the coming of our Savior
   "and so to entrust to His beloved spouse, the Church…"
   the intrinsic connection always to be presumed and experienced between liturgy and the church
   "a *memorial* of His death and resurrection…"
   recall the treatment of biblical memorial in chapter 1
   "a sacrament of *love*, a sign of *unity*, a bond of *charity*…"
   descriptions of God's gifts to the church through the Eucharist
   "a *paschal banquet*…"
   all liturgy is paschal, about Christ's paschal mystery and our paschal victory through, with, and in him
   "in which Christ is eaten, the mind is filled with grace, and a pledge of future glory is given to us."
   taken from St. Thomas Aquinas's antiphon for the Feast of Corpus Christi about the past, present, and future of the paschal mystery.

No. 48: "The Church, therefore, earnestly desires that
Christ's faithful, when present at this mystery of faith,
should not be there as strangers or silent spectators; on
the contrary, through a good understanding of the rites
and prayers they should take part in the sacred action
conscious of what they are doing, with devotion and
full collaboration…"

> emphasizes participation as a key theological factor
> as opposed to the kind of passivity in terms of voice,
> gesture, and movement encouraged by the Tridentine
> liturgies; again, active participation should reflect
> that we "take part in the mystery of God" through
> Christ in the power of the Holy Spirit in the liturgy.

"They should be instructed by God's word…"

> emphasis on the proclamation of the word at every
> Mass in such a way as to make it comprehensible
> and accessible to all participating

"and be nourished at the table of the Lord's body…"

> important emphasis that the Eucharist is a sacred
> meal

"they should give thanks to God; by offering the
Immaculate Victim, not only through the hands of the
priest, but also with him…"

> a very important reminder that the ordained and
> baptized priests offer the Mass together, through
> their different roles and ministries; the baptized laity
> is not passive

"they should learn also to offer themselves…"

> the offering at Mass should also be reflected in the
> offering of self as a living sacrifice (see Rom 12:1)

"through Christ the Mediator…"

> important reference to "Christ" as opposed to
> "Jesus," since our worship is always in and through
> the risen Christ, who is our eternal high priest and
> mediator of all grace (recall that the title of Pius XII's
> encyclical is *Mediator Dei*)

"they should be drawn day by day into ever more perfect union with God and with each other…"

important emphasis on union with God and each
other: theology and ecclesiology always operative in
the sacraments

"so that finally God may be all in all."

ends with eschatology again when this world has
come to an end, and we are all called to the kingdom of heaven forever

b. Specific Reforms of the Mass

Liturgy of the Word (nos. 51–53)

- These paragraphs led to the creation of a lectionary
  with a three-year cycle of Scripture readings for
  Sundays and a two-year cycle of Scripture readings
  for weekdays, as well as special readings for solemnities and feasts (most also on a three-year cycle)
  and proper weekdays for saints' feasts (when they
  are celebrated on weekdays).

- The restoration of the homily at Mass (and all sacraments) has been one of the major and noted revisions of the Mass.

Communion (no. 55)

- This section reiterates what had been taught by
  popes since Benedict XIV and in all post–Vatican II
  documents on the Mass: the lay faithful are to
  receive communion from hosts consecrated at the
  same Mass in which they participate.

- It indicates tentative first steps toward reviving the
  practice of receiving communion under both
  species. These examples led to a much wider experience of distributing under both forms in the *General
  Instruction of the Roman Missal* 283, which has been
  supplemented by the U.S. Bishops Document
  Norms for the Distribution and Reception of Holy
  Communion under Both Kinds in the Dioceses of
  the United States of America (see nos. 27–54), which
  expands the practice even further.

Word and Eucharist Together (no. 56)

- This statement that Word and Eucharist form one

act of worship is very important theologically, liturgically, and pastorally.

- It is important theologically because it emphasizes the importance of the act of proclaiming the Sacred Scriptures at Mass and in all liturgies. The word is not to be seen as an appendage before the sacrament occurs. The word is now seen to be constitutive of the act of sacramental liturgy.

- It is important liturgically because the revision of all liturgical and sacramental rites after the Council involved research into what readings had been used at what liturgies and then assessment of what should be in the revised books of readings at the sacraments, for example the *Lectionary for Mass*. This also led to the restoration of the role of reader at Mass (and all liturgies) so that the priest himself is not seen to be the only one who enacts the liturgy, but that the liturgy is enacted by a number of people in the gathered assembly who have specific ministries.

- It is important pastorally because it overcomes the post-Tridentine practice that understood the three principal parts of the Mass to be offertory, consecration, and (priest's) communion. If anyone was present for these three parts of the Mass, they would have fulfilled their Sunday obligation. Knowing that much of the rhetoric during the Reformation concerned the proclamation of the word puts this in context: after the Reformation, the essential parts of the Mass did not include the word, although non-Roman Catholic worship services did, so much so that it was not uncommon for the churches of the Reformation to celebrate the Eucharist only four times a year and at Christmas and Easter.

Concelebration (nos. 57–58)

This very ancient practice is here revived. The indications of when it could be done have been greatly enhanced to the extent that it is commonplace today.

2. The Sacraments (nos. 59–78)

    a. Theology of the Sacraments

- As we saw above from the Dogmatic Constitution on the Church, so here the Constitution on the Sacred Liturgy begins with some general comments about the sacraments (no. 59):

- The purpose of the sacraments is to sanctify men, to build up the Body of Christ, and finally, to give worship to God; because they are signs, they also instruct. They not only presuppose faith, but by words and objects, they also nourish, strengthen, and express it; that is why they are called "sacraments of faith." They do indeed impart grace, but in addition, the very act of celebrating them most effectively disposes the faithful to receive this grace in a fruitful manner, to worship God duly, and to practice charity.

    Disposition and Sacramentality (no. 61)

- Paragraph 61 deals with proper dispositions in an invitational, pastoral way. The background here is how sacraments function with intention — they are not automatic or magic.

- It underscores how we use things from creation in worship.

    b. Specific Reforms of the Sacraments

    Adult Initiation (nos. 64–66)

- The restoration of the catechumenate for adults recalls the common practice in the early church, as described in chapter 3 regarding St. Cyril of Jerusalem. In 1966, in fact, Pope Paul VI gave permission for a proposed rite to be used on an experimental basis in fifty "catechumenal centers" in Japan, Mali, Togo, the Ivory Coast, Upper Volta, Rwanda, Congo, Zaire, Belgium, Canada, France, and the United States. In 1968, the group charged with this revision met to discuss reports from these centers, and their insights helped shape the final version of the Rite in use today. This recalls the premise that throughout history the church has *adopted* and *adapted* rites.

- The scope and practice of the Order for the Christian Initiation for Adults varies. But along with the progressive assimilation of other Christians into the Catholic church (no. 66) through formation sessions and rites, this stands as a major shift in how "converts" are welcomed into the church, emphasizing communal belonging from the very beginning.

Infant Baptism (no. 67)

- In the history of the church, there was never a rite composed for the baptism of infants. It was always a condensed version of adult baptism with the emphasis on the godparents. This new rite is based on ancient sources and practices but puts the emphasis on the child's parents first and foremost, then on the godparents.
- That there are several forms of the new rite indicate a number of things about the theology of the sacrament, including the recommendation that baptism should be celebrated at a communal celebration that includes a Liturgy of the Word and the participation of a number of ministers.

    (1) Rite of Baptism for Several Children; (2) Rite of Baptism for One Child; again presumes a communal celebration; (3) Rite of Baptism for a large number of children; (4) Rite of Baptism administered by a Catechist when no Priest or Deacon is available; (5) Rite of Baptism for Children in Danger of Death when no Priest or Deacon is available.

- That it can be celebrated at a Mass is a clear liturgical demonstration of the theology that baptism leads to Eucharist.
- When not celebrated at a Mass, the procession from the baptismal font to the altar area and the recitation in common of the Lord's Prayer is another pastoral demonstration of this theology.

Confirmation (no. 71)

- The new rite for confirmation is celebrated for

those baptized as infants. That it has been revised to reflect that confirmation is closely connected with initiation draws on the patristic data and experience of celebrating this as part of the baptism-confirmation-Eucharist sequence (recall chapter 3 on St. Cyril of Jerusalem).

- This changes the focus from the medieval emphasis on confirmation as a means of strengthening one to defend the faith. When the rite was revised, however, pastoral provision was made to defer the celebration of the sacrament from between baptism and Eucharist to adolescence. This means that there are varying ages for the celebration of confirmation depending on the diocese in which one resides.

Penance (no. 72)

- The revision of the rite for penance contains four forms, and each contains the word *reconciliation*, judged to be more apt to describe the effect of the sacrament.

  (1) Rite of Reconciliation of Individual Penitents; (2) Rite of Reconciliation for Several Penitents with Individual Confession and Absolution; (3) Rite for Reconciliation of Several Penitents with General Absolution; (4) Various (biblical and liturgical) texts used in a celebration of (nonsacramental) reconciliation.

- That three out of the four rites here are communal makes a statement about the value of communal celebration of sacraments (noted in no. 27 above).

- That all of the four rites contain a celebration of the word as constitutive of the celebration makes a theological statement about the value of the proclamation of the word in sacramental liturgy. Penitents, however, do not always engage in such a proclamation and reflection when they celebrate the first of these rites (for individuals), this is something that needs pastoral attention in many places.

Anointing of the Sick (nos. 73–75)

- The change from the term *extreme unction* to *anointing of the sick* for this rite and the revision of the rites marks another major adjustment in sacramental practice. The name for the revised rite, *Pastoral Care of the Sick: Rites of Anointing and Viaticum,* is significant theologically and pastorally: it means that other ministers besides the priest can conduct visits to the sick (by using chapters 1–3).
- The communal character of the sacraments, such as penance, is demonstrated by the fact that the anointing of the sick (chapter 1) is envisioned to take place outside of Mass, or within Mass, and at a hospital or other institution.
- The value of understanding this sacrament primarily as a liturgy, and by exception for individuals alone, is underscored by the inclusion of a proclamation of the word and additional prayers.
- That chapter 2 is designed for the pastoral care of the dying and the celebration of viaticum demonstrates how important the Eucharist is, especially at the end of life. Two forms of viaticum are offered, one at Mass and one outside of Mass. The second form begins with a rite of sprinkling with holy water, thus indicating the close connection between baptism and Eucharist, here with viaticum as the last time one receives the Eucharist.
- The chapters on the commendation of the dying and prayers for the dead are rich in their paschal theology and can be used by anyone who is with the dying, including family members.
- The last chapter of the revised rite acknowledges emergencies that call for adapted rites for the commendation of the dying; among these rites are the celebration of penance and anointing together and Christian initiation for the dying (including baptism, confirmation, and viaticum).

Ordination (no. 76)

- The very modest suggestion that the "ceremonies

and texts for ordination rites should be revised" led to a number of revised rites (in the Roman Pontifical).

- In the Dogmatic Constitution on the Church (no. 29), the council fathers called for the restoration of the permanent diaconate. This required a revised rite to suit this new church order.
- What also occurred was that while investigating the history of holy orders, it was discovered that what was called the first of the major orders (subdeacon, deacon, priest) was, in fact, not always judged to be a major order and that the more ancient evidence was that the major orders were really diaconate, presbyterate/priesthood, and episcopacy. Those in charge of revising the ordination rites (more on the process below) requested and received the Holy See's approval to eliminate the subdiaconate and present new rites for the ordination of deacon, presbyter/priest, and bishop.
- The rite for the ordination of permanent deacons— that is, deacons who will not be ordained presbyters/priests—is distinguished from the rite for the ordination of transitional deacons, or deacons who will later be ordained presbyters/priests.

Marriage (nos. 77–78)

- The fairly straightforward statement (no. 77) that "the marriage rite now found in the Roman Ritual is to be revised and enriched in such a way that the grace of the sacrament is more clearly signified and the duties of the spouses are taught" is followed by the allowance that "the competent territorial ecclesiastical authority...is free to draw up its own rite suited to the usages of place and people....But, the rite must always conform to the law that the priest assisting at the marriage must ask for and obtain the consent of the contracting parties." This is an example of the kind of inculturation envisioned earlier in the Constitution, especially in no. 40.
- The theological value of the proclamation of the

word leading to the specific sacramental rite is affirmed by the placement of the rite of marriage after the homily and before the presentation of the gifts when celebrated at Mass and after the Liturgy of the Word when Mass is not celebrated. This conforms to all the other revised rites described above. (This will be discussed more fully in chapter 13).

- The church's pastoral concern for Catholics wishing to enter into matrimony in an ecumenical or interreligious context is demonstrated by the provision, in the revised rite for marriage, for a marriage between a Catholic and an unbaptized person (chapter three of the rite).

POST–VATICAN II PROCESS FOR THE REVISION OF THE SACRAMENTS—THE CONSILIUM

The implementation of these directives from the Constitution on the Sacred Liturgy took place over the decade following its promulgation, by which time all the *liturgical* rites of the church had been issued in Latin and most translated into the vernacular. At the risk of oversimplifying what was a complex and not always uniform process, the following outlines the phases for these revisions.

In 1964, Pope Paul VI established an agency to oversee the revision of the liturgy called the Consilium—technically *Consilium ad exsequendam Constitutionem de sacra Liturgia*. Under the Consilium, forty study groups (Latin: *coetus*) were assigned to study a sacrament or a part of a liturgical book in the work toward its revision. Those chosen to work on these study groups were, by design, experts in a variety of fields: liturgy, sacramental theology, Scripture, canon law, and pastoral practice. In addition, several study groups gleaned important insight from others whose work and pastoral ministry were related to the proposed revisions: for example, nurses and doctors for the rite for the anointing of the sick. Among others, the following aspects of this work should be kept in mind.

An evolving process. No one could have predetermined the number of study groups that would be required to implement the Constitution on the Sacred Liturgy's request to revise all the liturgies. Nor could one have predicted the number of times a particular study group had to meet. At times, "sub" study groups were created for part of a revised rite. For example, the group charged with the revision of the Order of Mass added members to consider the possibility of adding Eucharistic Prayers to the Mass, whereas before there was one Eucharistic Prayer, often called the Roman Canon. At times, the membership of the study groups would change for a variety of reasons, such as health, prior commitments, or inability to travel to meetings that were largely held in Europe.

An interrelated process. Some topics and revisions would influence all liturgies, such as the revision of the Roman calendar. At other times, members of study groups would meet with members of other study groups for advice and collaboration.

A collaborative process. Because of the complex nature of the work and the specializations it required more often than not, more than one study group was constituted to deal with parts of the revised rite. For example, for the revision of the Roman Missal and the *Lectionary for Mass*, the following study groups were at work:

Group 1—The Roman calendar

Group 10—The Order of Mass (*Ordo Missae*)

Group 11—Scripture readings at Mass

Group 12—The Prayer of the Faithful ("the universal prayer")

Group 13—Revision of Votive Masses

Group 14—Music at Mass

Group 15—Overall structure of the Mass

Group 16—Concelebration and communion under both species

Group 17—Revision of particular rites, such as Holy Week

Group 18—The Common of the Missal and the Breviary

Group 18a—Revision of the prayers and prefaces with special attention to the prayers for Good Friday and the Chrism Mass

Trial Uses. An example of "trial uses" prior to implementing the reform was the fact that several Masses were celebrated with invited guests and experts, as well as Pope Paul VI himself.

Dates for Implementation. The timeline for revising and implementing the revised rites from Vatican II was not uniform and contains a number of stories, each proper to the specific rite at hand. For example, while it was hoped that the new Missal would be published in Latin in 1969, in fact it was promulgated in 1970, four hundred years after the publication of the Tridentine Missal. This led to the process of translating the rites into the vernacular languages. Sometimes this was done by a committee under a particular (geographical) conference of bishops—Italy or Germany, for example. (Spain was different because of the number of Spanish-speaking countries requiring different translations.) To oversee the translation of the Latin revised liturgies into English, the English-speaking bishops decided to collaborate and form one agency, the International Commission on English in the Liturgy.

Revising the Revisions. Almost all the revised liturgical rites since Vatican II have seen a subsequent revision that nuanced the prior rite. These are adaptations derived from the revision; they are not completely new books. For example, the Roman Missal published in 1970 went to a second edition in 1975 and then to a third in 2002, which was translated into English and promulgated in 2010.

VATICAN II—A NEW CONTEXT FOR SACRAMENTAL THEOLOGY

During and after Vatican II, sacramental theologians continued to work on new approaches to the discipline that would respect the tradition as well as open up fresh insights. For example, Raymond Vaillancourt and Kenan Osborne have elaborated on the contributions of both Schillebeeckx and Rahner. That Christ is the original sacrament (*Ursakrament*) and the church is the ground sacrament (*Grundsakrament*) of the seven ecclesial acts is commonly asserted today. The language of encounter and phenomenology also characterizes contemporary reflection on the dynamism of sacraments. Such an approach signals a shift from emphasizing Christ's presence in sacraments to the community's transformation through sacraments; it also marks a shift from emphasizing sacraments as things to sacraments as events.

Another recent avenue of approach to sacraments is symbolism. That sacraments are essentially symbolic actions that affect participants on many levels with their ambiguity and polyvalence is an important contribution in some contemporary theories, such as those of Louis-Marie Chauvet and David Power. The development of secularization theologies helped move theological reflection about grace and sacraments away from a cultic understanding to one wherein sacraments are viewed as strong moments of God's self-disclosure that occur throughout human life. This is influenced by Rahner's incarnational approach to theology, which holds that human nature has been redeemed and that grace is always available to redeemed creation through Christ. In this perspective, sacraments are not the exclusive channels of God's grace; yet they are central moments and privileged means of encountering God through Christ. Such an approach returns to the wide context of how God acts in creation, in the incarnation, and in the paschal mystery as the appropriate context for experiencing and interpreting sacraments as unique signs of God's grace and favor.

Another critique of a cultic notion of sacrament comes from liberation theologians such as Juan Luis Segundo, who try to determine the life relation of sacramental participation. They argue that a too-facile celebration of sacraments can numb consciences to the social and political realities of living the Christian life. The challenge that engagement in sacraments entails is to love the justice and peace of God's kingdom that is experienced in sacraments. The liberating power of sacraments is thus to be channeled into a way of living life that reveals the liberating power of God's justice and peace.

Inquiry into the human phenomenon involved in individual sacraments—for example, initiation, reconciliation, or taking on a new identity—has led some theologians to follow the seminal work of

Arnold van Gennep, in his book *Rites of Passage,* in emphasizing sacraments as rites of passage. While exact parallels between some of the sacraments and rites of passage are often hard to establish—for confirmation, for example—this avenue of inquiry is useful in emphasizing the life relations that sacraments articulate.

The fact that some Christians no longer participate in sacraments regularly because they see little or no value in them ("believers, not belongers" and "spiritual, but not religious") has led some theologians to reflect on this pastoral phenomenon and to attempt to articulate the importance of sacraments—for example, Raymond Vaillancourt, Henri Denis, and Raymond Didier. The relationship between evangelization and sacramental practice is raised as the relationship between sacramental celebration and a vibrant experience of church life. This also raises the delicate question of prerequisite faith for admission to sacraments, especially initiation. Some pastoral approaches, such as those by Christianne Brusselmans, find the method employed in the Order of the Christian Initiation for Adults (catechumenate, immediate ecclesial preparation, celebration, and mystagogy) a helpful model to follow in other sacraments.

The post–Vatican II proliferation of bilateral and multilateral ecumenical dialogues on the sacraments has ushered in a new era of speaking about them in ways that are often grounded in the tradition and yet had been neglected in the post-Reformation era. For example, the revival of the meaning of the Greek term *anamnesis* ("memorial") as a way of describing the memorial experienced in sacraments has occurred largely because of this ecumenical impetus. Max Thurian, among others, saw this as a way of transcending the terms of disagreement over the Eucharist between Protestant and Roman Catholic Churches.

Many liturgists argue that the tools of social science (for example, sociology and anthropology) should be utilized to interpret the data collected from observation in sacramental celebration in history to interpret the past (the work of Martin Stringer, for example; see the bibliography for all references in these paragraphs) and present (for example, Mary Collins) impact of the rites in order to develop an adequate method to deal with sacraments as enacted phenomena.

Contemporary writing on Spirit Christology and the role of the Holy Spirit in sacraments (by Edward Kilmartin, for example) has helped overcome the absence of such an emphasis in conventional understandings of sacraments. The example of the Eastern tradition in understanding sacraments as the work of the Holy Spirit helps Western theologians today to address this lack in its interpretation of sacraments.

Feminist voices such as those of Susan Ross and Susan Roll are not absent from sacramental conversations in contemporary monographs on the subject. At times, these approaches call for a more egalitarian approach to leading (or presiding at) the liturgies. That the language we commonly use in liturgy and sacraments can be heard differently by different people participating is an important caution, lest using the same terminology be perceived to mean the same thing for everyone.

While a completely satisfactory approach to the study of the sacraments has yet to emerge in the postconciliar church, the evidence of recent decades, particularly since and in light of Vatican II, attests to a growing maturity in the liturgical celebration of and theological reflection on sacraments.

That liturgical celebration can ground a helpful avenue for understanding sacraments is the thesis of part 2 that follows. Part 3 fleshes out the method argued there.

DISCUSSION QUESIONS

1. Explain the important relationship between the Vatican II constitutions on the Church and on the Sacred Liturgy.
2. How does an understanding of the liturgy and theology of sacraments in the patristic era (chapter 3) help to explain many of the liturgical reforms implemented after Vatican II?
3. The present post–Vatican II Rite of Penance contains rites for the reconciliation of penitents. What are the similarities and differences in meaning of the words *penance* and *reconciliation*?

Part Two
METHOD

9

LITURGICAL SACRAMENTAL THEOLOGY

Precedents and Present Rites

The purpose of this chapter is twofold: (1) to note some of the historical precedents and magisterial teachings for the liturgical theology of the sacraments that we will articulate in part 3 of this book, and (2) to present a summary of the contemporary liturgical sources on which this theology is based.

HISTORICAL PRECEDENTS

PATRISTIC ERA

The classic source for establishing the relationship between liturgy and theology is found in the phrase ascribed to Prosper of Aquitaine (390–455), who was a disciple of St. Augustine—"The law of prayer grounds [or establishes] the law of belief" (*ut legem credendi lex statuat supplicandi*). Yet it is commonly agreed that this is the first succinct articulation of what had, in fact, already been an accepted premise of theological argument. Evidence as early as Hippolytus's *Apostolic Tradition* and the positions argued by Tertullian, Origen, Cyprian, and Augustine are commonly cited as examples of recourse, prior to Prosper, to the church's liturgy to ground the articulation of its faith. Such recourse was had in a variety of ways, including ritual structures, sacramental practices, and prayer texts. For example, Hippolytus's argument in the *Apostolic Tradition* came to establish the outline to be followed for praying the Eucharistic Prayer, which is the source text for Eucharistic Prayer II in the Roman rite; Tertullian referred to the church's penitential practices in order to distinguish pardonable from not pardonable sins; and Augustine frequently referred to the church's actual liturgical practice—specifically, initiation rites or parts of the eucharistic rite such as prayers of the faithful, the Our Father, or texts of final blessings—to counter the Pelagian heresy, which claimed that we could "earn" grace and therefore salvation. In addition, the exploration of the meaning of such central theological tenets of Christian belief as the mystery of the Trinity, the divinity of Jesus, original sin, and the need for grace were very frequently derived from their articulation in the church's liturgy.

Prosper's dictum in its original setting means that the liturgy expresses the church's belief and manifests its faith. The statement's reference to the apostolicity of liturgy means that liturgy is a theological source to the degree that it is founded on Scripture and is the expression of the faith of the praying church beginning with the prayer and belief of the apostles. Prosper's reference to liturgical texts also implies an appreciation of such texts as poetic, symbolic, and more fully existential than rational in composition and style (which is what we commonly find in the church's official magisterium). A proper interpretation of the liturgy rests on the presumption that the church's engagement in *rites*, not just in texts that are spoken and heard, grounds the articulation of the church's belief. Prosper's argument is also in line with much other patristic evidence that reflects flexibility in liturgical rites and variety in interpreting them.

Sometimes commentators on Prosper's text and subsequent expositions of what this text means will shorten it to read *lex orandi, lex credendi*—the "law of prayer" is the "law of belief." In this context and in what follows, the word *lex*, "law," carries the connotation of "principle" or "foundation," as opposed to a legal statute (*ius*) enacted or promulgated to insure good order in society.

As already noted, patristic literature reflects the *lex orandi, lex credendi* relationship in a number of ways, three of which are of particular import here. The first, and for our purposes the most important, concerns the tradition of *mystagogia* (see chapter 3) enshrined in the mystagogic catecheses—that is, patristic explanations of the sacraments tied directly to what was spoken and what occurred in the liturgy. The second concerns homilies preached by the fathers on liturgical feasts, which offered explanations that helped to form the theological understanding and meaning of feasts and seasons, as well as the theology they express or that underlie them—for example, St. Leo the Great's Christmas sermons on the theology of the incarnation. The third concerns theological writings rooted in liturgical practices—for example (see again chapter 3), Augustine's use of liturgical rites in articulating his argument in *De baptismo*.

The authority of the liturgy in the patristic era was not that of a simple deposit transmitted intact. The *lex orandi* both reflected a living theology and supported a response to liturgy in Christian living. Hence, the use of the liturgy in mystagogic catecheses to explain the meaning of sacraments resulted in a rich and pluriform sacramental theology, including what may be termed "liturgical/sacramental ethics." At the same time, the very variety found in such catecheses invites creativity today in the way that mystagogia can and should function since these catecheses did not (and could not) result in a uniform liturgical/sacramental theology.

For example (generally speaking), the structure of the eucharistic liturgy in the patristic era included (some form of) an entrance rite, proclamation of Scripture readings, homily, intercessions, presentation of gifts, proclamation of the Eucharistic Prayer, distribution of communion, and conclusion. The mystagogic catecheses based on the Liturgy of the Eucharist concerned commentaries on the rites, including Scripture texts (particularly those associated with the Eucharist), the Eucharistic Prayer, and the eucharistic species. This is clear in the example of the catecheses of St. Cyril of Jerusalem. At the same time, instances of liturgical pluriformity in this period included the shape of the introductory and dismissal rites, the choice of Scripture readings, and the structure, length, style, and theological themes of the Eucharistic Prayer. This liturgical pluriformity was usually more easily seen in the structure of the Eucharistic Prayer and the comparatively more elaborate content in these (longer) texts in prayers from the Christian East, which more fully developed themes noted only briefly in the West. Structurally, this meant greater emphasis on the parts of the prayer invoking the Holy Spirit (the *epiclesis* [more on this in chapter 15]) in Eastern liturgical sources than in the Roman Canon used in the West, which contained no explicit invocation of the Holy Spirit. Theologically, the themes receiving greater emphasis in the prayers from the East included, for example, praise for creation, more elaborate exploration of the mystery of the Trinity, and greater emphasis on soteriology (the "theology of redemption") and the paschal mystery. However, liturgical variety was not limited to the East; the varied parts of the Roman Canon attest to the same phenomenon in the West. In fact, the differences in the text of the Canon on which Ambrose based part of his catechesis in the *De Mysteriis* and *De Sacramentis* exemplify Western liturgical variety. One application of this historical data for today is that the present Roman Rite contains a number of choices for prayer text and rites that should lead to a rich sacramental theology based on a number of texts and rites (see part 3).

Recalling the presentation and discussion of St. Cyril's mystagogic catecheses, we can say that the kind of liturgical theology that derives from such a complexus of liturgical elements can be characterized as (1) *biblical-theological* in the sense of interpreting the Scripture texts with which each of the five catecheses begins; (2) *systematic* in terms of the theology of initiation that results from commenting on the rites—for example, illumination and ecclesial belonging; and (3) *ethical* in terms of the kind of new life that results from sacramental initiation and that ought to be reflected in the way the initiated live their lives.

What is important to note from the methodological point of view in the patristic era is that Prosper's adage captured the sense that the liturgy grounded much of the theology, particularly what we have conventionally called "sacramental theology," through this period.

Two tentative applications for our task at hand can be derived from studying this period, one methodological, the other theological. Methodologically, from this period, we learn that it is liturgy as *enacted rites* containing words and gestures (among other things) taken together that serves as the primary source for theology. This means that we should not interpret a word, phrase, or a particular sacramental sign, symbol, or gesture apart from the whole enacted rite. The theological insight derived from this era concerns a theology of sacraments that is rich and multifaceted. Illumination, adoption, purification, enlightenment, filiation, cleansing, renewal, rebirth, incorporation into the paschal mystery, and incorporation into the life of the Trinity are based on and derived from the liturgy. This suggests that the more that contemporary theologies of initiation use both the liturgy as its primary source and appropriate insights from previous eras that interpreted such rites (principally the patristic era), the richer they will be in developing initiation theology. What was codified in Prosper of Aquitaine's adage is clearly a reflection of the important liturgical theology of the whole patristic era.

The influence of the church's orthodox faith on the liturgy was also in evidence in this period. Scholars point to the way heresies needed to be taken into account and, at least in a subtle way, corrected by the liturgy. A prime example is the heresy called "Arianism," taught in the early fourth century by Arius, a presbyter from Egypt, which taught that Christ was not divine. To counteract this teaching, the doxology (from the Greek word *doxa*, meaning "to give glory") was changed from "Glory to the Father, through the Son, in the Holy Spirit" to read "glory to the Father, and to the Son and to the Holy Spirit," whereby the preposition *to* indicates equality of the three persons in God, as opposed to prepositions that might diminish that equality: *through* and *with*.

In effect, *lex credendi* needed to be preserved in the *lex orandi*, and sometimes this caused changes to the church's *lex orandi*.

THOMAS AQUINAS

For a variety of reasons, including the increased lack of vernacular usage for the liturgy and the distancing of the community from active engagement in the enacted rituals of the liturgy, after the patristic era, the church's *lex orandi* was less appreciated as a central source for the theology appropriated by most Christians. At the same time, however, the church's *lex orandi* continued to function as a source for theology, especially sacramental theology, but in a different way. Medieval authors such as Peter Lombard continued to recognize that sacraments were a source of healing. No less a figure than Thomas Aquinas held that they were integrally related to the work of the incarnate Word. To the specific question of how Aquinas understood liturgy as a source for theology, it is clear that Aquinas regarded liturgy as one of the church's "authorities" (*auctoritates*) for church teaching. He distinguished among three such authorities: (1) the doctrine and the practice of the church; (2) the apostolic tradition, that is, the teaching of the fathers transmitted in the Church's life; and (3) Sacred Scripture. He understands the liturgy to be a major part of the first of these *auctoritates*, along with councils and papal teachings. He argues that this is an appropriate understanding of the liturgy since in the liturgy, the faith and life of the church is manifested.

In order to establish the real-life context in which Thomas did theology, it is important to recall that he was a Dominican friar and that he lived and worshiped among a community of fellow mendicants. His daily participation in the Liturgy of the Hours (as it is now called), his daily celebration of the Mass (with extreme devotion, reverence, and awe, as attested in his writings), and his written commentaries on so many of the books of the Bible attests to the supreme value that the Bible and the liturgy had for him and, by extension, for his theology.

The clearest expression of Aquinas's liturgical interest is found in his discussion of the relationship between Christian cult and the Trinity, the action of the Spirit, the mystery of Christ, and the ecclesial reality of sacraments. Despite the experienced diminishment of popular participation in sacramental liturgy, especially when compared with the patristic era, Aquinas repeatedly asserts the ecclesial reality of sacraments from objective and subjective perspectives, emphasizing the "faith of the church" (*fides ecclesiae*), the "enactment [act] of the church" (*actus ecclesiae*), the intention of doing what the church intends (*intentio ecclesiae*), and the church's rite(s) (*ritus ecclesiae*) in sacramental activity. Here Aquinas's claim that the prayer of the church takes priority over the private prayer of individual believers would not be surprising considering his own mendicant observance, which emphasized daily communal celebration of the Eucharist and the hours.

Just as they did in the patristic era, the scriptural word proclaimed at sacramental liturgy and the scriptural basis for some teachings on the sacraments continue to have an important role in Thomas's theology of sacraments. Thus the close association of word and rite that we have seen in patristic liturgy and catecheses was sustained, at least to some extent. Thomas stands in line with Augustinian sacramental teaching in emphasizing that it is the incarnate Word who gives power to sacramental words. However, Aquinas gives particular attention to the "sacramental words" spoken by the priest at the core of the rite, most usually in connection with such sacramental symbols as water, bread, and wine. He sees these words as a spiritual factor that gives precision to the significance of the symbolic action or material element in use. It is in this way that he adopts the terminology of *matter* and *form* to describe the Augustinian contention that the element and the word together comprise a sacrament.

To the specific question of how the liturgy served as a source for sacramental theology, some measure of influence continued, but in a manner different from the patristic era. For example, initiation theology reflected the contemporary emphasis on *who* was initiated, *when*, and *how*. The comparatively complete and elaborate descriptions from patristic sources of the catechumenate, initiation liturgy, and liturgical theology now waned because adult initiation ceded to the more common practice of children's initiation. Hence, the Lenten rites of the catechumenate and their catechetical instructions were telescoped into a baptismal rite for children held at one time. In the West, the separation of water baptism from chrismation influenced the development of a theology of confirmation that was at least distinguished, if not separated, from baptism. (This was not the case in the East, where the sacraments of initiation were kept together, both ritually and theologically, whether for adults or for children.) Similarly, Aquinas's theory about confirmation was clearly influenced by the thirteenth-century practice of administering confirmation in late childhood, and his approach to anointing of the sick ("extreme unction") reflected the contemporary practice of delaying this anointing until one was near death.

While it is clear that medieval theologians were preoccupied with a systematization of sacraments that was less influenced by the rites themselves than was the case in the patristic era, the sacramental practices of the day continued to play an important role in medieval understandings of sacraments. The *lex orandi* was not absent; it was understood in a different way. It is important to be fair to Aquinas's teaching in that it reflected the needed systematization of theology at the time and yet sustained some measure of reference to liturgical practice, if not the full liturgical reality that was assumed in the patristic age. Just as the liturgy was not the sole source for theology in the patristic era—one recalls the use of Scripture, the teaching of other fathers, and Neoplatonism—so, for Thomas, liturgy was regarded as one of the *auctoritates* for theology alongside Scripture and Aristotelian philosophy. It is often argued that commentators on Aquinas and later Thomists did something of an injustice to the careful, balanced, and measured Scholastic theology he produced. Somewhat later descriptions of the mechanistic understanding of the priest's role in sacraments and the devotional practice of eucharistic adoration, as opposed to sharing in eucharistic communion, would affect medieval eucharistic theology and piety. Not all prayers, hymns, and texts associated with commemorating "eucharistic miracles" had the same theological breadth and depth as those authored by Aquinas for the Feast of Corpus Christi (recall chapter 6). Eucharistic practices such as the private Mass and the stipend system were hardly prime examples of what eucharistic liturgy should be. Yet it was these practices above all that would influence both the sacramental theology and piety of this era. Liturgy continued to influence theology, but more as rites performed *for* the people than *by* and *with* the community.

REFORMATION AND TRENT

The risk of generalization about what are very complex matters is invariably inherent in dealing with the Protestant Reformation and the Catholic (once called the Counter-) Reformation as exemplified at Trent. Yet, it can be asserted that one concern important to the Reformers was a "cleansing" of the medieval Catholic doctrine about and liturgical celebration of the Eucharist. The basis for this was that some liturgical practices were judged not to be found in the Scriptures (that is, *sola scriptura*) and that the theology of eucharistic sacrifice was judged to be at least limited, if not bad theology. This means that scriptural data and theological ideas came to dominate how the liturgy was to be celebrated. In effect, *lex orandi, lex credendi* can be understood to mean that liturgy can influence theology and theology can influence liturgy—for example, the way Reformers removed references to sacrifice in the prayers of the liturgy. While in the patristic era changes were made to the *lex orandi*–based *lex credendi*, it is often argued that the Protestant tradition gave (appropriate) priority to *lex credendi* when it came to forms of existing worship that needed correction, especially when the Reformers purged the existing liturgical rites of nonscriptural assumptions, usages, and references.

The Catholic liturgy at the time of the Reformation was clearly in great need of reform—specifically, it needed adjustments that were theologically accurate and authentic. Therefore Pope Pius V issued the Roman Breviary (1568) and the Roman Missal (1570), in hopes of unifying the church after the Reformation (but see chapter 6 for certain exceptions to this reform.)

It was especially after the Council of Trent that a clear separation developed between the liturgy and sacramental theology. In the wake of the Tridentine concern for rubrical precision in performing the liturgy, as demonstrated by the printing of rubrics in the Roman Missal and Ritual, liturgy became equated with the external performance of the church's rites. Sacramental theology was incorporated into manuals of dogmatic theology that paid little attention to the rites themselves as a theological source. The sacramental discussions in such manuals focused on the Reformation debates about causality, the number of sacraments, and their institution. The divorce between the *lex orandi* and *lex credendi* was exemplified in the division of what had been a single area of study into two: liturgy and sacramental theology.

The result was a rather legalistic understanding of liturgy, with sacramental theology assigned to dogmatic tracts. Most theological manuals after Trent were highly apologetic in tone and many were merely compilations of Tridentine decrees with some commentary. This resulted in imbalanced tracts whose content was severely limited since Trent dealt with ad hoc issues regarding sacraments. In fact, as we saw in chapter 6, its decrees were never intended to be a complete sacramental theology or to disclose a complete theology of a particular sacrament. Given the need to reassert Roman Catholic teaching, however, it was understandable that subsequent theological manuals would reiterate and sometimes explain, but rarely go beyond, the parameters set by Trent's decrees. Given the pervasiveness of this attitude after Trent, it is not surprising that some authors in the early evolution of the liturgical movement can now be criticized for an almost exclusively apologetic approach to liturgical sources whereby liturgical texts were used as "proofs" and doctrinally authoritative statements. In fact, what they were doing was imitating a post-Tridentine approach to Catholic theology derived from the manuals.

MAGISTERIUM

That the "law of prayer" finds its way into the papal magisterium after Trent, at least on occasion, is clear, for example in the pronouncements of Popes Sixtus V (d. 1590), Pius IX (d. 1878), Pius XI (d. 1939), Pius XII (d. 1958), Paul VI (d. 1978), John Paul II (d. 2005), and Benedict XVI. It is notable that both in 1925 and in 1928, Pope Pius XI stated that the liturgy is the most important organ for the ordinary magisterium of the church.

Not surprisingly because of his theological acumen and experience as a professor and author, Pope Emeritus Benedict XVI engaged these terms and ideas fully in his apostolic exhortation *Sacramentum Caritatis* (2007) following the worldwide Synod of Bishops on the "Eucharist in the Life and Mission of the Church" (2005). The document itself is divided into three parts:

Part 1. The Eucharist: A Mystery to be Believed
Part 2. The Eucharist: A Mystery to be Celebrated
Part 3. The Eucharist: A Mystery to be Lived

In this exhortation, the pope says with regard to *lex orandi, lex credendi,*

> The Synod of Bishops reflected at length on the intrinsic relationship between eucharistic faith and eucharistic celebration, pointing out the connection between the *lex orandi* and the *lex credendi,* and stressing the primacy of the *liturgical action.* The Eucharist should be experienced as a mystery of faith, celebrated authentically and with a clear awareness that "the *intellectus fidei* has a primordial relationship to the Church's liturgical action." (no. 34)

This brief survey of historical and contemporary sources indicates that the liturgy has been used as a primary source for delineating the theology of sacraments at different times and places. There are a number of reasons why the liturgy can and should be used as a primary source for understanding what sacraments are and what they do. Among them is the very breadth of the liturgical rites as revised after Vatican II in terms of Scripture readings, liturgical prayers, signs, and gestures, as well as the fact that almost always the sacraments are celebrated in the vernacular, making them readily understandable and comprehensible.

LITURGICAL SOURCES

In the Constitution on the Sacred Liturgy, the council fathers decreed, "The liturgical books are to be revised as soon as possible; experts are to be employed on the task, and bishops are to be consulted, from various parts of the world" (no. 25). This seemingly modest and straightforward statement set in motion the first revision of all the Catholic Church's liturgies at one time, a task involving forty committees of acknowledged experts from all over the world.

The following outline contains the liturgical books that are presently used in the church's liturgy to celebrate the sacraments. Given our approach to sacramental theology as based on the liturgy, these rites should be regarded as the primary sources for sacramental theology. (Note that the Roman Missal is treated last simply because it is the most familiar sacramental ritual we have and is, in many ways, the most complex.)

The Roman Ritual (formerly one volume, now several volumes, as noted in the introduction)

Rite of Baptism for Children
Rite for the Christian Initiation for Adults
Order for Christian Funerals
Rite for the Pastoral Care and Anointing of the Sick
Rite of Marriage
Rite of Penance

Each of these sacramental rituals contains the following:

A "decree" for the promulgation of each of these revised liturgies, sometimes an Apostolic Constitution by the pope.
　　For example, in his Apostolic Constitution on the Roman Missal, among other things, Pope Paul VI stated,

The recent Second Vatican Ecumenical Council, in promulgating the Constitution *Sacrosanctum Concilium*, established the basis for the general revision of the Roman Missal: in declaring "both texts and rites should be drawn up so that they express more clearly the holy things which they signify" and in ordering that "the rite of the Mass is to be revised in such a way that the intrinsic nature and purpose of its several parts, as also the connection between them, can be more clearly manifested, and that devout and active participation by the faithful can be more easily accomplished"; in prescribing that "the treasures of the Bible are to be opened up more lavishly, so that richer fare may be provided for the faithful at the table of God's Word"; in ordering, finally, that "a new rite for concelebration is to be drawn up and incorporated into the Pontifical and into the Roman Missal."

An "Introduction" and/or a "General Instruction" for the partic-
ular rite, which is extremely important for understanding the liturgy of the sacrament(s) and the rites for the sacraments themselves.

The document called the General Instruction to the revised rites sets out the theology of what the revised rites mean and the protocols of what should be followed when celebrating the liturgy. This is where we find helpful indications for "why" and "what" we celebrate in and through the liturgy. Everything we say, do, and use in the liturgy has a theological meaning. This "Instruction" helps in understanding what these are. The protocols also contain helpful information about the theological meaning behind and contained in the way we celebrate the sacraments. This is a "handbook" for the rite that follows.

The rites themselves—rites and prayers—divided up into chap-
ters dealing with different possible celebrations with the texts of the prayers and the protocols to be followed (that is, the "rubrics," from the Latin for "red" because in many liturgical rites the "directions" for the celebration are printed in the books of rites in red ink).

An example of the chapter divisions in each of the rites comes from the Rite of Baptism for Children:

Chapter 1—Rite of Baptism for Several Children
Chapter 2—Rite of Baptism for One Child
Chapter 3—Rite of Baptism for a Large Number of Children
Chapter 4—Rite of Baptism for Children Administered by a Catechist when No Priest or Deacon Is Available
Chapter 5—Rite of Baptism for Children in Danger of Death when No Priest or Deacon Is Available
Chapter 6—Rite of Bringing a Baptized Child to the Church
Chapter 7—Various Texts for Use in the Celebration of Baptism for Children

THE SACRAMENTS

1. Scriptural Readings
2. Other Forms of the Intercessions
3. Another Form of the Prayer of Exorcism
4. Blessing and Invocation of God over Baptismal Water
5. Acclamations and Hymns
6. Forms of the Final Blessing
Appendix
Litany of the Saints
Special Invocations

The Roman Pontifical (Liturgies Celebrated by the Bishop)

Ordinations (bishop, presbyter/priest, deacon)
Rites of Installation to the Ministries of Reader and Acolyte
Rite of Election for the Rite for the Christian Initiation of Adults
Rite for Confirmation
Rite for the Dedication of an Altar and a Church
"Station" Masses (when the diocesan bishop visits a parish or other institution in the diocese)

Each of these is divided up into the same structure of chapters as found in *The Roman Ritual* for the sacraments (above).

The Roman Missal (Third English Edition, 2011)

The Missal is really a collection of books. The present Missal contains the following introductory documents:

General Instruction of the Roman Missal (1970ff.)

As in other sacramental rituals, this document describes the protocols to be followed in the Mass and theological descriptions of the parts of the Mass. It is the "handbook" that guides all the ministers of the liturgy in what they do at Mass. A summary is found below.

• *Norms for the Distribution and Reception of Holy Communion under Both Kinds in the Dioceses of the United States of America*

The first part of this document contains a theological description of what the Eucharist is. The second part of the title concerns the protocol for the distribution of communion, including ministers who distribute and postures for communicants.

• *Universal Norms for the Liturgical Year and the General Roman Calendar*

"Apostolic Letter" (*Paschale Mysterium*): By Pope Paul VI, explaining and endorsing the revised calendar.

"Universal Norms on the Liturgical Year and the Calendar": Summarizes the rank given to each day, week, and (seasons of) the year.

"The Calendar": Describes the kinds of celebrations (e.g., memorials, feasts, solemnities) and the proper day for celebrations.

"Table of Liturgical Days According to Their Order of Preference"

"The General Roman Calendar": A month-by-month listing of all the saints and solemnities celebrated.

• *Proper of Time*

Mass texts (also called a Mass formula) for each day of each liturgical year starting with the First Sunday of Advent. These are the entrance antiphon, collect, prayer over the offerings, communion antiphon, and prayer after communion. Almost all of these are derived from traditional, mostly ancient sources. These books are called the following:

Antiphonal (Entrance and Communion Antiphons): Verses often from the Scriptures to accompany the entrance and communion processions and suggested verses of psalms.

Sacramentary (Collect, prayer over the gifts, prayer after communion): Prayers for the presiding bishop or priest.

• *The Order of Mass*

Texts of the "ordinary" of the Mass and, rubrics, meaning directions, in the text of a "Mass formula" that describes what is to be done during the Mass.

- *Proper of Saints*
  Same sources as for the Proper of Time for all the saints in the Calendar.
- *Additional Masses*
  Commons, Ritual Masses, Votive Masses, Masses for the Dead

Lectionary and The Book of the Gospels (2002, 2000)

Scripture readings to be proclaimed at Mass.
Structure of Scripture readings for Sundays (according to a three-year cycle):

Old Testament reading (during Easter season from the Acts of the Apostles)
Responsorial Psalm
New Testament reading
Gospel acclamation
Gospel reading
The Gospel is chosen according to a semicontinuous reading from an evangelist each year, that is, Year "A," Gospel of Matthew; Year "B," Gospel of Mark; Year "C," Gospel of Luke. Each year for parts of Lent and the Easter season the Gospel of John is proclaimed.
Structure of Scripture readings for weekdays (according to a two-year cycle):

First Reading (continuous reading from an Old Testament or New Testament book)
Responsorial Psalm
Gospel Acclamation
Gospel (continuous reading of Matthew, Mark, Luke over a one year cycle)

AN EXAMPLE—THE ROMAN MISSAL

Because of the importance of the introductory document to all the sacramental rituals called the *General Instruction*, the following outline and brief description of the *General Instruction of the Roman Missal* is as follows:

Introduction (nos. 1–15)

> explaining how the "new" Missal is in continuity with the liturgical and theological tradition that preceded it. (Note the many references to the Council of Trent.)

Chapter 1—"The Importance and Dignity of the Celebration of the Eucharist" (nos. 16–26)

> This contains a rich explanation of the theology of the Mass.

Chapter 2—"The Structure of the Mass, Its Elements and Its Parts" (nos. 27–90)
Each of the parts of the Mass is described in terms of what it means and its implication for our spiritual lives.
> Example: The purpose and theological meaning of the entrance rites (nos. 46–54).
> Example: The theological meaning and principal parts of the Eucharistic Prayer (nos. 78–79).

Chapter 3—"Duties and Ministries in the Mass" (nos. 91–111)

> This is a particularly important chapter given the expansion of liturgical roles from the Tridentine Mass, which concerned the priest and server(s) only.

Chapter Four—"The Different Forms of Celebrating Mass" (nos. 112–287).

> This contains directives for Mass with the people (the most common form of Mass, Sundays and weekdays, nos. 115–98). This contains protocols for Masses with a deacon and without a deacon.
> Concelebrated Masses (nos. 199–251)
> Mass at which only one minister participates (nos. 252–72). This was formerly called a "private Mass."

Some General Norms for All Forms of Mass (nos. 273–87), among which are theological explanations for gestures such as the veneration of the altar and *Book of the Gospels*, genuflections and bows, incensation, purification (of vessels); the twentieth century may be said to have revised the study of manuscripts and prayer texts (often called "euchological" from the Greek term *euche*, meaning "to bless") for the sake of the vitality of both the communion under both kinds.

Chapter 5 — "The Arrangement of Churches for the Celebration of the Eucharist" (nos. 288–318)

General Principles (nos. 288–94)
- Arrangement of the Sanctuary for the Sacred Synaxis (*synaxis* is a Greek term meaning "coming together" or "assembly," frequently used to refer to "the sacred liturgy") (nos. 295–310)
- Arrangement of the Church: places for the gathered assembly, musicians, and for the reservation of the Eucharist (i.e., where the tabernacle should be located and who decides) (nos. 311–18)

Chapter 6 — "The Requisites for the Celebration of Mass" (nos. 319–51)

Bread and wine for celebrating the Eucharist (nos. 319–24)
Sacred Furnishings in General (nos. 325–26)
Sacred Vessels (nos. 327–34)
Sacred Vestments (nos. 335–47)
Other Things Intended for Church Use (nos. 348–51)

Chapter 7 — "The Choice of the Mass and its Parts" (nos. 352–67)

- "Pastoral effectiveness" of the celebration relating liturgical texts with the needs of the participants (no. 352)
- Overall instruction about the choice of Mass texts where they are not assigned and others, for example, in solemnities like Christmas, Easter, Ascension, and Sundays (nos. 353–55)

- Choice of Texts for the Mass: the readings, orations, Eucharistic Prayer (and preface), and chants (nos. 356–67)

Chapter 8 — "Masses and Prayers for Various Needs and Occasions and Masses for the Dead" (nos. 368–85)

Particularly notable here are the directives for Mass texts contained in this new Missal not found in the tradition but that were judged to be important to meet contemporary needs, for example, "For the Unity of Christians," "For the Evangelization of the Peoples," "For Persecuted Christians," "For a Spiritual or Pastoral Gathering," and several for civil needs.

Chapter 9 — "Adaptations within the Competence of Bishops and Bishops' Conferences" (nos. 386–99)

This chapter is the most notable addition to this, the third edition of the *General Instruction of the Roman Missal,* compared to its two predecessors where it was not present. The chapter is largely inspired by the document *Varietates Legitimae* (the Fourth Instruction on the Implementation of the Roman Missal, 1994) about liturgical adaptation and inculturation.

DISCUSSION QUESTIONS

1. Discuss how a reading of the *GIRM* nos. 1–15 helps to explain the continuity between the Missal published after the Council of Trent and that published after Vatican II.
2. Why does an appreciation of the "historical precedents" discussed in the first part of this chapter help to lay a foundation for the approach to sacramental theology in the balance of the chapter (and in the rest of this book)?
3. Review the Scripture readings assigned for this week and discuss how they reflect the arrangement of the Lectionary for Mass presented above.

10

LITURGICAL SACRAMENTAL METHOD AND AGENDA

The purpose of this chapter is (1) to present an overview of the kind of liturgical theology that will be argued in part 3, (2) to delineate four of the elements that furnish the data on which a contemporary sacramental theology derived from the revised liturgical rites can be based, as well as to make observations about the theological value of this data, leading to (3) listing the eight elements that will be delineated in part 3 that, taken together, can comprise what constitutes a liturgical theology of the sacraments.

TWO METHODOLOGICAL PREMISES

1. Each and every thing that we use in the liturgy—every word we say, every action we engage in, every object that we use or touch, and every gesture we perform—has a theological meaning, and sometimes more than one. One of the purposes in the arguments throughout part 3 is to raise up these theological meanings.
2. Each and every act of liturgy is an immediate and direct experience of the saving mysteries of our salvation, mediated to us through the complexus of words, gestures, signs, and silences (among other things) that comprise the sacred liturgy. The phrase *mediated immediacy* (coined by Edward Kilmartin) is the theological touchstone for all that follows in part 3. The theological center of mediation is Christ our Lord. What facilitates our immediate engagement in God through Christ is the liturgy.

As noted toward the end of the last chapter in the quote from Pope Paul VI, liturgical scholarship from after the Council of Trent through the twentieth century unearthed numbers of manuscripts containing ancient liturgical sources. Many of those ancient prayers and rites have been restored to use in the sacramental liturgies revised after Vatican II. This can lead to a wealth of data and liturgical experiences on which to base the kind of liturgical theology that will be argued here.

The phrase *lex orandi, lex credendi* is often used to describe this kind of theology. In recent (post–Vatican II) years, enormous strides have been taken in methods of doing liturgical studies toward appreciating the whole liturgy both as articulated prayers and as an enacted set of rites and symbolic acts, all of which need to be interpreted theologically—hence the value of appreciating the inherent symbolic nature of the liturgy. For the sacramental theology articulated on the basis of the revised liturgy, the church's *lex orandi* is found in the sources summarized in chapter 9. This is in accord with the assertion of the Constitution on the Sacred Liturgy (no. 48) that we should have a good understanding of the "rites and prayers" (*per ritus et preces*) of the sacred liturgy.

As noted in chapter 8, one of the pioneers arguing for what we here call a *liturgical theology of the sacraments* was Dom Odo Casel (1886–1948), a Benedictine monk of the Abbey of Maria Laach in Germany. In his then-groundbreaking book *The Mystery of Christian Worship*, he argued that through the liturgy, we have direct access to the founding mysteries of our salvation, particularly Christ's saving life, death, resurrection, and ascension. Through the words and rites of the liturgy, this is accomplished at God's initiative and sustaining action among us, until the coming of the kingdom. What follows in part 3 of this book is one way to follow in the footsteps of Casel and of many like him, especially Benedictines, to draw out the meaning of what the liturgy says and does.

Lex orandi, lex credendi emphasizes the intrinsic interrelationship of liturgical prayer and orthodox belief. In addition, the phrase *lex vivendi* ("the law of living") is often added in order to bring out the relationship between the liturgical celebration of the sacraments and our living of the Christian life. Terms such as *spirituality* or *ethics* have also been used to describe the real-life implications of the celebration of sacraments. Therefore a study of the church's *lex orandi* always implies a continuum: from human life to the liturgy and from the liturgy to human life. This is to suggest that the (sacramental) liturgy as the "summit and source" of the Christian life always implies and refers to daily human life, its challenges and opportunities, its failures and successes, its suffering and glory.

Thus "what we pray" and experience in and through the liturgy is "what we believe," and both what we pray and what we believe have essential ramifications on how we view life and live the Christian life.

THEOLOGY FROM THE RITES

In light of the thesis and method of what follows in part 3, the following four sources for theology drawn from the liturgy should be collected, studied, and prayed over for any inquiry into the theological meaning of sacraments in general, an individual sacrament, or any part of the rite of a sacrament. These four sources offer the data on which a liturgical theology of the sacraments can be based. The elaboration in part 3 is meant to help explore the theological meaning and depth of this data and other things used in sacramental celebration. They are presented here by way of an introduction and an overview. In addition, they are placed here "upfront" in order that it be clear that the lens through which we view the liturgy is theological—what the liturgy means and is—as opposed to rubrical—how one celebrates it.

1. Scripture readings (more in chapter 13)

> Study of and reflection on all the Scripture texts assigned in the Lectionary list for a particular sacrament.

> More often than not, for many sacraments, a number of choices for readings are provided in a chapter of the revised ritual. In pastoral practice, this is often done in consultation with the couple to be married for weddings and with family members for funerals. At other times, for example, for communal services for the sacrament of penance or the anointing of the sick, the parish staff will select texts from among the options provided.

For example, see the Rite for Reconciliation with Several Penitents in the Rite of Penance, which contains "Sample Penitential Services." The suggested first reading is 1 Corinthians 10:1–13, recalling the exodus with the subtitle "all this that happened to the people of Moses in the desert was written for our benefit." The suggested responsorial psalm is Psalm 106 with the refrain "Lord, remember us, for the love you bear your people." The sample service for Lent suggests the proclamation of Luke 15:11–32, the parable of the prodigal son with the subtitle "Your brother here was dead, and has come to life." Study of and reflection on these texts would be a way to enter into this sacrament during Lent more fully. One of the most poignant things about this Gospel parable is that while we know that the younger son returned to his father and that the elder son resented this and was "angry," we do not know whether the elder son joined in the festivities. The full meaning of the rite of reconciliation is that we are reconciled with God and one another.

For the Mass, the assigned Scripture readings are contained in the *Lectionary for Mass*.

2. Prayers of blessing, consecration, and absolution (more in part 3, chapter 14)

> Study of and reflection on the prayers of blessing (for example, the blessing of water at baptism or at the Easter Vigil, below) and prayers of consecration (for example, the blessing of chrism at the Chrism Mass on Holy Thursday) or the Eucharistic Prayer (including the preface) at Mass (below).

When sacraments are celebrated within Mass, a prayerful reflection on and study of the preface for that day and the Eucharistic Prayer is an important part of the *lex orandi*. This would mean, for example, the preface used at an ordination and the proper prayers in the Roman Canon for Masses at which ordinations take place.

Especially important is reflection on the Scripture texts embedded in all such blessing prayers. For example, for the sacrament of penance, this would mean reflection on the formula for absolution, noting especially its scriptural basis:

God, the Father of mercies (2 Cor 1:3)

Emphasis is on mercy from the beginning of the prayer; naming God as "Father" introduces the Trinity as always active in all liturgy.

through the death and resurrection of his Son

All liturgy is paschal; our reconciliation, salvation, redemption and sanctification are all possible because of Christ's death and resurrection into which we are incorporated in every liturgy.

has reconciled the world to himself (2 Cor 5:19; also see Rom 11:10; Col 1:14)

This reiterates the emphasis in all the rites of penance on reconciliation. A useful complement to this for reflection would be 2 Corinthians 5:16–31.

and sent the Holy Spirit among us for the forgiveness of sins;

This phrase reiterates what is bedrock liturgical theology — that all we do and say in the liturgy is effective only through and in the power of God's Holy Spirit abiding and working in the church.

through the ministry of the church (2 Cor 5:18–20)

All liturgy is ecclesial; whether this sacrament is celebrated in common or individually, this is a brief but important statement that the priest always acts *in persona Christi* ("in the person of Christ," not in his own person) and *in nomine/persona ecclesiae* ("in the person/name of the church").

may God give you pardon and peace (Luke 7:50; Col 1:14)

Liturgical prayers and texts almost always use the deprecatory form "may," which puts the emphasis not on the minister but on God acting in the sacraments.

The text reiterates the emphasis on harmony and peace as a result of the sacrament. A useful complement to understanding this text would be the appearance of the risen Christ to the apostles and to "doubting Thomas" with the key phrases "peace be with you," "receive the Holy Spirit," and about the forgiveness of sins. A shortened version of this text, John

20:19–31, is used in all three cycles of the Sunday Lectionary; the shorter form is used on the Solemnity of Pentecost (John 20:19–31, again in all three Lectionary cycles).

and I absolve you from your sins (Matt 16:18; 18:18)

In the Roman Catholic tradition, the power to absolve from sins is reserved to the ordained priest or bishop; these citations from the Gospel of Matthew are often invoked as bases for the "power of the keys," among which privileges is the power to absolve.

in the name of the Father, and of the Son, and of the Holy Spirit.

That the priest or bishop acts in and through the power of the Trinity is reiterated at the end of this powerful prayer of absolution.

3. Other prayers of the liturgy (more in chapter 14)

For all sacramental liturgies, this means the opening prayer/collect and the concluding prayer. Sometimes it also includes a special blessing at the dismissal. One example from the Rite of Penance is the following opening prayer/collect (no. 99):

Almighty and merciful God,
you have brought us together in the name of your Son
to receive your mercy and grace in our time of need.
Open our eyes to see the evil we have done.
Touch our hearts and convert us to yourself.
Where sin has divided and scattered,
may your love make one again;
where sin has brought weakness,
may your power heal and strengthen;
where sin has brought death,
may your Spirit raise to new life.
Give us a new heart to love you,
so that our lives may reflect the image of your Son.
May the world see the glory of Christ
revealed in your Church,
and come to know
that he is the one whom you have sent,

Jesus Christ, your Son, our Lord.
Amen.

If sacraments are celebrated at a Mass, then the prayer over the offerings, the preface, and Eucharistic Prayer—especially when the latter contains special parts of the prayer assigned because of the sacrament being celebrated, such as baptism—and the prayer after communion, which would take the place of the "concluding prayer" from the rite for the sacrament itself, are proclaimed (see chapter 14).

4. Sacramental signs, gestures, and postures (more in chapters 11 and 12)

Every sacrament involves the use of the means of human communication through the senses—sight, sound, smell, taste, and touch. These are all involved in every sacramental action. Some sacraments involve primal elements, such as water for baptism (see chapter 11). Others involve things that are the result of combining nature and human work, such as bread and wine (see chapter 14). What the sacramental rite says about these signs and how they are to be used is another important factor in understanding sacraments (see the *General Instruction* and indications throughout the rite itself).

An Example of this would be gestures and the handling of bread and wine at Mass. The rite of the Mass itself is an elaboration on the words in the Last Super account as proclaimed in the Eucharistic Prayer: "He took *bread, blessed* and *broke* it and *gave* it to his disciples" (Matt 26:26–29; Mark 14:22–25; Luke 22:15–20).

The four essential parts of the Liturgy of the Eucharist are derived from these four verbs:

take—at the presentation of the gifts and the preparation of the altar;
bless—consecration during the Eucharistic Prayer;
break—at the Lamb of God;
give—at communion.

Each of these actions involves the bread and wine used at Mass. The actions are as follows:

> the presentation of the gifts and the preparation of the altar, and those who are involved in this rite;
> how and where they are placed on the altar and the vessels used, that is, patens for the bread and chalices for the wine;
> the priest taking the bread and wine in his hands during the words of institution and consecration and showing them to the people;
> the breaking of the bread at the "Lamb of God;"
> the placing of a part of the consecrated bread in the chalice;
> the raising of the consecrated species at the invitation to communion;
> the act of distribution of communion, who is involved in the distribution;
> the procession of the assembly to communion;
> the showing of the host/chalice to the communicant while the minister says, "Body of Christ," to which the communicant says, "Amen."

Each of these gestures has a theological meaning, some of which are described in the *General Instruction of the Roman Missal* as well as the Missal itself. Again, study of what these liturgical texts say and reflection on these actions form part of the theology of any sacrament.

For example, with regard to the presentation of the gifts and the preparation of the altar, these are contained in the *GIRM* nos. 73–77 and the Roman Missal, "The Liturgy of the Eucharist," nos. 21–30. More precisely, it is important to note what these sources say about the theological meaning of who is involved and what this rite represents.

With regard to the procession of the gifts, the *GIRM* states,

The offerings are then brought forward. It is praiseworthy for the bread and wine to be presented by the faithful. They are then accepted at an appropriate place by the priest or the deacon and carried to the altar. Even though the faithful no longer bring from their own possessions the bread and wine intended for the liturgy as in the past, nevertheless the rite of carrying up the offerings still retains its force and its spiritual significance.

It is well also that money or other gifts for the poor or for the Church, brought by the faithful or collected in the church, should be received. These are to be put in a suitable place but away from the Eucharistic table. (no. 73)

Regarding this rite, the Roman Missal says, "It is desirable that the faithful express their participation by making an offering, bringing forward bread and wine for the celebration of the Eucharist and perhaps other gifts to relieve the needs of the Church and of the poor" (no. 22).

This is made even more explicit in the directives for the Evening Mass of the Lord's Supper on Holy Thursday, which states, "At the beginning of the Liturgy of the Eucharist, there may be a procession of the faithful in which gifts for the poor may be presented with the bread and wine" (no. 14).

What is summarized here for the bread and wine at Mass is said about each and every other element of what is used in the celebration of Mass: the location of the altar, ambo, presider's chair, the vesture, books used in the celebration, and so on. These are all contained in the GIRM as well as in the Missal itself.

As stated above, everything we say, do, and use in the liturgy has a theological meaning. Each is worth reflection and discussion from the authoritative liturgical sources.

While these four things can be drawn from the liturgical rites found in books (which will be more extensively described in chapters 13 and 14), nonetheless there are two things to be noted about the revised liturgies. First, they contain a wealth of prayers, Scriptures, and variables in the actual celebration of the liturgy, such as the number of prefaces and Eucharistic Prayers that can be used at the Eucharist. All of these should be studied as constitutive of the reformed liturgy. Second, the actual celebrations of sacramental liturgy are most often the way we hear and experience what the liturgy says and does. In other words, there are variables in the way the liturgy is celebrated, and sometimes the description of a liturgical ritual is one thing, and what actually happens when that rite is celebrated is another. This requires being attentive to what is actually done in the celebration. Obvious examples of what influences how we experience what the rituals and prayer books say are the church buildings themselves (and what is contained in them) and music. The council fathers did not want to impose uniformity regarding church buildings or music (see Constitution on the Sacred Liturgy nos. 112–21 for music and nos. 122–30 for "art" more generally). They left it to bishops' conferences to delineate guidelines for each.

ACTUAL CELEBRATIONS OF THE LITURGY

One of the more notable parts of the revised liturgy for sacraments is the variety of prayers and rites that can be used. At the same time, given the present structure of the reformed liturgy with its variety and flexibility, there is the issue of whether what is experienced at liturgy conforms to what the ritual books envision. For example, with regard to the use of water, the initiation rites always place immersion, meaning to plunge the candidate into the baptismal pool, before infusion, meaning pouring water on the candidate's forehead, as the way to celebrate water baptism. When infusion is normally used, one needs to ask the question about whether what is envisioned in the symbolic action of initiation is really happening.

Another example would be *what* the presider "says" when given the opportunity to use "these or similar words." In fact the question needs to be raised as to how "similar" the words spoken are in relation to what is envisioned. This most often happens after the sign of the cross and the greeting at the beginning of any sacramental liturgy.

Given the symbolic richness of the act of liturgy, any approach to articulating the theological value of the *lex orandi* needs to be attentive to the languages of liturgy, among which are the Scriptures, symbols, euchology (a term derived from the Greek word *euche*, meaning prayers proclaimed at the liturgy), and the arts, as well as an evaluation as to whether what is experienced at liturgy actually reflects what the component elements of the reformed liturgy can and should articulate theologically.

One important exercise in this regard would be to review the texts provided in the Missal or other sacramental rituals at the entrance and communion processions and compare them with what was actually sung at those moments. It would also be instructive to compare what the *Lectionary for Mass* sets out as the responsorial psalm and Gospel acclamation for a given day's liturgy and what was actually sung at those parts of the Liturgy of the Word.

CHURCH BUILDINGS

In the United States, the guidelines for churches are contained in the USCCB document *Built of Living Stones: Art, Architecture and Worship*. In addition, most often local dioceses have their own supplementary guidelines, given the fact that the *General Instructions* for the sacraments often reserve some decisions to the local bishop about the conduct of the liturgy—such as whether to kneel at the invitation to communion or to stand—and the location of some of the things in the church (such as the placement of the tabernacle, *GIRM* 311–14).

Historically, the Catholic Church has never adopted one style of church architecture. Because we belong to the "catholic" (meaning "universal") church, our faith has been inculturated in a variety of times and cultures in history and the present—that is, it has been influenced by and "adapted" to suit different cultures. This inculturation allows for a variety of styles of art and architecture to flourish today.

MUSIC

In the United States, the guidelines for music are found in *Sing to the Lord*. In actual practice, this document allows for variety and great flexibility in what is sung or listened to at the liturgy of the sacraments.

While the actual rites of the church do provide antiphons for different parts of the liturgy—that is, the entrance and communion antiphons at Mass—these are not always sung or recited. A rule of thumb would be to see whether or to what extent what is actually sung coincides with what the antiphons say. The principle here is that the *lex orandi* does provide texts that should be acknowledged. When what is sung does not correspond to the church's *lex orandi*, a rule of thumb is not to factor them into a liturgical theology of the sacrament.

For example, the antiphon for Christmas Day says,

> A child is born for us, and a son is given to us;
> his scepter of power rests upon his shoulder,
> and his name will be called Messenger of great counsel. (from
> Isa 9:5)

There is a rich theology of the Feast of the Nativity contained here. The reference to "a child for us" indicates that Christ will die "for us and our salvation." In other words, the incarnation necessarily leads to his death and resurrection. The reference to "a son" reflects the notion of filiation—that Christ is from the Father and is the Father's son. This is extended to us who at baptism become brothers and sisters in Christ. The notion of "name" in the Scriptures carries with it associations of identity and role. Here Christ is God's unique messenger of Good News.

SOME OBSERVATIONS ON THIS DATA

AUTHORITATIVE SOURCES

When theology is derived from the liturgy, there is a sense in which it is authoritative because the church's liturgical rites are published with the authority of the Holy Father in the name of the whole church. This endorsement comes two ways. The first is in the form of a "Decree" from the Sacred Congregation for Divine Worship, which invariably ends with the assertion that the rite is being promulgated with the authority of the pope. In addition, there are revised rites that are introduced by what is called an *Apostolic Constitution* written by the pope himself, often indicating changes from the former rite and authoritatively endorsing the revision. This is the case, for example, for the revised Rite for Confirmation.

A REVISED/REFORMED LITURGY OF THE SACRAMENTS

As has already been noted, the present reformed liturgy reflects traditional practices and texts as well as adaptations and new compositions. Often in the Apostolic Constitutions introducing the "new" rites, the Holy Father explains the major changes in a summary way. In the Apostolic Constitution on the Mass (*Missale Romanum*), Paul VI summarized the major changes in the Mass and endorsed them. These include the following:

> The addition of three Eucharistic Prayers to the traditional Roman Canon and more than ninety prefaces "from the earlier tradition of the Roman Church or now newly composed so that through them particular parts of the mystery of salvation may become more clearly evident and more and richer motives for thanksgiving." The advantage here is that no one prayer can say it all. Having a number of prayers helps to reflect the breadth of the mystery of salvation being celebrated.
> The rites for parts of the Mass have been simplified with "due care being taken to preserve their substance." This is particularly true "for the offering of the bread and wine and with regard to the rites for the breaking of the bread and Communion."
> In accord with the directives of the Constitution on the Sacred Liturgy, the "universal prayer" and the homily have been restored to the Mass. In addition, the "penitential act" has been revised (and simplified).
> More generous reading from the Sacred Scripture has been provided for, along with the use of the responsorial psalm between the proclaimed scriptures at Mass. (This will become the *Lectionary for Mass* and *The Book of the Gospels*.)
> The number of the prayers of the Mass has been increased based on ancient texts and some have been newly composed for contemporary needs.
> At the end of the document, the pope quotes Pope Pius V, who, when promulgating the Missal after the Council of Trent, saw

the Missal as "an instrument of liturgical unity and as a monument of true and reverent worship in the Church."

The publication of "decrees" for all the revised rites and an Apostolic Constitution for certain revised rites indicates that the liturgy is always "the prayer of the church" and is always officially endorsed by the church's highest authority.

In an extremely important paragraph in this document, Pope Paul VI acknowledged the value of making available in the liturgy the results of manuscript discoveries of recent centuries for their "doctrinal" and "spiritual" riches. He stated,

> However, it should in no way be thought that this revision of the Roman Missal has been introduced without preparation, since without any doubt the way was prepared by progress in liturgical disciplines these last four centuries. For if, after the Council of Trent, the reading and examination of "ancient manuscripts, both those in the Vatican library and others discovered elsewhere" helped not a little in the revision of the Roman Missal, as is confirmed by the Apostolic Constitution *Quo primum* issued by Our Predecessor Saint Pius V, subsequently on the one hand very ancient liturgical sources have of course been discovered and published, and on the other hand the liturgical formularies of the Eastern Church have been studied more deeply. As a result, it has been the desire of many that not only these doctrinal and spiritual riches not lie in the darkness of archives, but rather be brought out into the light to enlighten and nourish the minds and spirits of Christians.

This Apostolic Constitution was dated Holy Thursday 1969 and decreed that the new (Latin) Missal was to be promulgated on the First Sunday of Advent, 1969.

It is clear from this historical and contemporary overview that the liturgy has been used as a source for delineating a theology of individual sacraments. This review also admits of times when that reliance was more robust and full than in others. Among other reasons why the

201

liturgy can be used in such a way today is because of the scope of the reform—that is, all liturgies were revised; in their breadth they offer a host of prayers and Scripture readings and rites to reflect on, especially when compared to the previous Roman Missal and Roman Ritual; and most often the sacraments are celebrated in the vernacular, making comprehension and the embrace of the rite possible.

AGENDA IN PART 3

These two chapters in part 2 are intended to furnish the background to set up the consideration of the eight elements in part 3, which, taken together, can comprise a liturgical theology of sacraments. The delineation of them here indicates what they are. The purpose of part 3 is to give a theological explication of each of these elements as drawn from the liturgy and the rich theology that can be drawn from them based on the revised liturgy.

The *first four items* articulate the way sacraments work. They all deal with and explicate the "event" character of what happens in preparation for and during the celebration of the liturgy of the sacraments.

They are the following:

Sacramentality
Humans and human work
Word enacted
Prayer events

The *second four items* concern what always happens in the celebration of sacramental liturgy and provide rich theology about these sacred realities, in particular what humans "participate" in when celebrating them and through them so as to "participate" in God. While these are not exclusively liturgical, in that they can be found in other theological sources, these categories function in a particular and unique way in sacramental liturgy.

They are the following:

Experience of the Trinity
Paschal Memorial

Communio
"Already" and "not yet"

To illustrate how the eight elements in this liturgical theology of sacraments function, part three will most often discuss the celebration of the Sacred Paschal Triduum: the Evening Mass of the Lord's Supper, Friday of the Passion of the Lord (Good Friday), and the Easter Vigil in the Holy Night. The Easter Vigil is of particular note because it is the occasion for the celebration of the sacraments of baptism, confirmation, and the Eucharist for the catechumens and candidates coming into the Catholic Church. (It should be noted that on Friday and Saturday morning, many parishes, most religious communities, and all monasteries celebrate the Liturgy of the Hours. Because our concern here is sacraments, we will not comment on those liturgies. But for the sake of completeness, these should be participated in and understood to comprise the full liturgical celebration of these "three days.")

The *Universal Norms on the Liturgical Year and the Calendar* states,

> Since Christ accomplished his work of human redemption and of the perfect glorification of God principally through his Paschal Mystery, in which by dying he has destroyed our death, and by rising has restored our life, the sacred Paschal Triduum of the Passion and Resurrection of the Lord shine forth as the high point of the entire liturgical year. Therefore the preeminence that Sunday has in the week, the Solemnity of Easter has in the liturgical year. (no.18)

With regard to the Easter Vigil specifically, when baptism, confirmation, and the Eucharist are celebrated in their most solemn fashion, the *Norms* continues,

> The Easter Vigil, in the holy night when the Lord rose again, is considered the "mother of all holy Vigils," in which the Church, keeping watch, awaits the Resurrection of Christ and celebrates it in the Sacraments. Therefore, the entire celebration of this sacred Vigil must take place at

night, so that it both begins after nightfall and ends before the dawn on the Sunday. (no. 21)

The celebration of baptism, confirmation, and the Eucharist during the Easter Vigil are situated in a very full act of liturgy that comprises the elements found in the celebration of the liturgy of the sacraments. Hence it can be considered as paradigm or a model liturgy whose elements of sacramentality, human work, word enacted, and prayer events function in terms of the way sacraments "work." The Easter Vigil is also a paradigm or model liturgy in which the theological themes of all sacramental liturgy are found and expressed in their fullness. They are trinitarian theology, paschal theology, communion, and the "already" and "not yet" (see chapters 15–18 for elaborations on them).

The way the liturgy invites us to "participate" in and be renewed by the celebration of the dying and rising of Christ is exemplified at the Easter Vigil when new members of the church are initiated ("catechumens") and are brought into the church ("candidates"), are confirmed, and share in the Eucharist for the first time. The ritual setting for all of this is the church's annual "passover," our annual "passing over" from death to life, from darkness to light, from bondage to freedom, from sin to forgiveness, from isolation to communion in the triune God.

In preparation for this, secure a copy of the Easter Vigil liturgy containing the data outlined above, and parts of the Rite for the Christian Initiation of Adults and the Rite of Confirmation that will be discussed. (It would also be helpful to review the introduction and "Scriptural Foundations" [chapter 1] as these will be presumed in understanding a liturgical theology of sacraments to support what follows in part 3.)

From what has been discussed in part 2, one has the sources needed to delineate a liturgical theology of all the sacraments. The purpose of part 3 is to draw out some of the depth of the way sacraments work and the major theological insights that are gleaned from the celebration of the liturgy of the sacraments. The intention here is to offer as broad a range of possibilities for delineating that kind of theology based on the liturgy's inherent multivalence. What follows are descriptions of ways to appreciate the theology of the sacraments and not definitions of them, given that the experience of the various elements that comprise the liturgy is always broader in range and scope than a single definition of the sacred liturgy of sacraments. And even then, what the liturgy itself offers to engage us in sacraments and allow us to reflect on them theologically can only tether the imagination of those who partake; they cannot determine exactly what one experiences. Sacramental celebrations are just that, celebrations in communities of faith, whose appropriation of what is celebrated cannot be predetermined or preprogrammed.

AGENDA IN LIFE

Part of what is argued above and is intrinsic to part 3 concerns *lex vivendi*, a concept that raises more questions than it offers answers. At the very least, one should ask oneself, what are the implications for daily life that derive from the celebration of the sacraments? At the same time, a delicate balance needs to be struck in order that the liturgy not be seen to be utilitarian, that is, how it can be used to serve predetermined purposes. Nor should we so insist on the ethical living dimension of our faith that the liturgy would seem to be tangential, not to say even unnecessary for our faith and belief. A part of the thesis to be argued here is that there are ethical challenges and demands that derive from the liturgy and doctrine of our church. But they are best seen as a continuum, one leading to the other as intrinsically interrelated. This interrelationship prevents the liturgy from not being grounded in the real lives of those who celebrate and the real challenges that we in the twenty-first century face in our world. At the same time that these ethical challenges are inherently linked to the celebration of the liturgy, to reflect and sustain Catholicism's nature as "a sacramental church" means that liturgy and sacraments matter a great deal, and the fact that we believe, how we pray, and the way we act are part of each other. That every act of sacramental liturgy derives from human life is the premise of part 3, especially chapters 11 and 12. The way we celebrate and with what means is the subtext. That the liturgy sends us back to life should be on our minds as we read and study the chapters that follow.

This is summarized in the dismissals that end almost all of our liturgical celebrations:

> Go forth, the Mass is ended.
> Go and announce the Gospel of the Lord.
> Go in peace, glorifying the Lord by your life.

In some of the chapters that follow, this "agenda in life" will make specific reference to how that particular element can and should influence how we view life and live the Christian life in the world. In effect, this is meant to underscore the fact that sacramental ethics—the way we view life and live our day-to-day lives—comprise part of sacramental theology or the understanding of what the liturgical rites say and do.

DISCUSSION QUESTIONS

1. Pray over and discuss the Scripture readings and Mass texts to be used for next Sunday's Mass (1) as an example of the material needed for a liturgical theology of the Mass, and (2) as a way to prepare spiritually for next Sunday's Mass.

2. Review the prefaces for a liturgical season in the Roman Missal, for example, Advent, Christmas, Lent, or Easter, and pray over and discuss what these texts assert about the theology and spirituality of that particular season.

3. Pray over and discuss the formula for absolution cited above (in "Theology from the Rites," liturgical source no. 2), noting especially the scriptural sources for this prayer.

Part Three
THEOLOGY

11

SACRAMENTALITY

The purpose of this chapter is (1) to articulate the reality underlying the celebration of all liturgy and sacraments—that is, the principle of sacramentality or sacramental principle—and the closely allied principle of mediation; (2) to exemplify these arguments by exploring the way primal elements are used during the Easter Vigil; and (3) to indicate, by way of example, the relationship of the celebration of the liturgy and living the converted, Christian life in the world.

A SACRAMENTAL WORLDVIEW

One of the purposes of part 1 of this book was to describe the evolution and practice of the liturgy of the sacraments at several important moments in Christian history. As those sacramental practices evolved, it became clear that the experience and descriptions of what have become the cherished "seven sacraments" in Catholicism derived from a rich and broad tradition of naming and celebrating sacramental realities in and through the liturgy. St. Augustine, among others, assigns the term *sacrament* to hundreds of sacred realities. It was only with Peter Lombard in the twelfth century that the Western church decided on the number seven for the sacraments, which was declared as doctrinally binding at the Council of Trent. It was also St. Augustine who left us the definition of *sacrament* as "a sign of a sacred thing," a definition that has ensured in the Western theological tradition right up to the *Catechism of the Catholic Church*, which calls them "efficacious signs of grace perceptible to the senses" (no. 224).

What underlies the descriptions of the evolution and practice of sacraments per se is the rather broad and wide principle of *sacramentality*, the meaning of which reflects St. Augustine's assertions about "a sign of a sacred thing" and the *Catechism*'s reference to "signs" "perceptible to the senses." Many of the signs used in the sacred liturgy are taken from ordinary daily life as lived in this world. Sacramentality is based on the belief in the goodness of creation and the engagement of humans in the act of honoring God and growing in sanctification through the celebration of (sacramental) liturgy. Sacramentality is also based on the value of human labor and productivity (see chapter 12). While on the one hand the act of liturgy takes us out of the everyday world in order to worship God in a ritualized way, on the other hand in the act of worshiping God, we use the things of this world, either directly from creation or from "the work of human hands"; therefore the act of liturgy engages us to see the world and all that dwells in it as revelations of the glory of God.

Sacramentality is a worldview, a way of looking at life, a way of thinking and acting in the world that values and reveres the world. Sacramentality acts as a prism, a theological lens through which we view creation and all that is on this good earth as revelations of God's presence and action among us here and now. The premise of sacramentality means that in fact we do not live in "two different worlds," the sacred and the secular, but that we live in one graced world named "good" by God in Genesis 1:3. At the same time, this principle admits that there are moments of particular sacrality in the liturgy that enable us to experience the divine in the human and on this good earth by the use of things and actions from daily life, such as dining and bathing, to worship God. Sacramentality is a worldview that invites us to be immersed fully in the here and now, on this good earth, and not to shun matter or avoid the challenges that such earthiness will require of us, even as we pray through liturgy and sacraments (and other means) to enter into heaven when this earthly pilgrimage has ended. Since the human being is the pinnacle of God's creation (Gen 1:26–27), part of what is called "dominion" (Gen 1:18–19) is to value and revere the things God has created and to see human beings as part and parcel of that created world who carry particular responsibility to care for the world and all that dwells in it. In the liturgy, the theology of the goodness of creation and of human beings in light of the incarnation is reflected by the fact that we "use" them as the very "stuff" of the liturgy. Created human beings use other aspects of the created world to worship the God of creation, the God of the covenant, and the God of redemption. It is all of a piece and is a continuum.

TETHERED MULTIVALENCE

A term that is often used to describe the many possible ways to understand the many and varied meanings inherent in the things we use in sacraments is *multivalence* or *polyvalence*, which means "having many meanings." The more we experience and appreciate the multivalence of the things we use in sacramental liturgy, the richer will be our experience of them. For example, as will be seen below, the prayer to bless water for baptism refers to a number of things in addition to "cleansing," among which are the "power to sanctify" and "an end to vice and beginning of virtue."

Also, there is an inherent ambiguity in the doctrine of sacramentality in that the use of things from creation can be both positive and negative at the same time. We use water in baptism to signify a number of things about life and vitality. The only element, except air, without which we cannot live is water. Yet, too much water can kill vegetation. One can drown in water. What can seem to be a serene body of water may well have currents underneath that cause death by drowning. In a sense, these inherent tensions reflect precisely why and how they are used in liturgy because their use does not mean that their meaning is always apparent or obvious or even definable. Their ambiguity invites reflection on the ways in which we live what we celebrate in terms of conversion and Christian witness in the world, and how we do not. The value and importance of the prayers used with primal elements in sacramental liturgy is that they offer numerous possibilities for understanding what these elements mean and reveal.

Sacramentality is based on the goodness of creation and the engagement of humans in worship, especially through the primal elements of earth, air, fire, water, and light/darkness. These are constantly used in worship as means of naming God, experiencing God, and worshiping God. But they are used in worship in relation to words and texts, lest their use be perceived to be a pantheism of any sort (see chapter 14). The point to be made here is that our appreciation of creation and all created reality is not unfettered or a psychological "free fall." Rather, part and parcel of humans engaging in the act of worship is the use of all our human faculties of mind and heart. In worship, we use and experience things of this world—for example, water, food, oil—in themselves. We also use and experience things of this world—for example, bathing, dining, anointing—in sacramental actions. We make reference to things of this world when we combine their use with prayer texts, which most often are a review of salient moments in salvation history when God used these self-same elements to reveal and save (see chapter 14).

One of the purposes of prayer texts in sacramental liturgy is to *tether the sacramental imagination*, even as in hearing them we are directed to experience a range of their possible meanings (multivalence), offering rich avenues for reflection and deeper appropriation of what is occurring. The God of creation, of the covenant, of revelation, and of redemption is the very same God we worship through the liturgy. One needs all of these dimensions of sacramentality to try to be grasped by God and to attempt to "grasp" God. *Lex orandi, lex credendi* means that we "say" many things in and through the liturgy—sometimes with words.

CREATED AND DIVINE

Inherent in the sacramental principle is the theological reality that we use our bodies in worship. It is the genius of the liturgy of sacraments that we celebrate the mystery of faith with the very flesh and blood that God created as "good" in Genesis. In the Prologue of the Gospel of John, we are reminded that "the Word became flesh" (1:14). It was Tertullian, as discussed in chapter 2, who asserted that the flesh is the instrument of salvation. Among other things, this means Christ's taking on our own flesh and blood and our using our flesh and blood to worship God (see chapter 12).

At the same time, liturgy is also both "heaven on earth" and "the threshold of heaven." It is the most sacred thing we do because through and in it, we humans literally participate in God and are embraced by God. Liturgy is the breaking into our world of all that is of God and of the kingdom of heaven. It is the fullness of the divine offered to us, but precisely because it is sacramental, it is offered through created means and human beings. Until we are called from this good earth to a new heavens and a new earth (Rev 21:1), we use the things of this earth and of human life to commune with God through the liturgy. Sacramentality presumes engagement in the world and the use of the things on this earth; and this engagement in and through the sacred liturgy leads us to experience that which transcends this world, the transcendent yet immanent triune God.

The genius of Catholicism, and of all the churches that use the liturgy as its central form of prayer, is that the very use of the things from and of creation itself offers a symphony of praise to God our Creator and Redeemer. It is also a theology of creation in action. By using and revering the things of this earth, we show honor to the God who created and redeemed us. This is also to suggest that there is a primalness, an earthiness to the act of sacramental worship. And the act of sacramental liturgy puts the world into proper perspective. Like many other of the paradoxes in sacramental worship, it is paradoxical that we are divinized (made like God by sharing in his divine life) by the ritual use of the things of this earth. To paraphrase Pope John Paul II, who says in his encyclical *Ecclesia de Eucharistia* that the Eucharist is always celebrated "*on the altar of the world*" (no. 8), every sacrament has a "cosmic character." It is also at every Mass that we acclaim,

> Holy, Holy, Holy Lord God of hosts.
> Heaven and earth are full of your glory.
> Hosanna in the highest.
> Blessed is he who comes in the name of the Lord.
> Hosanna in the highest.

This acclamation has been a traditional part of the Eucharistic Prayer since the middle of the fifth century. It is taken from Isaiah's vision (Isa 6:3; also in Rev 4:8) acclaiming the glory of God revealed by and on the earth and from the acclamation that greeted Jesus as he entered Jerusalem for his passion (Matt 21:9, taken from Ps 118:26; also in Matt 23:39). It is notable theologically that it combines the praise of God for creation and for his Son's act of redemption.

We celebrate sacramental liturgy using the blessings of this good earth, the blessings of creation on this good earth, and human beings on this earth made in God's very image and likeness. Holiness, salvation, and redemption are given to us in sacraments because of the principles of sacramentality and mediation. We live in a graced world: the liturgy sets us in proper order and reshapes us in God's image and likeness through this act of redemption so that we can be sent forth to live in the world that we worship.

MEDIATED EXPERIENCE

At the risk of oversimplification, it can be said that there was a certain presumed robustness in the way liturgies in the patristic period were celebrated, and that at their heart, they "used" the things of creation and "the work of human hands" in recognizably engaging ways. Reading the mystagogic catecheses of Sts. Cyril of Jerusalem, Ambrose, and Theodore of Mopsuestia (see chapter 3), among other great mystagogues, reveals instructions on the sacraments based on the use of light/darkness, water, bread and wine, oil, and chrism by human beings in the community of the church. Clearly these were unselfconsciously used to worship God and to explore how God works through them. These rites evolved and changed in later centuries, so that by the time of the Scholastics, a number of distinctions were made and a certain condensing of the rites had taken place. But even then (and since), Catholicism upheld the importance of "signs" in the liturgy by insisting, at its barest minimum, on the "matter" and "form" of sacraments. Another way of saying this is that "matter matters." And Catholicism never wavered from ensuring that in and through liturgy and sacraments, the world and all that God created was part of praising, thanking, interceding, and being sanctified by that ever steadfast God of creation, of the covenant, and of redemption.

The Catholic liturgical experience is always a *mediated experience*. This means that our direct experience of God is accomplished through the use of created and manufactured things from and on this earth. By its very nature, sacramental liturgy mediates salvation and sanctification by the things of this world (human and otherwise) to those engaged in its celebration. Our direct encounter and experience with the saving deeds of our salvation is through creation, created things, and human beings. Recall again St. Augustine's famous adage (see chapter 3) that we add the "word" to the "element" and we have a sacrament.

As noted above, the phrase *mediated immediacy* is one that Edward Kilmartin, SJ, used to describe the way we humans experience God and all that is divine through the celebration of the liturgy. This can be understood to be a contemporary way of asserting St. Leo the Great's important teaching—"What was visible in our Lord has passed over to the sacraments." The way sacraments incorporate us into the saving mysteries of his passion, death, resurrection, and ascension is by the principles of sacramentality and mediation.

PRIMAL ELEMENTS: EARTH, AIR, FIRE, WATER AT THE EASTER VIGIL

EARTH, AIR, FIRE

There is always a cosmic context and a cosmic character to the celebration of the Easter Vigil. One of the many theological meanings of the Easter Vigil is that it is an act of re-creation. In the Northern Hemisphere, this is experienced by the coming of the spring. What was once given to us as "good" in the Book of Genesis is re-created each year at the Vigil liturgy, which is celebrated at night. The liturgical assembly gathers outside the church in another place, preferably in the open air. They do so in the presence of "a blazing fire" (Easter Vigil Liturgy no. 8) that has been prepared beforehand. There are obvious cosmic overtones struck at the very beginning of this liturgy. Historians of religions remind us of light festivals at the spring equinox that provide part of the cosmic character to our celebration of the vigil. Therefore, a rich theology of creation is a fundamental substratum, exemplified by the use of fire outdoors in the open air.

The fact that this liturgy begins in darkness reminds us that Christ has overcome any darkness in this world. The opening rites of the Vigil demonstrate this by being conducted with the blessing of a fire out of doors.

The priest's introduction speaks of "this most sacred night" and the text of the prayer to bless the fire immediately combines a reference to fire itself to refer to Christ, who

> *bestowed upon the faithful the fire of your glory...*
> Then with the sign of the cross (note the use of bodily gesture)
>   he says,
> *sanctify this new fire, we pray,*
> *and grant that, by these paschal celebrations*
> *we may be so inflamed with heavenly desires*
> *that with minds made pure*
> *we may attain festivities of unending splendor...*

The candle, made of beeswax (this in itself is an example of the "earthiness" of the liturgy), is inscribed with the Greek letters *alpha* and *omega*. These are the beginning and ending letters of the Greek alphabet to signify totality, beginning to end. The priest then inscribes the number of the calendar year on the candle. This shows the interrelationship of this particular annual celebration of Easter (this calendar year of Our Lord) with Easters celebrated in the past and the eternal Easter we will one day celebrate in the kingdom of heaven.

The inscription of the date reminds us that once again in this year of Our Lord the resurrection marks a definitive break in human history, an event that graces and illumines all that happens to the believer in the next twelve months, until the end of calendar time and until the end of time. The annual enactment of this rite reminds us that each year we enter into this mystery of Christ until that day of the Lord when time will end and all will be eternity, an enduring and abiding union with God that cannot be bound by time or space. At the same time, the date on the candle reminds us that this year is truly blessed and consecrated by Christ's resurrection.

The addition of placing five grains of incense into the candle (a feature derived from the Gallican liturgy, which is noted for its allegorizing tendencies) reminds us that death is the price Jesus paid for this victory over sin and death. The grains of incense refer to the wounds endured by Christ.

The priest then lights the paschal candle from the new fire saying,

> *May the light of Christ rising in glory dispel the darkness of our hearts and minds.*

The deacon (or other minister) holds the lighted paschal candle and follows the thurifer, who carries the thurible with incense burning from the flame of the new fire, in procession from the darkness outside the church into the darkened church, stopping three times to sing "Light of Christ," to which we respond "Thanks be to God." While the deacon is processing with the paschal candle, all who participate in the liturgy light smaller handheld candles from the paschal candle. Normally, this procession with three stops imitates the procession on Good Friday when the deacon, or other suitable minister, carries the veiled cross into the church, stopping three times.

The act of processing from place to place is one of the ways in which we use our bodies in worship. Almost all sacramental liturgies begin with an "entrance" procession with the ministers of the liturgy (such as at Mass) or with some members of the assembly (as at weddings or funerals). One of the meanings attached to this act of movement is that we are pilgrims on this earth, always on the way to eternity. Another more specific meaning for processions taken from liturgical history is called "the stational liturgy." This refers specifically to liturgies in which the local bishop celebrates liturgy in different churches in his diocese. The historical precedent for this is that in the early church, the Bishop of Rome (the pope) celebrated Mass daily during Lent in a different church. Each day the liturgical procession would begin where the Eucharist had been celebrated the previous day. The procession would go to the stational church for that day, then the next and the next, until the celebration of the Easter Vigil at the cathedral church of St. John Lateran. Obvious meanings here include that Lent was a communal experience in which the celebration of the liturgy figured prominently.

Through this procession following the paschal candle from outdoors into the church, and through other actions and movements in the Vigil liturgy, we experience our following of the Lord.

In the light of the candle, we see that Christ has come to shatter the darkness of sin and death:

and from the gloom of sin,
leading them to grace
and joining them to his holy ones.

The light/darkness motif, poignantly emphasized at the Easter Vigil, is intrinsic to a number of sacramental liturgies, especially the Rites of Christian Initiation that at times in liturgical history were celebrated at the Easter Vigil, and at the vigils of Epiphany and Pentecost. The light/darkness motif is central to the celebration of Evening Prayer, which itself is derived from the daily synagogue evening services that often began with a *lucernarium* hymn praising God for light in creation and for the light that illumines our minds and hearts. That this is sung at nightfall reflects and reiterates what happens at the Easter Vigil, which takes place "at night." But again we have here the ambivalence of light/darkness. While we welcome the light that triumphs over darkness, we also realize that in our lives, sometimes the darkness is never completely overwhelmed and extinguished.

Once the deacon has led the community by the light of the Easter candle, he places the candle in the stand prepared for it in the middle of the assembly and sings the traditional Easter proclamation, the first word of which in Latin is *Exsultet*, a verb inviting us to "rejoice." This proclamation has a privileged place in liturgical tradition and in the present reform of the Easter Vigil because it is a kind of overture to so many of the themes that will be raised up in the rest of the liturgy, especially in the readings, most obviously that it recounts major events of salvation history when God intervened to redeem and sanctify his chosen people. The format of the proclamation includes elements of a preface prayer, like that used at the Liturgy of the Eucharist, and a blessing prayer, such as the Eucharistic Prayer itself.

The deacon invites "all creation" to "rejoice" and "exult." The phrase *Let the trumpet of salvation sound* recalls the first reading on Ash Wednesday from Joel 2:15, which contains the exhortation to sound a trumpet, to "proclaim a fast," and to "call an assembly." The assembly gathered this night has come full circle, the fast of Lent and the Triduum now turns to a solemn feast of the Lord's salvation. Employing the cosmic symbolism of this evening liturgy, the text acclaims that darkness vanishes forever and that now, once again this year at this season, the risen Savior shines upon you. The biblical imagery of the fall explicitly refers to Adam and to Christ overcoming Adam's sin: "Who for our sake paid Adam's debt to the eternal Father / and, pouring out his own dear Blood / wiped clean the record of our ancient sinfulness." The Exodus and Passover feast is recalled when the deacon sings, "These then are the feasts of Passover / in which is slain the Lamb, the one true Lamb / whose Blood anoints the doorposts of believers." Salvation history reaches its culmination here in that what happened in the Exodus event—specifically, the marking of the homes of the Israelites—is the paradigm and the expression in the first covenant of Christ's sacrifice and the sanctification we inherit from him in the new covenant. The particularly poignant, repeated text and musical motif that support the texts, *This is the night,* lead to a rapid succession of references to light in the "pillar of fire" (also recalling the account of Israel's history read in the office of readings from the Book of Exodus during Lent), to baptism in the phrase *washes faults away,* and to resurrection in *when Christ broke the prison-bars of death.* The Easter Vigil is the night

> *that even now, throughout the world,*
> *sets Christian believers apart from worldly vices...*

The repeated use of *This is the night* and *O blessed night* combines the memorial of important moments of saving history with the event that is occurring at this Vigil. It also refers to O *truly blessed holy night, the sanctifying power of this night,* and of fire and light:

> *the praises of this pillar,*
> *which glowing fire ignites for God's honor,*
> *a fire into many flames divided,*
> *yet never dimmed by sharing of its light....*

The imagery of Adam's sin and Christ the new Adam is again referred to in the statement, "O truly necessary sin of Adam, / destroyed completely by the Death of Christ! / O happy fault / that earned so great, so glorious a Redeemer!" The Adam/Christ typology, especially seen in the euchology of Good Friday, is reiterated with the understanding that the redemption and grace of Christ far outweigh the fall and sin inherited from Adam. Hence the deacon can acclaim, "O truly blessed night, / when things of heaven are wed to those of earth" and we are wed "divine to human."

The symbol of this union is the Easter candle itself: "But now we know the praises of this pillar, which glowing fire ignites for God's honor, a fire into many flames divided, yet never dimmed by sharing of its light." The reference to the pillar of fire that led Israel to the promised land strikes a note of fulfillment. The new fire is Christ, hence it fulfills the old. It is also eschatological in the sense that the fire that led Israel to its promised homeland is now the flame of Christ who will lead us one day to our heavenly homeland. We ask that it might "overcome the darkness of this night." And that God might "receive it as a pleasing fragrance, / and let it mingle with the lights of heaven."

In the next section, nature and night symbolism refer to the union of this liturgy with the morning to follow:

> *May this flame be found still burning*
> *by the Morning Star:*
> *the one Morning Star who never sets....*

At the very end, the text combines creation with eschatology when it acclaims,

Receive it as a pleasing fragrance,
and let it mingle with the lights of heaven.

At the conclusion of the Easter proclamation, the deacon takes his place and the service of light is completed. Rich in its symbolism and full in its theology, this part of the liturgy offers something of an overture and a summary of what follows. By movement, sign, and symbol, the community is drawn into an experience professing that Christ has come, spent his life in obedience to God the Father, was betrayed, suffered, died, rose from the dead, and now shares his life with and among us in a privileged way through the liturgy.

The light symbolism is also evoked later at the liturgy of baptism (the third part of the Easter Vigil), at which time candles for the newly initiated are again lighted from the Easter candle. What occurs in this third part is the association of the light symbolism with water baptism and new life in Christ. In the meantime, however, the individual candles are put aside and the second part of this night liturgy, the Liturgy of the Word, begins (see chapter 13 below).

WATER

We have already noted that, besides air, water is the only element without which we cannot live. It signifies life and vitality for all God's creatures. For humans, ethical debates about the end of life are often about hydration as well as nutrition. Therefore it is appropriate that we use water for baptism and for the renewal of our baptismal promises at the Easter Vigil. It is also appropriate that we use water at the beginning and the end of the funeral Mass and, where it is the custom, at the end of the funeral liturgy at the rite of commendation. Water used at baptism is fittingly used when the baptized leave this world in fulfillment of what baptism signifies and accomplishes, our union with Christ risen from the dead.

One of the features of the present rite of baptism is that we bless water each time we celebrate the sacrament. The prayer does not define what baptism is and does. Rather it offers a host of metaphors for us to think about as the water is blessed. The multivalence contained in the prayer reflects what liturgical prayers regularly do. This same prayer is used at the Easter Vigil.

The prayer with some commentary follows:

O God, who by invisible power
accomplish a wondrous effect
through sacramental signs
and who in many ways have prepared water, your creation,
to show forth the grace of Baptism;

The use of terms such as *sacramental signs* and *your creation* reflect the sacramental principle. Blessing prayers are always about praising God for creation and redemption.

O God, whose Spirit
in the first moments of the world's creation
hovered over the waters,
so that the very substance of water
would even then take to itself the power to sanctify;

This is an explicit reference to Genesis 1:2, accommodated to the trinitarian belief of our theological tradition. The fact that the spirit moves over the water in Genesis is an important reminder of the action and life-giving attributes of God. "Water" is again addressed directly. Here it is referred to as having the power to make holy. Recall that the first reading at the Easter Vigil is Genesis 1:1—2:2.

O God who by the outpouring of the flood
foreshadowed regeneration,
so that from the mystery of one and the same element of water
would come an end to vice and a beginning of virtue;

The text continues to reflect the Book of Genesis, specifically chapters 6—9. These deserve prayerful reflection as they deal with sin, alienation from God, the covenant relationship, all God's creatures being saved, and human reproduction. The prayer again explicitly refers to water. Here its death-dealing qualities are noted as well as its life-giving properties. The fact that water can destroy as well as sustain life is paramount here and offers insight into the struggle between life and death in all our lives. Putting an end to vice and living the virtuous life is always a struggle, if not an outright fight.

> *O God who caused the children of Abraham*
> *to pass dry-shod through the Red Sea,*
> *so that the chosen people,*
> *set free from slavery to Pharaoh,*
> *would prefigure the people of the baptized;*

The reference to Abraham and his progeny and, by extension, to us who now share in a covenant relationship is an important introduction in the prayer's move from Genesis (chapters 11ff.) to Exodus. As in the preceding section, here, too, the possible destructive qualities of the Red Sea are turned on their side to refer to Israel's being sustained in life through this event of salvation accomplished in water. The call of Abraham in Genesis 2:1–22 is the Vigil's second reading. Exodus 14:15 — 15:1 is the third reading, accompanied by the canticle from Exodus 15.

> *O God, whose Son,*
> *baptized by John in the waters of the Jordan,*
> *was anointed with the Holy Spirit,*

The reference to filiation ("son/daughtership") is very important for underscoring the personal relationship enjoyed by the baptized with the three persons of the Trinity. The anointing of Jesus with the Holy Spirit in the Jordan stands as a moment of demarcation for his role as Messiah. The fact that these texts (Matt 3:13–17; Mark. 1:7–11; Luke 3:15–16, 21–22) are read on the now restored Feast of the Baptism of the Lord is very significant.

> *and, as he hung upon the Cross,*
> *gave forth water from his side along with blood,*

These references to John 19:34 and 1 John 5 are very important because they have been used in a number of ways, especially by patristic authors, to describe the saving effects of Jesus' death and resurrection

223

as commemorated in the sacraments. The classic reference is Augustine's comment that the church is born from the wounded side of Christ.

> *and after his resurrection, commanded his disciples:*
>   *"Go forth, teach all nations, baptizing them*
>   *in the name of the Father and of the Son and of the*
>   *Holy Spirit,*

This reference to the end of the Gospel of St. Matthew offers a number of interpretations, including that the baptized now share in the life of the Trinity and that all the baptized are to be evangelizers and are to go forth and witness in the world to the life-giving saving mysteries of the ascended Christ who intercedes for us at the Father's right hand, principally through the liturgy.

> *look now, we pray, upon the face of your Church*
> *and graciously unseal for her the fountain of Baptism.*

The recounting of significant moments of salvation history now turns to the experience of the same gracious intervention by the God of the covenant and to the three-personed God in whom we live and move. The reference to the "fountain" of baptism can serve as a reminder that baptism is often referred to as "the fountain of life."

> *May this water receive by the Holy Spirit*
> *the grace of your Only Begotten Son,*
> *so that human nature, created in your image*
> *and washed clean through the Sacrament of Baptism*
> *from all the squalor of the life of old,*
> *may be found worthy to rise to the life of newborn children*
> *through water and the Holy Spirit.*

The prayer again explicitly refers to water (twice) and to humans being created in God's image—both taken from Genesis, the Easter Vigil's first reading. The use of *only begotten Son* is important here when we pray that those to be baptized will be begotten by God and from above (recall the Nicodemus dialogue in John 3). That within six lines the Holy Spirit is referred to twice is again significant of the Spirit's role in baptism and in sustaining the life of God given to those who are baptized in the communion of the church.

> *May the power of the Holy Spirit,*
> *O Lord, we pray,*
> *come down through your Son*
> *into the fullness of this font,*

Again the Holy Spirit is invoked in the classical way of liturgical prayers—from the Father through the Son. This trinitarian mediation is important as it underscores how through the Trinity we experience the presence and action of God in our lives. The reference to *font* for water baptism is significant; it recalls that patristic authors have capitalized on this as both a "womb" and a "tomb." The multivalence of these words should not be lost here. It is a womb to give birth as does a mother's womb, and it also begets new members in the church. It is a tomb because it recalls the days Jesus spent in the tomb between his death and resurrection and is a tomb in which we are to place all that is death-dealing in our lives.

> *so that all who have been buried with Christ*
> *by Baptism into death*
> *may rise again to life with him.*

This explicit reference to Romans 6 recalls the first New Testament reading from the Easter Vigil and reiterates a classical understanding of what baptism accomplishes. The use of the word *may* is interesting, again because of its possible multivalence. One meaning is that we ask that God accomplish this now, namely, that we have new life with Christ here and now. But when read against the actual text of Romans 6, there is an eschatological motif here, namely, "that we shall also live with him," not only here and now but in heaven forever. A play on the *already* and *not yet* of all Christian liturgy is operative here.

> *Who lives and reigns with you in the unity of the Holy Spirit,*
> *one God, for ever and ever.*

The prayer's conclusion reiterates that it is through the power of the Holy Spirit that we can do anything liturgically. It also affirms the unity and diversity of the church as it is incorporated into the Trinity ("in the unity of…").

Take the blessing prayer for water and the liturgical fact that fresh and clean water is blessed at every baptism (except during the Easter season). The very fact that we bless water each time we use it in initiation and (can) bless oil for the anointing of the sick every time we use it for the sacrament, as well as bread and wine for the Eucharist, is itself theologically significant: blessing prayers matter, liturgically and theologically. They matter ritually in that they bless ever fresh elements from the earth for humanity's sanctification. So, when the prayer of blessing lyrically recounts how water has been used in salvation history as a rich symbol of God's graciousness, what occurs here and now is that the contemporary community is drawn into the sweep of saving history in this act of blessing God. Blessing prayers thus remind us of what God has done through these paradigmatic acts. They also thus remind us that this same God acts in these same ways here and now. Reliance on saving history reminds us that our own personal and collective histories are similarly blessed by God's presence and action.

The prayer is thus effective in drawing us more fully into the paradigmatic events of salvation history while at the same time through this blessed water, it makes present an act of recreation and redemption here and now through creation's gift of water. The refreshing and life-sustaining properties of water do not diminish. Through the act of blessing, they are in fact magnified. Hence when persons are immersed in it for sacramental initiation, the chosen ones are cleansed and refreshed through creation's gift of water itself. This liturgical act and the liturgical theology derived from it place the emphasis less on what sacraments *cause* than on the fact that the blessed water reminds us of all creation as God's blessing and that its use here in baptism effects a new act of blessing, now of this person. The water retains its intentionality—as that which gives life, without which we cannot live. When used liturgically, water does precisely what it is intended to do. It does not become something else. It sanctifies by being what it is, declared so by the prayer of blessing.

AGENDA IN LIFE

The celebration of the liturgy of baptism presumes the blessing of fresh water. However, the reality of how water is allocated and used in our world may well challenge and even diminish some of the liturgical theology that can be derived from these liturgical rites. Today the state of water is both tragic and paradoxical. Water covers nearly 75 percent of the earth's surface, but only 3 percent of it is fresh water and less than 1 percent of the earth's fresh water is accessible and usable by humans. But one billion people on the planet (one out of eight) do not have access to clean water. This results in 3.5 million deaths each year from water related illnesses, of which 84 percent are children (as of this writing, approximately one child every twenty seconds). The use and costs of water are also unequally distributed. For example, a person in the United States uses more water in a five-minute shower than a person in the developing world uses all day, and the urban poor often pay five to ten times more per liter of water than their wealthy neighbors in the same city. The crisis is compounded by competing interests (agriculture, industry, and domestic use), ineffective management by governments, increased efforts to privatize water supply and distribution, war and political instability, and a general lack of political will to address the crisis. Water is poised to be a major source, if not *the* major source, of international conflict for the next century, which will result in failed states, intra- and interstate conflict, famine, migration, and global economic pressures.

One of the principal debates surrounding the global water crisis is whether water is a human right or a commodity. Water is a basic necessity for human existence as are food, air, shelter, and health care. Without water, people die. Thus classifying water as a human right seems accurate. But what is often overlooked in the "human right or commodity debate" is that water requires expensive infrastructure (purification and a delivery system) and labor in order to be useable. Some of the basic necessities of human existence, such as air, are readily available and are freely distributed, while others, such as food, clothing, shelter, and health care are labor intensive and require

227

infrastructure. While water at first seems more like air in that it is often available free of charge from rivers, lakes, and rain, usable/potable water is not free. As such water is more like the other basic necessities that are treated as both rights and commodities. The Catholic Church's teachings on water reflect a more nuanced understanding of water as both a right and a commodity.

The *Compendium of the Social Doctrine of the Church* describes water as "a gift from God" to which "everyone has a right" and decries treating water as "just another commodity among many" or as "merely an economic good." Pope Benedict XVI, on World Water Day 2007, clarified the Church's understanding of water by describing water as "a common good of the human family" and "an essential element for life." He went on to say, "Access to water is in fact one of the inalienable rights of every human" that ought to be managed according to the ethical principles of subsidiarity, participation, and the preferential option for the poor. Important to note here is that Catholic social teaching on water describes *access* to water as a right and decries treating water exclusively as a commodity, but it does not preclude the privatization of water. Instead it engages the Church's teaching on private property, which distinguishes between "use" and "ownership."

The focus here is the intersection of water, ethics, and sacrament. In Catholic social thought, water is both a *common good* (given by God intended for all to use) and a *material good* that can be privately owned, so long as "access to safe water and sanitation for all" is guaranteed. If the water crisis were simply about questions of access and sanitation, then this would be principally a matter of social justice. But water ethics spills over into sacramental theology because water is used in liturgy and sacrament. The global water crisis is redefining water's meaning. What was once a symbol of purification and life has for many become a commodity they cannot afford and a symbol of filth and death. This makes the global water crisis not only a social justice issue, but one of sacramental stewardship as well.

It ought to be obvious that care for the environment should be a presumed consequence of liturgical celebration. This is concretized in how we use water and how water rights are determined. There is an important connection between using water in sacraments and how peoples on this earth are enabled to have sufficient and potable water for their very survival.

The theology of stewardship is also implied for it is the genius of the human person to praise God for the gifts of creation and thereby to restore creation to its legitimately exalted place as icon of all of God's blessings toward us. Human beings bless God over things and persons, and these blessings keep their intentionality but also, through the act of blessing, make explicit God's presence among us. The theological issue rests on what it means to bless God. The church's *lex orandi* gives us a major insight into understanding through our present blessing prayers, in which persons and things are held in relationship, retain their intentionality and make explicit God's presence.

Thus the act of liturgy and engagement in sacraments is seen to be central, even pivotal, for any proper appreciation of creation's sacramentality. If one of the Catholic contributions to the burgeoning ecological consciousness is our liturgical and theological tradition as brought to bear for a theological vision of environmental concerns, then it is imperative to review and disclose what our liturgical prayers say, enact, and do. Our thesis is that they make explicit and direct the theology of creation and of sacraments toward revering God's presence in all of creation before, during, and after the liturgy. From the perspective of the way the liturgy integrates belief, thought, and prayer on the basis of the sacramental imagination, it would seem that a Catholic way of articulating this sacramental vision and lens on creation might well be through what we term the *liturgical imagination*.

DISCUSSION QUESTIONS

1. Review the liturgy for the Easter Vigil, noting all of its cosmic elements, for example, the act of assembling outdoors, the blessing of the new fire, light, darkness, water, chrism, bread, and wine. Discuss where these are found in other liturgies and what they mean in them.

2. Discuss the positive and negative properties of fire and water and how that affects your understanding of their use in sacramental liturgy.
3. In light of the teaching from St. Leo the Great mentioned earlier, reflect on the ways in which what Christ accomplished on earth are now found in the sacraments.

12

HUMANS AND HUMAN WORK

The purpose of this chapter is to complement the previous chapter on sacramentality to consider (1) the engagement of our human bodies in the liturgy, (2) things manufactured by "the work of human hands" that are also intrinsic to the enactment of the sacraments, and (3) an indication of how the human work intrinsic to the celebration of sacraments influences the way we live our lives.

"SACRAMENTS ARE FOR HUMANS"

The phrase *sacramenta sunt propter homines* ("sacraments are for humans") has often been used, especially in Catholicism, to describe the obvious—that sacraments are celebrated for the benefit of those who participate in them. In effect, this is to say that sacraments are not "things." They are events and special means of participating in acts of salvation and redemption.

We saw another related classic phrase from Tertullian (see chapter 2), who stated that "the flesh is the instrument of salvation." This can refer to Christ, the incarnate Word, who as "the Word of the Father" took on our human flesh and became one of us in order to save us. Another meaning of the phrase is that we who are human participate in the liturgy and sacraments by the use of our bodies and our human faculties. This reflects the assertion that every action and gesture we perform in sacraments has one or more theological meanings (see chapter 10). One of the sparks that make sacraments "work" precisely as sacraments is the interrelationship of words, symbols, and gestures enacted through our bodies and engaging our human faculties. The faculties of sight, sound, smell, taste, and touch, as well as bodily movement, are presumed to be involved in the liturgy. The "bodiliness" of worship means that our human bodies and faculties are respected and presumed to be engaged in and through the liturgy.

There is therefore a "sacramental appropriateness" in the way we worship God, in that our humanity and the things that humans do in daily life are used in sacraments for the worship of God and our sanctification. In other words, this means that the sacraments comprise an ensemble of things to see, hear, touch, taste, and smell.

Sacraments presume that we use our bodies to move from place to place in procession and that these processions mean something theologically. At the Easter Vigil, for example (see chapter 11), those who comprise the liturgical assembly gather outdoors and process indoors to the church (movement). The primal nature of the liturgy is also reflected here in the people's assembling in the dark and the blessing of the new fire (light). It also refers to leaving the outdoors to enter the church to celebrate the sacraments whereby catechumens become Catholic Christians and candidates become Catholics. The rather extensive Liturgy of the Word involves sight and sound. After the homily, those to be baptized process to the baptismal font (movement). The candidates step into the baptismal pool where the presider pours water over their heads and bodies (gesture), after which they emerge from the waters (movement). The commentary on this gesture from the patristic era rings true here. The font is a womb and a tomb—a womb that gives new life, and a tomb from which Christ emerged after three days. The newly baptized then receive confirmation by having their heads anointed with chrism (a mixture of olive oil and balsam; see further). They then join the assembly for the presentation of the gifts (movement, gesture) and the Eucharistic Prayer (sight, sound), after which they partake in the Eucharist for the first time (taste, movement).

For those already baptized in another Christian church, their initiation involves a profession of faith and the rites as described above from confirmation onward (procession and gesture).

In the case of infant baptism outside of the Easter Vigil, the liturgy of the sacrament begins at the door of the church with rites in which the presider (priest or deacon), parents, and godparents engage in a dialogue (sight, sound) about what the parents are requesting and the assistance the godparents will provide, as well as in the action of tracing of the sign of the cross on the infants' foreheads (gesture). The location again is important—at the door from outside and then processing into the gathered assembly of the faithful. After the Liturgy of the Word (sight, sound), the families process to the baptismal font (movement). At the font, the infants will either be immersed in the water or water will be poured on them. As noted in the previous chapter, that action is accompanied by the blessing prayer, which contains rich imagery of what the sacrament enacts through gesture and movement. The fact that immersion is the first preference given in the rite for infant baptism indicates the church's concern to engage bodies in their fullness. The immersion of naked babies in the baptismal font speaks very expressively in a nonverbal way about the life-giving qualities of water baptism. This is followed by the anointing with chrism, a mixture of olive oil and balsam (more on this further), whose fragrance is notable and sweet smelling (sense of smell). The families then process (movement) to the altar area where they will together say the Lord's Prayer. The move to the altar signifies that the child will one day partake of the Eucharist, bread and wine consecrated at the altar and communion received from the altar.

"THE WORK OF HUMAN HANDS"

It is important to recall here part of our discussion about St. Augustine's theology of sacraments (chapter 3). Against the Pelagian heresy, which taught that humans could "earn" their salvation by performing good works, Augustine argued that while good works were important, it was God's initiative and action that always offered salvation to the human race and that humans responded to God's initiative in a number of ways, including good works, among which are the sacraments.

The traditional prayer of blessing prayed by the priest as he places bread and wine on the altar describes this carefully:

Blessed are you, Lord God of all creation,
for through your goodness we have received
the bread/wine we offer you:
fruit of the earth and work of human hands,
it will become for us the bread of life/our spiritual drink.

Note how this prayer refers to God's gift that "we have received" as what we offer back to God.

One of the principal theological reasons why reflection on the work of human hands is important is that these manufactured (literally, "made by human hands") signs and symbols respect human ingenuity in that they require planning and the expenditure of humans' time to produce what is needed for the sacraments—that is, before any act of liturgy or sacrament takes place, human ingenuity, artistry, and time have been offered to God outside of and leading to the liturgy. The adage *No work, no Mass* is understood and expanded to mean that every sacramental sign, symbol, and thing presupposes the sacrifice of time, talent, and treasure brought to the liturgy in order for us to be continually transformed by the paschal sacrifice of Christ.

One of the factors that the church has presumed, and about which the recent popes John Paul II and Benedict XVI reminded us, is that the things destined for the worship of God should be good, true, and beautiful. One of the reasons is that God is all true, good, and beautiful, and anything that is designed to honor God should have those same qualities. This adds a criterion beyond the utilitarian when it comes to sacramental liturgy. Put differently, if what we use and do in the liturgy is to honor God, then it should be dignified, beautiful, and in itself should pay homage to God. The strictly utilitarian, the functional, not to say the cheap or the trite should have no place in sacramental worship. At the same time, this need not mean opulence or money squandered, a caution that would fit in well with the repeated exhortations from Pope Francis, especially from his encyclical on ecology, *Laudato Si'*: On Care for Our Common Home (2015).

The word *liturgy* comes from a Greek word and literally means "public work." Among the meanings connected with this term are "the work of the people," "a work that takes place in public according to a fixed ritual," or a "public act to honor God." Underlying all of these meanings is that what we humans do in and through the liturgy is really initiated and sustained by God's invitation and sustaining, life-giving grace. The third Eucharistic Prayer puts it this way:

> *Listen graciously to the prayers of this family,*
> *whom you have summoned before you:*
> *in your compassion, O merciful Father,*
> *gather to yourself all your children*
> *scattered throughout the world.*

Therefore we understand everything we do before and during the enactment of the sacraments as inspired and sustained by God, through Christ, in the power and communion of the Holy Spirit.

It is that same Holy Spirit who endows all believers with gifts and talents, which, taken together, offer a symphony of praise and thanks to God, both before and at the liturgy itself. St. Paul speaks of the *charisms* ("gifts") given to everyone for the sake of the common good. In the Letter to the Romans, he calls them "gifts that differ" (12:6) and lists several charisms in other letters (see Eph 4:11–16 and 1 Cor 12:4–11).

The act of sacramental liturgy presumes on these and is enacted because of these. We will discuss "liturgical roles" later (chapter 15), but what is important to note here is the varied talents and human work that precede and accompany the celebration of sacraments.

Even before moving to particular things used in the celebration of the sacraments, human artistry and the use of beautiful things are noteworthy, specifically with regard to the churches or other places in which we worship God and the music used in the liturgy.

BREAD AND WINE

The central elements of the Eucharist—bread and wine—are not "natural" symbols like water and light, but are manufactured symbols, the result of human ingenuity and hard work. The sacred meal that becomes the Eucharist involves the cycle of planting, harvesting, milling wheat into flour, and baking bread, and planting, harvesting, crushing grapes, and fermenting them to become our spiritual food and drink. There is something very fitting about this cycle of dying and rising to produce the bread and wine, consecrated to become the means for our participating in the dying and rising of Christ, the paschal mystery; note the biblical metaphor for this in John 12:24: "Unless a grain of wheat falls into the earth and dies." The human actions involved in making the bread and wine for the Eucharist are *paschal* processes—they involve dying and rising—just as we take part in the paschal mystery of Christ through our participation in the Eucharist (see chapter 15). This means that the "bread-ness" of bread and the "wine-ness" of wine make significant theological statements about what the Eucharist is.

The *General Instruction of the Roman Missal* says the following about the bread and wine:

> The bread for celebrating the Eucharist must be made only from wheat, must be recently made, and, according to the ancient tradition of the Latin Church, must be unleavened.
>
> By reason of the sign, it is required that the material for the Eucharistic Celebration truly have the appearance of food. Therefore, it is desirable that the Eucharistic Bread, even though unleavened and made in the traditional form, be fashioned in such a way that the Priest at Mass with the people is truly able to break it into parts and distribute these to at least some of the faithful. However, small hosts are not at all excluded when the large number of those receiving Holy Communion or other pastoral reasons call for them. Moreover, the gesture of the fraction or breaking of bread, which was quite simply the term by which the Eucharist was known in apostolic times, will bring out more clearly the force and importance of the sign of the unity of all in the one bread, and of the sign of charity by the fact that the one bread is distributed among the brothers and sisters.
>
> The wine for the celebration of the Eucharist must be from the fruit of the vine (cf. Lk 22:18), natural, and

unadulterated, that is, without admixture of extraneous substances.

The rite of presenting bread and wine is central to the celebration of the Eucharist. This is the meaning of the prayer at the very end of the Roman Canon (referring to a variety of foodstuffs):

> *Through whom you continue to make all these good things,*
>   *O Lord,*
> *you sanctify them, fill them with life,*
> *bless them, and bestow them upon us…*

Among the important theological meanings that the *GIRM* attaches to the bread at the Eucharist is reflected in the design and size of the host used by the priest. That it should be large enough to break into pieces for the communion of at least some of the faithful indicates the importance of sharing in the same broken bread at Mass. The bread broken and shared is a dramatic evidence of the fact that we partake together in the one bread as the Body of Christ to build us as the Body of Christ, the church. A parallel to bread broken and shared occurs when the chalice from which the priest drinks at Mass is one of the chalices (when two or more are required) used for the distribution to the congregation.

HOLY OILS AND CHRISM

The use of olive oil for anointing in sacramental liturgy derives from the Mediterranean basin, where to this day the human manufacture of oil and its use in daily life, especially cooking, is presumed, although another plant oil can be used as a substitute, according to local circumstances.

Three oils are used in sacramental liturgy. They are blessed by the diocesan bishop each year during the days preceding the Evening Mass of the Lord's Supper. While Holy Thursday is the traditional day for the oils to be blessed, and this is done by the pope in Rome and in some dioceses, it is not uncommon for this so-called Chrism Mass to take place some days earlier, so that as many priests and representatives from the (arch)diocese as possible may be present to participate.

Oil of the Sick. This is used whenever the sacrament of the anointing of the sick is celebrated—for example, in common at a parish Mass, in a hospital chapel, or at the bedside of an individual. This oil is traditionally blessed at the very end of the Eucharistic Prayer, before the bishop sings or says the doxology ("through him…"), but sometimes it is blessed outside of Mass or at another place during the Chrism Mass, such as after the homily.

Oil of Catechumens. This is used to anoint adult catechumens during the process of reception into the Catholic Church and to anoint infants at their baptism. It is usually blessed during the Chrism Mass after the prayer following communion, unless, like the other oils, it is blessed at a different point in the liturgy.

Sacred Chrism. The fact that the prayer used over the sacred chrism is a prayer for *consecration* and not simply *blessing* indicates that it is revered as the most important and precious of the oils used in sacramental liturgy. As noted above, chrism is used in the celebration of infant baptism and confirmation, the ordination of priests and bishops, as well as in the rite for the dedication of a church and an altar (when, in effect, the building is "baptized").

BOOKS

The invention of the printing press was a major development in the ability to transmit information and ideas. But with it came less need for scriptoria in monasteries and calligraphers for the production of Bibles and books for the liturgy. The present major revolution that has shifted attention from the printed word in printed books to the printed word on computer screens and tablets of a variety of types is certainly another major revolution in the way print material is disseminated.

However, the books used for the liturgy are of another sort. They have been and ought to be made of the finest materials and contain the best of Christian art. These books have their origins from the

Jewish tradition of scrolls containing the Torah, and covers for the scrolls made of precious materials and sometimes bejeweled, all to reflect respect for the fact that this is God's revelation. The phrase *the work of human hands* extends here to the book designers and manufacturers. Liturgical books should be recognizably beautiful books.

The *General Instruction of the Roman Missal* directs,

> Special care must be taken to ensure that the liturgical books, particularly the Book of the Gospels and the Lectionary, which are intended for the proclamation of the Word of God and hence receive special veneration, are to be in a liturgical action truly signs and symbols of higher realities and hence should be truly worthy, dignified, and beautiful. (no. 349)

It also describes the importance of this book and the proclamation of the Gospel itself:

> The reading of the Gospel constitutes the high point of the Liturgy of the Word. The Liturgy itself teaches the great reverence that is to be shown to this reading by setting it off from the other readings with special marks of honor, by the fact of which minister is appointed to proclaim it and by the blessing or prayer with which he prepares himself; and also by the fact that through their acclamations the faithful acknowledge and confess that Christ is present and is speaking to them and stand as they listen to the reading; and by the mere fact of the marks of reverence that are given to the Book of the Gospels.

Thus, among the books for the liturgy, the *Book of the Gospels* has prominence. At the beginning of Mass, it is carried in procession, usually by the deacon who will proclaim it during the liturgy, and placed on the altar. The *Book of the Gospels* is then carried in procession, sometimes accompanied by candles and incense, for the proclamation of the Gospel, which takes place from the ambo. In Masses where the bishop presides after the deacon proclaims the Gospel, the deacon carries the Gospel book to the bishop, who kisses it at the place of the Gospel text for that day. Then, "In more solemn celebrations, if appropriate, a Bishop may impart a blessing to the people with the *Book of the Gospels*" (GIRM 175).

All of this suggests that liturgical books are to be very carefully designed with the greatest artistry and should be treated with great care. (Recall that these are among the "variables" in the celebration of the sacraments, as stated in chapter 10.)

VESTURE

Every sacrament is enacted with liturgical ministers, many of whom wear special clothing. The term *vestment*, which is often used to describe these, means an outer garment signifying a robe of office or for a ceremony—for example, the judicial robes worn by judges in courtrooms. In the liturgy, the vestment that may be worn by all liturgical ministers is the white garment called the *alb* (from the Latin, meaning "white"). The alb takes its origin from the baptismal ceremonies in the early church, when at the Easter Vigil the newly baptized would emerge naked from the baptismal font and be clothed in these white garments. They would have worn them for the week following their sacramental initiation and then put them aside on the Second Sunday of Easter, which is called the "octave day of Easter"; the number eight signifies the new creation, that is, the addition of one day to the seven days of creation to signify entrance into the "new creation." One of the classic commentaries on what happens at baptism is from St. Augustine: "Let us rejoice and give thanks. We have not only become Christians but Christ himself....Stand in awe and rejoice: we have become Christ." Because the alb is associated with baptism, all baptized ministers may wear it. The GIRM states, "The sacred garment common to ordained and instituted ministers of any rank is the alb, to be tied at the waist with a cincture unless it is made so as to fit even without such" (no. 336) and then continues, "In the dioceses of the United States of America, acolytes, altar servers, lectors, and other lay ministers may wear the alb or other suitable vesture or other appropriate and dignified clothing" (no. 339).

The *GIRM* points out that other vestments are proper to ordained ministers only:

> In the Church, which is the Body of Christ, not all members have the same function. This diversity of offices is shown outwardly in the celebration of the Eucharist by the diversity of sacred vestments, which must therefore be a sign of the function proper to each minister. Moreover, these same sacred vestments should also contribute to the decoration of the sacred action itself. The vestments worn by Priests and Deacons, as well as the attire worn by lay ministers, are blessed before being put into liturgical use according to the rite described in the Roman Ritual. (no. 335)

The vestments proper to the priest are the stole and the chasuble; the vestments proper to the deacon are the stole (worn over the left shoulder) and the dalmatic. The *GIRM* asserts

> It is fitting that the beauty and nobility of each vestment not be sought in an abundance of overlaid ornamentation, but rather in the material used and in the design. Ornamentation on vestments should, moreover, consist of figures, that is, of images or symbols, that denote sacred use, avoiding anything unbecoming to this. (no. 344)

Words such as *beauty* and *nobility* are important statements about the artistry and creativity that go into conceiving and designing vesture. "The work of human hands" is also involved in the making of the cloth and the sewing of the vesture.

The word *chasuble* comes from the Latin *casula*, which means an outer garment worn in the Late Roman Empire. The word *dalmatic* comes from the late Latin *dalmatica*, signifying a tunic, another kind of outward garment. The Latin *stola* gives us the word *stole*, whose liturgical use probably comes from the time when Constantine gave permission for church officials to wear clothing originally designed for imperial officials, with its shape and color designed to reflect status in Roman society. The stole was (and is) worn around the neck.

Another vestment that may be worn when celebrating sacraments outside of the Mass is called the *cope*, which "is worn by the Priest in processions and during other sacred actions, in accordance with the rubrics proper to the individual rites" (*GIRM* 341).

The *GIRM* continues, "Diversity of color in the sacred vestments has as its purpose to give more effective expression even outwardly whether to the specific character of the mysteries of faith to be celebrated or to a sense of Christian life's passage through the course of the liturgical year" (no. 345). It then lists the liturgical colors in use today. It is common for the minister presiding at a sacramental celebration to wear white or a color to reflect the feast or season. While the "Introduction" to the *Rite of Penance* indicates that the liturgical vestments in the celebration of penance are laid down by the local bishop (no. 14), most commonly the priest wears an alb and purple stole, purple indicating penitence, the same color of vesture as is used during Advent and Lent.

CHURCH BUILDINGS

The very design and construction of a place for the celebration of the sacraments presumes artistry, imagination, and creativity on the part of the architect or designer. It also presumes an outlay of natural resources from the earth to build the building, as well as the effort of the laborers who construct it. Another factor is that the Catholic Church has always been supportive of the arts as destined for liturgical use, as reflected in chapter 7 of the Constitution on the Sacred Liturgy, part of which follows:

> Very rightly the fine arts are considered to rank among the noblest activities of man's genius, and this applies especially to religious art and to its highest achievement, which is sacred art. These arts, by their very nature, are oriented toward the infinite beauty of God which they attempt in some way to portray by the work of human hands; they achieve their purpose of redounding to God's praise and glory in proportion as they are directed the more exclusively to the single aim of turning men's minds devoutly toward God.

Holy Mother Church has therefore always been the friend of the fine arts and has ever sought their noble help, with the special aim that all things set apart for use in divine worship should be truly worthy, becoming, and beautiful, signs and symbols of the supernatural world, and for this purpose she has trained artists. In fact, the Church has, with good reason, always reserved to herself the right to pass judgment upon the arts, deciding which of the works of artists are in accordance with faith, piety, and cherished traditional laws, and thereby fitted for sacred use.

The Church has been particularly careful to see that sacred furnishings should worthily and beautifully serve the dignity of worship, and has admitted changes in materials, style, or ornamentation prompted by the progress of the technical arts with the passage of time. (no. 122)

The Constitution on the Sacred Liturgy reiterates that the church authorities have never chosen one school of architecture over another:

The Church has not adopted any particular style of art as her very own; she has admitted styles from every period according to the natural talents and circumstances of peoples, and the needs of the various rites. Thus, in the course of the centuries, she has brought into being a treasury of art which must be very carefully preserved. The art of our own days, coming from every race and region, shall also be given free scope in the Church, provided that it adorns the sacred buildings and holy rites with due reverence and honor; thereby it is enabled to contribute its own voice to that wonderful chorus of praise in honor of the Catholic faith sung by great men in times gone by. (no. 123)

The bishops of the United States have given directives about church buildings and their contents in the document *Built of Living Stones* (2000). The sections of this document on the celebration of the sacraments are of particular relevance for our purposes. In addition, it should be noted that buildings designed for liturgical purposes should envision the celebration of all the sacraments, not only the Eucharist, and should allow adequate space for the processions and movement intrinsic to the celebration of the liturgy.

For the effective celebration of the revised liturgies of the sacraments, a number of things within the worship space deserve special attention and care in design and scale.

Baptistery. With the revision of rites for infant baptism and adult initiation, the *baptistery* receives special attention. It is very important that it be designed to allow for immersion of infants and the generous pouring of water on adult candidates so that the movement and gestures of the liturgies can be effectively seen and participated in.

Ambo. Because all of the revised sacramental rituals contain a liturgy of the word and the ministry of preaching has received increased attention, it is important that the ambo be well designed, visible for all to see, and have effective sound amplification.

Presider's chair. This should be situated in such a way that the presider can be seen and heard by all. In cathedral churches it is called the *cathedra*, which means the chair where the bishop sits and from which he presides. Its meaning goes as far back as the Jewish liturgical tradition where rabbis are seated when they preach and teach. This is a sign of their authority to teach and their responsibility to be well schooled in what they teach. (This is why Jesus sits down to articulate the Beatitudes in the Gospel of Matthew 5:1–11.)

Altar. From the patristic era to today, the phrase *the altar is Christ* has been used to indicate its centrality and the place where Christ's sacrifice is enacted. When a church is dedicated (see *Rite for the Dedication of a Church*) the altar is anointed with chrism and the bishop prays,

> *O God, sanctifier and ruler of your Church,*
> *it is right for us to celebrate your name*
> *in joyful proclamation;*
> *for today your faithful people desire*
> *to dedicate to you,*
> *solemnly and for all time,*
> *this house of prayer,*

where they worship you devoutly,
are instructed by the word,
and are nourished by the Sacraments.

This house brings to light the mystery of the Church,
which Christ made holy by the shedding of his blood,
so that he might present her to himself
as a glorious Bride,
a Virgin resplendent with the integrity of faith,
a Mother made fruitful by the power of the Spirit.

Holy is the Church,
the chosen vine of the Lord,
whose branches fill the whole world,
and whose tendrils, borne on the wood of the Cross,
reach upward to the Kingdom of Heaven.

Blessed is the Church,
God's dwelling-place with the human race,
a holy temple built of living stones,
standing upon the foundation of the Apostles
with Christ Jesus its chief cornerstone.

Exalted is the Church,
a City set high on a mountain for all to see,
resplendent to every eye
with the unfading light of the Lamb,
and resounding with the sweet hymn of the Saints.

Therefore, O Lord, we beseech you:
graciously pour forth from heaven your sanctifying power upon
    this church and upon this altar,
to make this for ever a holy place
with a table always prepared for the Sacrifice of Christ.
Here may the flood of divine grace
overwhelm human offenses,
so that your children, Father,
being dead to sin,
may be reborn to heavenly life.

Here may your faithful,
gathered around the table of the altar,
celebrate the memorial of the Paschal Mystery
and be refreshed by the banquet
of Christ's Word and his Body.

Here may the joyful offering of praise resound,
with human voices joined to the song of Angels,
and unceasing prayer rise up to you
for the salvation of the world.

Here may the poor find mercy,
the oppressed attain true freedom,
and all people be clothed with the dignity of your children,
until they come exultant
to the Jerusalem which is above.
Through our Lord Jesus Christ, your Son,
who lives and reigns with you in the unity of the Holy Spirit,
one God, for ever and ever.
Amen.

MUSIC

The Constitution on the Sacred Liturgy devotes all of chapter 6 to this issue:

> The musical tradition of the universal Church is a treasure of inestimable value, greater even than that of any other art. The main reason for this pre-eminence is that, as sacred song united to the words, it forms a necessary or integral part of the solemn liturgy.
>
> Holy Scripture, indeed, has bestowed praise upon sacred song, and the same may be said of the fathers of the Church and of the Roman pontiffs who in recent times, led by St. Pius X, have explained more precisely the ministerial function supplied by sacred music in the service of the Lord.
>
> Therefore sacred music is to be considered the more holy in proportion as it is more closely connected with the litur-

gical action, whether it adds delight to prayer, fosters unity of minds, or confers greater solemnity upon the sacred rites. But the Church approves of all forms of true art having the needed qualities, and admits them into divine worship.

Accordingly, the sacred Council, keeping to the norms and precepts of ecclesiastical tradition and discipline, and having regard to the purpose of sacred music, which is the glory of God and the sanctification of the faithful, decrees as follows... (no. 112)

The phrase "the glory of God and the sanctification of the faithful" has its roots in Pope Pius X's *motu proprio* on sacred music, in which he encourages active participation in the liturgy for these purposes. The phrase has been reiterated several times in recent papal teaching to indicate what is at the heart of liturgical participation.

In the rest of chapter 6 of the Constitution on the Sacred Liturgy, in subsequent papal magisterial statements, and in the US bishops conference document *Sing to the Lord* (see chapter 10), a number of guidelines are provided about what kind of music and texts are appropriate for the celebration of the liturgy, with several options left to national episcopal conferences or the discretion of the diocesan bishop. At the same time, all sacramental liturgies contain texts that are to be regarded as normative for the theology of what the sacraments celebrate. The closer the actual music used at the liturgy comes to these normative texts, the more reliable will be the liturgical theology derived from these rites.

AGENDA FOR LIFE

IN THE LITURGY

The Missal for the Evening Mass of the Lord's Supper, which begins the Easter Triduum, states, "At the beginning of the Liturgy of the Eucharist, there may be a procession of the faithful in which gifts for the poor may be presented with the bread and wine." This reflects the classic Roman liturgy when gifts for the poor were also brought in procession with bread and wine, and the role of deacons was to help that ritual action and then to distribute the food after the liturgy ended.

That food distribution is a hallmark of our charity reflects an inherent Catholic aspect of the Eucharist as always a celebration of the church and always concerned for those who do not have enough to eat. In light of Pope Benedict's addresses about food distribution and just wages, one can easily argue that this is part and parcel of the meaning of the celebration of the Eucharist. Related to this is land distribution and how equitably the world's resources are shared. This may also call into question our methods of farming and the need for newer technologies to support the world's increasing population and need for food. In and through the celebration of the Eucharist we are drawn into and experience the paschal mystery of Christ made possible by "the work of human hands." Clearly part of a creation consciousness about the liturgy is that we experience "the works of our redemption" through "the work of human hands," then sanctified and given as the bread of life and cup of eternal salvation.

These offerings are then brought forward in the liturgy. It is praiseworthy for the bread and wine to be presented by the faithful. They are then accepted at an appropriate place by the priest or the deacon and carried to the altar. Even though the faithful no longer bring from their own possessions the bread and wine intended for the liturgy as in the past, nevertheless the rite of carrying up the offerings still retains its force and its spiritual significance.

It is good also that money or other gifts for the poor or for the church, brought by the faithful or collected in the church, should be received. These are to be put in a suitable place but away from the eucharistic table.

THE SACRAMENTALITY OF HUMAN WORK

Given what we have said about human work earlier in the chapter, it is important to note at least the following three things about "the work of human hands."

First, when humans engage in work to craft things for their use in the liturgy, all that goes into their manufacture deserves attention

248

and reverence. Things used in the liturgy are the result of the sweat of brows for which those who manufacture them deserve just compensation. Liturgical objects are less "things" and more labors of love for the Lord, even before a liturgy begins. Reflection on the work of humans who enable the liturgy to happen is a sign and act of respect for other human beings.

Second, that many of the things used in worship are the result of the human imagination and the creativity of artists needs to be respected. Popes John Paul II and Benedict XVI have drawn our attention to the church's long-standing tradition as the patron of the arts and respect for artists. Each artifact in the worship space and each item used in the liturgy is the result of creativity and artistic care. Artists deserve to be well compensated financially for their contributions to sacramental liturgy precisely because what they have designed is for the celebration of sacraments through signs, symbols, and liturgical objects.

The "work" of the liturgy is carried out before any specific act of the sacred liturgy takes place and always underlies it. Part of the social teaching of the Catholic Church concerns human work and just wages for work. By the very composition of the elements comprising sacred liturgy and the human work involved in the celebration of the liturgy, the Christian community makes a number of statements about the dignity of the human person, the dignity of human labor, and just compensation for work. Just as the adage cited above summarizes this principle, so the phrase of liberation theologians, "You cannot celebrate Mass with stolen bread" means that just wages must be paid to all workers and that human labor can never be presumed or stolen.

DISCUSSION QUESTIONS

1. Recall the last celebration of the sacraments of initiation (baptism, confirmation, and Eucharist) you participated in, and compare how the ritual described the use of the human bodies in terms of movement and actions with what you actually experienced.

2. What recommendations would you make for teaching others about the value of things made by human hands and human work and their importance in understanding the meaning of sacraments?

3. List and discuss all the things that are "the work of human hands" that exist prior to the celebration of sacramental liturgy.

13

WORD ENACTED

The purpose of this chapter is (1) to articulate the way in which the proclamation of the Scriptures is a "word event" in sacramental liturgy, (2) to show how the liturgy organizes and structures our hearing of the word of God, and (3) to comment on the Scripture readings for the Easter Vigil to illustrate their importance as being proclaimed at the Vigil and as paradigmatic of the proclamation of the word at every sacramental liturgy.

WORD EVENTS

While the proclamation of the Scriptures was never entirely absent from the liturgy of the sacraments, since the Second Vatican Council, the Catholic Church clearly has reemphasized the value of the proclamation of the Scriptures as an intrinsic and constitutive part of the liturgy of the sacraments. As the Constitution on the Sacred Liturgy states about the Mass, the Liturgy of the Word and the Liturgy of the Eucharist form "one single act of worship" (Constitution on the Sacred Liturgy 56). The ritual books we use for this proclamation are the *Lectionary for Mass* (from Latin *lectio*, meaning "reading") and the *Book of the Gospels*. One of the most notable features of the revised liturgical rites is that all of them have a lectionary that selects the most appropriate Scripture readings to be proclaimed at that particular liturgy, for example, for marriage, funerals, ordination, and so on.

These books contain selected sections from the Sacred Scriptures in printed words on pages bound together within beautifully designed and appropriately decorated covers. What is contained on these pages and within these covers is the word of God that is meant to be proclaimed aloud in public. Unlike some other kinds of printed words with which we are familiar, for example the words of a legal contract or the words on the pages of a novel, the words in these books are intended to be spoken and, when spoken, are meant to be listened to and appropriated. When this dynamic occurs in the liturgy, the proclaimed word recreates us in God's image and likeness and reshapes us to adjust how we look at and live life.

Therefore these liturgical books are really not so much examples of the "print media" as examples of the "speech media." And for any speech medium to be really what it is intended to be, these readings require careful articulation by the speaker and the openness of the audience to want to listen, to be persuaded, and to change. That we have readers and a deacon to proclaim the Scripture readings and the priest to preach and preside over the Eucharist (and, on occasion, a deacon to preach) derives from a precedent reflected in the mid-second-century *First Apology* of St. Justin, in which he refers to what is contained in our liturgical books for proclamation as the "memoirs of the apostles and the writings of the prophets." The key here is to appreciate that when a Scripture text is spoken in the liturgy, something *happens*. Theologically, the principle is that *when God speaks, things happen*. When those who proclaim the Scriptures do in fact proclaim them, they give them new life in this time and place in the presence of the gathered liturgical assembly.

One of the expressions St. Augustine uses to describe the sacraments is "visible words." This refers to the power of God's word in the Scriptures, starting with Genesis 1:3, where when God speaks, something happens. God says repeatedly, "Let there be…" and things come to be. This idea of the creative word of God forms the basis for the understanding that when the word of God is proclaimed in the liturgy of the sacraments, things happen. (See below for more on this text and its place in the Easter Vigil.) The word is not proclaimed for information. In fact, because they are the Scriptures, we already know, or can find out, what they reveal by way of study, prayer, and instruction. Instead, when the Scriptures are proclaimed in the liturgy, they are performative—they "perform," "enact," and "do" the saving things among us that they describe. When the Scriptures are proclaimed in the liturgy, that proclamation joins us to the events or ideas they are recounting. They are always "symbolic"—the Greek verb *symballein* means "to throw together" or "to put in a relationship." Its opposite is *diaballein*, from the Greek root *diaballein*, meaning "to break apart" or "to separate." The proclamation of the word is a highly *symbolic* action.

Another fundamental biblical foundation for the Liturgy of the Word comes from the Jewish Passover service. A major part of this table ritual is to hear the story of the Exodus once more, again and again. And, in the words of the Midrash, we should consider that we, here and now, are similarly saved and redeemed by the hearing of this same foundational exodus story. (See chapter 15.)

For example, the parables of the lost sheep (Luke 15:4–7) and the prodigal son (Luke 15:11–32) are assigned in the Rite of Penance for the sample communal celebration of penance during Lent. Both reflect the overarching care that God takes to seek after and welcome us. Certainly, both parables are examples of overturning expectations. What seems illogical and unlikely becomes the gospel. What would be "bad economics" in expending such limitless efforts to find the coin and to kill the fatted calf for a banquet for the son becomes good religion. This forgiving and reconciling face of the gospel happens when these parables are proclaimed. When proclaimed, this gospel enacts what reconciliation means. Such texts function in the liturgy in a paradigmatic way in that their proclamation puts us in proper relationship with God, the whole church, each other, and the world. But for the proclamation to be truly effective, it requires our willingness to listen.

Another way to understand "word events" is to realize that all liturgy is an act of memorial. The Greek term *anamnesis* means "to make memory." More fully, it means to engage in a liturgical action in which, by word and action, such as Scripture reading and dining at the sacrificial meal of the Eucharist, we are contemporary with the saving events of our redemption, which are never relegated to the past but always perdure and are perpetuated in and through the liturgy. It is in and through the liturgy, celebrated in common in a covenanted people, that these saving events that happened once and for all in saving history are renewed and we are drawn into them by this very act of celebration. Hence, at the Passover, a crucial part of the ritual is hearing the story of Israel's liberation through the Exodus. In Christian liturgy, we hear stories from the Gospels that tell us of the words and deeds of the earthly Jesus leading to his death and resurrection, poignantly and profoundly commemorated at the Easter Vigil. There is an anamnetic nature and power to the Scriptures that we hear at every sacramental liturgy.

But this proclamation always presumes that what is proclaimed is welcomed by attentiveness and active listening. In its wisdom, the Roman Liturgy of the Hours each day begins with the admonition, "If today you hear his voice, harden not your hearts" (from Ps 95). Because it is a constitutive part of every act of sacramental celebration, the proclamation of the word of God should always be approached with this phrase taken to heart, literally. The first words of the Rule of St. Benedict are the invitation to "listen" "with the ear of your heart." In the words of Psalm 51:10, we pray that the Lord would create "a new heart" within us.

All of this is to suggest that the regular and repeated, active and committed listening to the word of God—as opposed to a passive "hearing"—is part of the enactment of sacraments. This leads to their complement in the more specifically sacramental action to follow, such as bathing for baptism or dining for the Eucharist. In the words of St. Augustine, these are "visible words" in the sense that what God says happens.

LITURGY OF THE WORD "STRUCTURES" OUR HEARING OF THE WORD

The Liturgy of the Word structures how we hear the word of God in at least four ways.

IN THE STRUCTURE OF THE LITURGY OF THE WORD ITSELF

Like many other things in the liturgy, the selection of the Scripture readings has already been done, either in terms of the exact selections for Sundays and weekdays for Mass or the collection of readings to choose from for individual sacraments. For example, it is common practice today for couples planning their wedding to choose the Scripture readings for their wedding or for families to choose readings for the funeral of a loved one (or the deceased may have done this on his or her funeral planning). Also, it is common that when confirmation, penance, or the anointing of the sick takes place, those who prepare the liturgies choose the Scripture readings from the assigned lectionary texts assigned to those sacraments. With regard to the celebration of the rites preparing for the Christian initiation for adults and at the rite itself, almost all of those rites take place in the context of the Sunday liturgy and finally at the Easter Vigil, where the readings are assigned and fixed.

What underlies this is the principle that we do not "pick and choose" what we want to hear. Rather, in the church's wisdom, the texts presented for us help to ensure that the "two-edged sword" of the Scriptures is retained. The texts can offer consolation—as in the parables of the lost coin and the prodigal son—as well as challenge (such as "love your enemies") or comfort ("come to me all you who labor and find life burdensome"), or they can require changes in how we view life or what we value in life ("Whoever wishes to come after me must deny himself, take up his cross, and follow me," Mark 8:34).

Structure of the Liturgy of the Word

Proclamation of First Reading*
Silence
Responsorial Psalm
(Proclamation of Second Reading on Sundays and Special Feasts and Sacramental Liturgies)
Verse before the Gospel
Gospel Procession
Proclamation of the Gospel
Homily
Silence

---

* At the liturgy, the lector proclaims the reading(s) from the ambo.

The way the Scriptures are proclaimed in the celebration of the liturgy demonstrates the "event" nature of the proclamation. From as far back as the call of Abraham (in Gen 11), through all the covenants in the Bible, the dynamic is the same—*call* and *response*. The classic text is from Exodus, summarizing the many times in Exodus when God took initiative to lead and save his people: "We will do everything that the LORD has told us" (Exod 24:3). The proclamation of the Scriptures requires that we welcome them and embrace them as the measure of our lives.

The reading ends with the acclamation, "The word of the Lord." This acclamation can have many meanings, including that the *proclamation* of the word, not the text on the pages, is the word of God. And when we hear it, we respond, "Thanks be to God." We say, in effect, we welcome it and revere it as God's revelation. Or, more profoundly, we are willing to obey it.

The Lectionary indicates that the reading should be followed by a period of silence, a time to let the proclamation "sink in" and to take deep root in our lives. This kind of penetration takes a lifetime, yet each time the Scriptures are read, we are invited once more to recommit ourselves to what has been proclaimed.

Then follows the responsorial psalm, whose title indicates exactly what it is—a prayerful response through the words of the Psalmist to what we have just heard and welcomed into our lives. As will be noted below, one of the options for the psalm that responds to the first reading at the Easter Vigil (about creation, Gen 1:1—2:2) is Psalm 104. This is a psalm of praise of God's act of creation with the refrain "Lord, send out your Spirit, and renew the face of the earth." This response captures the dynamic of the proclamation of the word since through it we hear familiar texts yet are always "renewed" by and through them. Depending on the occasion, there may be another reading from the New Testament.

The Gospel acclamation follows. On Sundays, this usually reflects the contents of the Gospel to follow: for example, the Gospel reading on the Third Sunday of Lent in the "A" cycle, about the woman from Samaria who asks Jesus for water (John 4:5–42), is preceded by the Gospel acclamation, "Lord, you are truly the Savior of the world; give me living water, that I may never thirst again."

While the verse before the Gospel is sung, the deacon or priest takes the Gospel book from the altar and carries it in procession to the ambo. Depending on the circumstances, the deacon or priest may incense the *Book of the Gospels*, which has now been placed on the ambo in preparation for the proclamation. In an action parallel to the end of the first reading, the deacon or priest proclaims, "The Gospel of the Lord," to which we respond, "Praise to you, Lord Jesus Christ" as a sign of commitment to what was just proclaimed. The homily follows, which in the celebration of the sacraments, often acts as a bridge between scriptural words and enacted rites that follow. Or, to paraphrase St. Augustine, for "audible symbols," meaning the Liturgy of the Word that engages us and prepares us for "visible words," meaning words enacted at the liturgy.

TEXTS IN RELATION TO EACH OTHER

At a minimum the Liturgy of the Word for the sacraments would consist of two Scripture readings—one of which is always a Gospel—normally with the responsorial psalm and the Gospel acclamation. The context for the celebration of a sacrament would provide a clear liturgical context for hearing these texts in relation to one another and what is to follow in the sacramental celebration. At other times, sacramental liturgies contain the fuller form of three readings plus psalm and acclamation.

On Sundays in Ordinary Time, the Gospel and first reading, which is taken from the Old Testament, are related: "The books of the Old Testament with all their parts...acquire and show forth their full meaning in the New Testament...and in turn shed light on it and explain it" (Dogmatic Constitution on Divine Revelation 16). The psalm, as always, is a response to the first reading. The second reading from the New Testament epistles is on a different weekly cycle and does not directly reflect the first reading and the Gospel. The three readings that comprise the Liturgy of the Word are proclaimed once every three years.

On weekdays during Ordinary Time, the Gospels are proclaimed in order, with Mark coming first, followed by Matthew and then Luke. These Gospels are the same year after year. However, the first readings for Ordinary Time, with their proper responsorial psalm, are arranged in two cycles that alternate each year. Thus the Gospel is juxtaposed with a different first reading every other year. For example:

Year 1, Week 1, Monday		Year 2, Week 1, Monday
First Reading	Hebrews 1:1–6	1 Samuel 1:1–18
Gospel	Mark 1:14–20	Mark 1:14–20

Thus each year, Ordinary Time begins with the first of a continuous series of readings from the Gospel of Mark, while every other year, it begins with the first of a series of readings either from the Letter to the Hebrews or from 1 Samuel.

TEXTS IN THE CONTEXT OF THE LITURGICAL YEAR

Some texts are assigned to particular times of the church's calendar. For example, the Gospel parables of the lost coin (Luke 15:4–7) and the prodigal son (Luke 15:11–32) are proclaimed at different times as assigned by the *Lectionary*, all of which cannot help but affect the way they are heard.

For example, Luke 15, with the parables of the lost coin, the lost sheep, and the prodigal son, is proclaimed on the Twenty-Fourth Sunday of cycle C in Ordinary Time. But in the weekday cycles, the parables of the lost coin and lost sheep (Luke 15:1–10) are proclaimed on Friday of week twenty-one, because these Gospel readings follow a continuous cycle, chapter after chapter. Returning to the Sunday cycles, the parable of the prodigal son (Luke 15:1–3, 11–32) is proclaimed on the Fourth Sunday of Lent during cycle C because this gospel is specially designated to reflect the fact that Lent is a penitential season, as the Constitution on the Sacred Liturgy points out: "The season of Lent has a twofold character: primarily by recalling or preparing for baptism and by penance, it disposes the faithful, who more

	Year A	Year B	Year C
First Sunday of Lent	Genesis 2:7–9; 3:1–7 Psalm 51:3–6, 12–13, 17 Romans 5:12–19 OR 5:12, 17–19 Matthew 4:1–11	Genesis 9:8–15 Psalm 25:4–9 1 Peter 3:18–22 Mark 1:12–15	Deuteronomy 26:4–10 Psalm 91:1–2, 10–15 Romans 10:8–13 Luke 4:1–13
Second Sunday of Lent	Genesis 12:1–4a Psalm 33:4–5, 18–20, 22 2 Timothy 1:8b–10 Matthew 17:1–9	Genesis 22:1–2, 9a, 10–13, 15–18 Psalm 116:10, 15–19 Romans 8:31b–34 Mark 9:2–10	Genesis 15:5–12, 17–18 Psalm 27:1, 7–9, 13–14 Philippians 3:17—4:1 OR 3:20—4:1 Luke 9:28b–36
Third Sunday of Lent	Exodus 17:3–7 Psalm 95:1–2, 6–9 Romans 5:1–2, 5–8 John 4:5–42 OR 4:5–15, 19b–26, 39a, 40–42	Exodus 20:1–17 OR 20:1–3, 7–8, 12–17 Psalm 19:8–11 1 Corinthians 1:22–25 John 2:13–25	Exodus 3:1–8a, 13–15 Psalm 103:1–4, 6–8, 11 1 Corinthians 10:1–6, 10–12 Luke 13:1–9
Fourth Sunday of Lent	1 Samuel 16:1b, 6–7, 10–13a Psalm 23:1–6 Ephesians 5:8–14 John 9:1–41 OR 9:1, 6–9, 13–17, 34–38	2 Chronicles 36:14–16, 19–23 Psalm 137:1–6 Ephesians 2:4–10 John 3:14–21	Joshua 5:9a, 10–12 Psalm 34:2–7 2 Corinthians 5:17–21 Luke 15:1–3, 11–32
Fifth Sunday of Lent	Ezekiel 37:12–14 Psalm 130:1–8 Romans 8:8–11 John 11:1–45 OR 11:3–7, 17, 20–27, 33b–45	Jeremiah 31:31–34 Psalm 51:3–4, 12–15 Hebrews 5:7–9 John 12:20–33	Isaiah 43:16–21 Psalm 126:1–6 Philippians 3:8–14 John 8:1–11

diligently hear the word of God and devote themselves to prayer, to celebrate the paschal mystery" (no. 109).

TEXTS IN A LITURGICAL SEASON

There is a "rhyme and reason" to the Scripture readings assigned in the *Lectionary for Mass* and for all the sacraments. On the Sundays of Lent, the "Introduction" to the *Lectionary for Mass* states (no. 97),

> The Gospel readings are arranged as follows: The first and second Sundays maintain the accounts of the Temptation and Transfiguration of the Lord, with readings, however, from all three Synoptics.
>
> On the next three Sundays, the Gospels about the Samaritan woman, the man born blind, and the raising of Lazarus have been restored in Year A. Because these Gospels are of major importance in regard to Christian initiation, they may also be read in Year B and Year C, especially in places where there are catechumens.
>
> Other texts, however, are provided for Year B and Year C: for Year B, a text from John about Christ's coming glorification through his cross and Resurrection and for Year C, a text from Luke about conversion.

The Sunday readings lead us to the celebration of the Paschal Triduum, in particular baptism, confirmation, and the Eucharist at the Easter Vigil.

The extremely rich Scripture readings assigned for the season of Lent are provided in a table on the next page.

For study and prayer over these texts (*lectio divina*), one could take several approaches. Pray over the readings assigned to be proclaimed together on an individual Sunday. Or, pray over the Gospels assigned for the three cycles—A, B, and C—for the first and second Sundays and compare and contrast them. Then, for the third, fourth, and fifth Sundays, pray over one of the cycles, for example the cycle A reading about baptism (water, light, and life) or the B cycle reading about identifying with Christ in his, and our, paschal mystery, or the C cycle reading about penance and reconciliation.

Alternatively, one could pray over the first readings for the Sundays as Old Testament foundations for what we are celebrating. One very poignant set of texts comes from the readings assigned for the A cycle, which is a series of texts about covenants that lead us to the commemoration of the new covenant in Christ's dying and rising for us and the covenant relationship he forged with us through the paschal mystery.

EASTER VIGIL LITURGY OF THE WORD

At the Easter Vigil, which St. Augustine called "the mother of all Vigils," there are nine readings, seven from the Old Testament and two from the New Testament. The directions for the liturgy state that "where more serious pastoral circumstances demand it, the number of readings from the Old Testament may be reduced, always bearing in mind that the reading of the Word of God is a fundamental part of this Easter Vigil." The stories of faith read this night recall the works of saving history in the Old Testament, their completion in the New, and our appropriation of them precisely through hearing them again in the liturgy. The dynamic of hearing the texts and responding in psalms and collect prayers is meant to foster abiding gratitude and awareness of how salvation is effected among us, especially through word and sacrament, particularly baptism and Eucharist. The use of collect prayers, almost all of which date from the eighth-century Gelasian sacramentary and thus are well attested in liturgical tradition, draws out the paradigmatic character of the readings and allows them to affect us in new and different ways.

The spoken introduction to this part of the liturgy brings out the importance attached to the reading of these texts:

let us listen with quiet hearts to the Word of God.
Let us meditate on how God in times past saved his people
and in these, the last days, has sent us his Son as our
    Redeemer.

> Let us pray that our God may complete this paschal work of
> salvation
> by the fullness of redemption.

Underlying this statement is an appreciation for the word of God as fundamentally anamnetic and sacramental, in the sense that God's active presence in creation and salvation history, as recorded and recounted in the Scriptures, is presently active and effective in the community that hears the word in faith. This Liturgy of the Word is another occasion when the words of the classic invitatory psalm at Vigils take on deeper meaning and offer us a significant challenge:

> Today, listen to the voice of the Lord:
> Do not grow stubborn, as your fathers did in the wilderness,
> when at Meribah and Massah
> they challenged me and provoked me,
> although they had seen all of my works.
>   (Ps 95:7–9) [Breviary translation]

The first reading from Genesis (1:1—2:2) about the creation of the world reflects the annual spring festivals of the re-creation of the world found in the rites of many primitive religions. These primitive religions would annually proclaim what were called "cosmogonic myths"—from the words *cosmos* for "the world" and *genesis* for "the beginning." The term *myth* does not mean something that is untrue; rather, it indicates what is the most true in terms of giving us a narrative to live by and in which to believe. In such religions, "myth" and "rite" combined for a religious festival.

Similarly, Israel's annual commemoration of becoming a people chosen by God coincided with the spring renewal of the earth, and the Easter Vigil's first reading from Genesis 1:1—2:2 places our Christian celebration within the same framework. We recall origins and beginnings, and in recounting them, we are remade and renewed. The evocative and sacramental power of the word is at work. In listening to the way God fashioned order out of chaos, we ourselves are remade and refashioned as his creatures, as were Adam

262

and Eve. Similarly, we are reminded of the stewardship required of us as we live on this good earth.

The darkness/light motif appears clearly at the beginning of the text, along with the subtle, but nevertheless important, notion that "days" begin with the evening: "Evening came, and morning followed—the first day" (Gen 1:5). This way of counting time and marking the passage of a day continues in Jewish and Christian liturgy. The celebration of Evening Prayer I of solemnities on the evening before what we usually call the feast day itself is based on this numbering. Hence, it is most appropriate that this reading about the days of creation should be the first proclaimed this evening, which is the beginning of the great day of rejoicing, the day of resurrection.

The motif of seven days is also significant liturgically, for after describing the separation of light from darkness, the creation of plants, animals, and then human persons, the reading ends by referring to the completion of creation on the seventh day: "On the seventh day God completed the work he had been doing; he rested on the seventh day from all the work he had undertaken" (Gen 2:2). Thus the Sabbath rest was established. This notion of a Sabbath day of rest is changed in Christianity in favor of Sunday, the day of the Lord, the day of the perfecting all of creation, since it was on this day that Christ rose from the dead to inaugurate the new creation. Our share in that absolutely new relationship with God through Christ is sustained and renewed weekly in the Eucharist. It is therefore most appropriate that at the Easter Vigil, we begin this Great Sunday by recalling all that preceded it in terms of God's acts—creation in the world and re-creation in Jesus Christ.

The use of Psalm 104 or Psalm 33 as psalm responses reflects well the creation motif so central to this reading. We now ask the all-powerful Spirit of God, which created all things, to renew and recreate us: "Lord, send out your Spirit, and renew the face of the earth" (Ps 104:30). It is also the mystery of God's divine action at work in the world that causes us to acclaim: "The earth is full of the goodness of the LORD" (Ps 33:5).

In the two prayers that follow, the goodness of creation is coupled with our being recreated by God and with the gift of redemption:

Almighty ever-living God,
who are wonderful in the ordering of all your works,
may those you redeemed understand
that there exists nothing more marvelous
than the world's creation in the beginning
except that, at the end of the ages,
Christ our Passover has been sacrificed.

O God,
who wonderfully created human nature
and still more wonderfully redeemed it,
grant us we pray,
to set our minds against the enticements of sin,
that we may merit to attain eternal joys.

Such concluding prayers function as particularly important summaries of how a reading of some aspect of saving history that leads us to experience the life of Christ is operative here and now in the liturgical gathering and in the lives of those who celebrate. Both prayers demonstrate how the main import of this reading concerns the continuing providence of God at work in our lives. The first deals with creation in general and its fulfillment in Christ. The second deals specifically with the creation of humankind but again looks to this fulfillment in the "more [wonderful]" work of redemption. Succinctly put, one can say that the chief function of the psalm prayers (prayers that follow the Psalms) is to point to christological implications of the psalm texts.

The second reading, also from the Book of Genesis (22:1–18), deals with the sacrifice of Isaac. Already proclaimed in the Lenten liturgy on the Second Sunday in cycle B (see table above), this text is a favorite of patristic authors and liturgical commentators as a way of illumining the attitude of Jesus as he went to death for us. Isaac's trust in his father Abraham is the model of Jesus' trust in his Father and of our trust in God. As Isaac obeyed and Jesus obeyed, so are we invited to obey our Father's will, even though this could mean the willingness to sacrifice what we hold most dear, as Abraham had to be willing to sacrifice his only son, or even death (Jesus). The responsorial psalm brings out this attitude of confidence and trust:

> *O Lord, my allotted portion and cup,*
> *you it is who hold fast my lot.*
>
> (Ps 16:5)

> *You will not abandon my soul to the nether world,*
> *nor will you suffer your faithful one to undergo corruption.*
> (Ps 16:10)

Once again the collect that follows helps to interpret this text christologically and also to apply it to our lives.

> *…who increase the children of your promise*
> *by pouring out the grace of adoption*
> *throughout the whole world*
> *and who through the Paschal Mystery*
> *make your servant Abraham the father of nations,*
> *as once you swore,*
> *grant, we pray,*
> *that your peoples may enter worthily*
> *into the grace to which you call them.*

The condition required here is acceptance of God's grace; the price we must pay is obedience to his will. The typology of Isaac and Jesus is completed when we ourselves become examples of those who have committed their lives to the Lord as our "portion and cup." The term *paschal mystery* is from the Latin *paschale sacramentum*, which refers to the liturgical appropriation of the whole paschal mystery, especially this evening.

The third reading is particularly significant because of its obvious liturgical reference to water, the key symbol used at baptism, and the act of freeing Israel from its bondage. This text (Exod 14:15–15:1) is frequently used as an Old Testament ground and support for theological and spiritual expositions on Christian baptism. Hence, its importance as a key reading directs us toward the baptismal emphasis of this liturgy. In fact, the rubrics direct that if not all the Old Testament readings for the Easter Vigil are actually used—if pastoral reasons dictate, it is allowed to choose a minimum of four of the seven readings—this reading from Exodus *must* be chosen because of the way God's freeing of the Hebrews from Egypt and thereby (subsequently) fashioning them into the people called Israel foreshadows Christ's freeing of us from the grasp of sin and death, by which he "won for [God] a holy people." The exodus event would seem to be the paradigm par excellence of the paschal event, as commented on by many patristic writings.

The response is taken from the text in Exodus (15:1–6, 17–18) that follows, the song of Miriam used at morning prayer on Saturday week one: "I will sing to the LORD, for he is gloriously triumphant; horse and rider he has cast into the sea" (Exod 15:1). Israel used this song to refer to the Lord's present action on their behalf as based on this significant intervention in their history. It is used in Christian worship to remind us that the same Lord who brought Israel through the Red Sea leads us through the waters of baptism to union with him. The baptismal reference inherent in the use of this reading on Easter is brought out in the two prayers that follow (the second of which was assigned to the vigil of Pentecost in liturgical tradition):

> For what you once bestowed on a single people,
> freeing them from Pharaoh's persecution
> by the power of your right hand,
> now you bring about as the salvation of the nations
> through the waters of rebirth…

> …so that the Red Sea prefigures the sacred font
> and the nation delivered from slavery
> foreshadows the Christian people

The waters of baptism thus become life-giving and the means of our experiencing redemption in Christ. (In the second prayer, the word *sign* translates the Latin *sacramenta*, which many commentators interpret as a reference to the paschal "sacraments" of baptism and eucharist celebrated this evening. Others argue that this phrase refers to the paschal mystery itself liturgically appropriated and experienced anew this evening through the celebration of the Vigil liturgy.)

The fourth reading applies even more directly to our situation as we celebrate the annual Liturgy of Easter, for it recounts a later intervention by God for Israel, long after Israel's victory at the Red Sea. In this section of Isaiah (54:5–14), the Lord calls to his people and brings them back to him. The covenant is thus reestablished, never to be broken again. There is a clear parallel here between God's act of calling a people to himself in baptism and in the renewal of the covenant in our annual celebration of Easter. The psalm response is a poignant reminder of our individual and personal relationship with God and our trust in him: "I will praise you, Lord, for you have rescued me" (Ps 30:2). In a particularly moving verse, the psalmist states, "At nightfall weeping enters in, but with the dawn rejoicing" (Ps 30:6). For our Christian celebration, this could be a reference to the death of Jesus and his burial at night leading to our celebration of his resurrection, which itself leads to rejoicing in the brightness of Easter day.

The relationship of Israel to the Christian church is emphasized in the collect that follows in which we ask,

> surpass, for the honor of your name,
> what you pledged to the Patriarchs by reason of their faith,
> and through sacred adoption increase the children of your
>   promise,
> so that what the Saints of old never doubted would come to pass
> your Church may now see in great part fulfilled.

God's initiative and sustaining grace is acknowledged, inviting us to participate more and more deeply in the divine life. In this context, "adoption" signifies God's unfailing call to us to the life of grace.

The fifth reading, also from Isaiah (55:1–11), speaks of the everlasting covenant we share with God and God's offer of salvation to all nations through the mediating power of God's word. The efficacy of the word of God has caused this particular text to be stressed in reflections on the importance of the revealed word:

> *It shall not return to me void,*
> *but shall do my will,*
> *achieving the end for which I sent it.*
>
> (Isa 55:11)

For those who have pondered the word of God in Lent and who have celebrated the liturgies of Lent as enactments of this announcement of salvation, this text functions as a fitting reminder of the importance of this liturgy as the fulfillment and completion of Lent. Lent leads to Easter as the catechumenate leads to baptism, and both of these are accomplished at this night vigil of the resurrection.

The response to this text also comes from Isaiah (12:2–6) with the implicit reference to initiation: "You will draw water joyfully from the springs of salvation" (Isa 12:3). The continuity of the Old and New Testaments and the place of the proclamation of the word in revealed religion is stressed in the collect:

> who by the preaching of your Prophets
> unveiled the mysteries of this present age,
> graciously increase the longing of your people…

The sixth reading, from Baruch (3:9–15, 32—4:4), proclaims the Lord as the fountain of wisdom and his revealed word as its clearest manifestation. In praise of the wisdom in the law of Moses, the prophet proclaims, "Hear, Israel, the commandments of life: listen, and know prudence" (Bar 3:9). The central place of the word for Israel is thus reiterated, and yet the history of Israel shows that fidelity was not always the response of those who heard this word. The God who addresses us through Baruch is the God of creation whom all are to obey. He is the Almighty One who has given life to Jacob and to Israel and to all his chosen ones. Hence to hear the precepts of the Lord and to follow them in our lives is the way to salvation. It is this pattern that marked the catechumenate in its various stages, always relying on the proclamation of the word and acting upon it in life as the criteria and means for conversion. The importance of the word is seen in the response to the psalm that follows this text: "Lord, you have the words of everlasting life" (taken from John 6:69; a similar response is used with this same psalm, Ps 19, on the Third Sunday for Lent in cycle B). The psalm itself deals with the familiar terms of covenant religion: laws, decrees, and precepts of the Lord, all of which we understand only from the perspective of the graciousness of the Lord's invitation to his people. It is on this basis that the invited can respond in faith and deed. This same psalm is used on Monday of the first week of Lent, a fitting way to begin this season of initiation preparation and renewal. The prayer that follows applies all of this to baptism by stating that the church calls all people to salvation; we pray that he will "graciously grant / to those you wash clean in the waters of Baptism / the assurance of your unfailing protection."

The seventh (and last) Old Testament reading is from Ezekiel (36:16–17a, 18–28) about the scattered people of Israel being brought again to one land by the Lord. Relying on Exodus terminology and imagery, the author assures the people that the Lord "will sprinkle clean water upon you to cleanse you from all your impurities" (Ezek 36:25), just as in Exodus blood was sprinkled on the doorposts of those to be saved. The Lord will continue to sustain this chosen people by giving them a new heart (Ezek 36:26) and by putting his spirit within them enabling them to live by his statutes and decrees (36:27). "You shall live in the land I gave your fathers; you shall be my people, and I will be your God" (36:28). This last statement is most important for it reiterates the foundation of the election of Israel and assures them of God's sustaining presence always with them. This abiding presence of God with Israel is fulfilled in and through Jesus. Again, this text has clear baptismal overtones that reflect the dynamic of the catechumenal process of responding to God's invitation and relying on his continued presence with us as we live according to his word.

The responsorial psalm can be either from Psalm 42:2, "Like a deer that longs for running streams, my soul longs for you, my God," or Psalm 51:12 (used frequently in Lent from Ash Wednesday on), "Create a clean heart in me, O God." Psalm 42 is sung if there will be baptisms at the Easter Vigil, but Psalm 51 is sung if there will be no baptisms. The prayer completes the proclamation of this reading by relating the text to our situation:

> O God of unchanging power and eternal light,
> look with favor on the wondrous mystery of the whole Church
> and serenely accomplish the work of human salvation,
> which you planned from all eternity;
> may the whole world know and see
> that what was cast down is raised up,
> what had become old is made new,
> and all things are restored to integrity through Christ,
> just as by him they came into being.

These significant images invite us to reflect on God's continual call for us to turn to him in true conversion and to rely on his presence and grace to sustain and complete this turning to him in faith and trust. An alternative collect refers to the paschal mystery (again, *paschale sacramentum*) and, more specifically, to our appropriation and experience of it in the sacrament of baptism.

With the readings from the Old Testament concluded, the congregation joins in the "Glory to God" hymn. On this Easter night, we are invited to pay close attention to and experience fully the meaning of the familiar text:

> Lord Jesus Christ, Only Begotten Son,
> Lord God, Lamb of God, Son of the Father,
> you take away the sins of the world, have mercy on us;
> you take away the sins of the world, receive our prayer;
> you are seated at the right hand of the Father, have mercy on us.

The reference to being freed from the "sins of the world" is an important way in which the liturgy relates the paschal mystery of Jesus Christ to our present situation. We who experience both intimacy with God in prayer and estrangement from him by our sins are once more brought near to this source of eternal life through the liturgy. It is here, especially in the sacraments of baptism and penance, that we experience most personally this salvation from God because our sins are forgiven and our hearts are washed clean in the blood of the Lamb of God. In the Easter Vigil, these ideas are most important to underscore because baptism will soon take place and the Eucharist will follow, baptism for the remission of our sins and the Eucharist as a continuation of our share in the paschal mystery "so that sins may be forgiven."

The association of baptism with the darkness/light motif already established in this liturgy is underscored in the prayer (from the former Roman Missal) that follows:

> *O God, who make this most sacred night radiant*
> *with the glory of the Lord's Resurrection,*
> *stir up in your Church a spirit of adoption,*
> *so that, renewed in body and mind,*
> *we may render you undivided service.*

In the letter to the Romans (6:3–11), St. Paul speaks eloquently of the resurrection of Christ. Here Paul uses the dynamic of Christ's dying and rising as a way of interpreting the rites of initiation. The symbolism of being immersed in baptismal waters and emerging as a new creation is used to remind Christians that this symbolic cleansing is a real participation in Christ's own death and resurrection. The baptismal font is truly a tomb like the tomb in which Christ lay for three days (recall the use of this metaphor by the church fathers; see chapter 3). In emerging from the font, the new Christian puts on Christ and shares intimately and fully in his resurrection (new life as from a "womb," another metaphor used by the fathers). Just as the death of Jesus led to his being raised to life with the Father, so our dying to self and to sin as symbolized by baptism leads to our being raised to the fullness of real life with God on earth as we look for its completion and perfection in the kingdom forever. The strong eschatological reference here should not be missed. Baptism is a pledge of union with God we will one day share completely. We who are baptized have forsaken sin and selfishness; in Christ, we emerge from the baptismal font to live fully alive in Christ Jesus forever (Rom 6:11).

Next follows the singing of the Easter alleluia and Psalm 118, a psalm frequently used during the Easter season. As an introduction to the Gospel and as a response to the reading from Romans, this text is pivotal. It marks the community's acknowledgment and ratification of all that is inherent in the rites celebrated this night. We proclaim that "the right hand of the Lord is exalted" (Ps 118:16) and that "the stone which the builders rejected has become the cornerstone" (Ps 118:22). Christ is our cornerstone and key stone in the structure of his body, the church.

The proclamation of the Easter Gospel now follows from one of the Synoptic Gospels (Matthew, Mark, or Luke, depending on the lectionary cycle—A, B, or C). From all that has gone before in the Liturgy of the Word we can say that this Gospel proclamation of Christ's resurrection is a synthesis and the fulfillment of salvation history. Creation is made new in Christ's resurrection; the Exodus is fulfilled in the paschal mystery. Passing through the Red Sea gives way to our leaving behind our old selves and putting on new life in the resurrection. The free offering of Isaac by Abraham fades now in comparison with the Father's offer of Jesus his Son whose dying and rising makes us free to live his risen life here and now on earth. He who was forsaken and condemned in the passion accounts now gloriously rises to life so that we who know well our weakness and sin may come to ever new experiences of union with God through the grace and love of his Son. Christ's resurrection is the way we come to new life through sacraments and symbols. His resurrected life enlivens and empowers the rituals we celebrate so that even in this passing world we might bear the beams of God's life and love. All this is possible for us and accomplished in Christ's resurrection.

DISCUSSION QUESTIONS

1. Read and pray over Romans 6:3–11. Discuss how this text can take on different meanings and applications when read at

Easter, or baptism, or a penance service, or a rite for religious profession, or a funeral.

2. Read the introduction and the first part of the *General Instruction* to the revised *Lectionary for Mass*. Discuss how this has helped you appreciate your own ministry in the Liturgy of the Word—for we *all* have one—whether you are a member of the faithful assembly (nos. 44–48) or a reader, cantor, or deacon (nos. 49–56).

3. Read Luke 4:16–30. The first part of this text contains Jesus' "homecoming" to Nazareth and contains the sense that the text he proclaims is fulfilled in their hearing. The second part concerns the resistance his proclamation causes among his own townspeople. Discuss how this helps you to realize the ways you both welcome and resist God's word proclaimed through the Scriptures.

14

PRAYER EVENTS

The purpose of this chapter is (1) to indicate the genre, structure, and contents of the prayers proclaimed by the presider in the sacraments (*lex orandi*) and (2) to exemplify how what they say and accomplish reflects the theological meanings of sacraments as well as what the sacraments accomplish—that is, relating *lex orandi* to *lex credendi* and *lex vivendi*—by commenting on a number of the prayers of the liturgy to glean their theological meanings. The chapter title, "Prayer Events," is meant to parallel the preceding chapter on "word events," both of which underscore that words always *do* something in sacramental liturgy.

The following principles should be kept in mind when reflecting on the prayers of the liturgy:

1. The prayers of the Roman rite never describe God or anything about God without describing how in and through the celebration of the liturgy God acts among us. Pay attention to the nouns describing God's attributes and the verbs indicating what we ask God to do for and among us.
2. The prayers of the Roman Rite are multivalent, in that words often have more than one meaning and those many meanings help to draw out the manifold, rich meanings of the liturgy.
3. Many of the prayers of the liturgy contain biblical references, some more than others.
4. The rhetoric of the liturgy is not description, rather it is rhetoric of incorporation into what is enacted uniquely in and through the sacred liturgy.
5. The meaning of any liturgical text is discovered in the context of the whole liturgy. No one prayer, or Scripture reading, or gesture, song, or symbol can be understood without appreciating the whole liturgical action, with these component elements,

among others. Specifically, this means appreciating texts in context, each in relation to the others and none in isolation. Again, this respects the liturgy as a number of prayers, rites, actions, and signs used in relationship to each other and in concert.

6. The working presumption for liturgical theology in general is that prayer texts in the liturgy always do something. (This parallels the theology of the proclaimed word in the previous chapter. Hence the chapter title.)

It is significant that almost all of the prayer texts in the Roman Missal come from ancient sources, whether that means sermons of the fathers of the church or collection of prayers from ancient sources called *sacramentaries, pontificals,* and *missals.* The fact that these texts are included in the present Missal means that they have important things to say to us today theologically to help us understand what the liturgy accomplishes.

When it comes to describing the theology of a particular feast or day within a season, pride of place goes to the presidential prayers, the prefaces, and the seasonal solemn blessings because they have been carefully chosen, edited, or adapted for use in the post–Vatican II Roman Missal. Our purpose here is to offer some comments about the theology contained in such prayers: consecration of the sacred chrism (used at the Easter Vigil and other occasions for baptism, confirmation, and ordination to the presbyterate and episcopacy), the prayers accompanying the use of chrism at the Vigil, and the presidential prayers (collect, prayer over the offerings, prayer after communion), prefaces, proper parts of the Canon, and final blessing for the Easter Vigil.

There are distinctions to be made among kinds of liturgical prayers for things used during the Paschal Triduum, specifically at the Chrism Mass and at the Easter Vigil.

Prayers of Consecration. In addition to the Eucharistic Prayer (and its Preface) to consecrate the bread and wine at the Easter Vigil Mass itself, the prayers to consecrate chrism and to consecrate a church and an altar have pride of place as well; they are about the prayer to consecrate chrism (and the prayers for the dedication of a church when chrism is also used) because they offer rich theological descriptions of what these things are and God's action on them.

Prayers of Blessing. The prayer to bless water for the celebration of baptism at the Vigil follows (as seen in chapter 11), as do the prayers to bless the oil of the catechumens and the oil for the anointing of the sick.

Presidential Prayers (at Mass). The presidential prayers include the collect, prayer over the offerings, prayer after communion, and solemn blessings.

BLESSING PRAYERS TO "BLESS" GOD

Among the most significant additions to the church's liturgy after Vatican II has been the restoration of additional prayers of blessing, praise, and thanksgiving used at all sacramental liturgy. From the point of view of the adage *lex orandi, lex credendi, lex vivendi*, these prayers are significant additions to the church's liturgy because they provide the basis for articulating a systematic explanation of what happens in the sacramental event and provide a rich field for reflection on what we believe and how we should live. Many of these prayers are rich in imagery and metaphors, the combination of which often has an impact on us on a variety of levels, intellectual and affective. No one prayer can "say" or "do" it all. One of the advantages of the post–Vatican II reform of the liturgy is the wealth of largely traditional prayers now used in the celebration of the sacraments. Theologically, these prayers derive from Jewish prayers of blessing. The Hebrew origin for this kind of prayer is the word *berakah* (plural *berakoth*). The Greek term *euche* derives from the Hebrew *berakah* and means "prayers of blessings." *Euchology* is the precise term used by liturgical scholars to describe these prayers in the liturgy. The aim of this structured prayer form is to praise, glorify, magnify, and thank God for the blessings of creation, human life, and God's sustaining covenant of love. Used in the Christian church, these prayers function in the same way—as bearers of theological meanings about creation, life, and God's all-encompassing presence. Theologically the point of *blessing* God is to thank God for all the *blessings* of life and for life eternal. Thus the emphasis in these prayers is not primarily on the "blessed" result of the act and declaration of blessing, but rather on the God who gives all good things, which gifts we call blessings.

One clear example of the way postconciliar liturgical texts advert to this truth is in the way blessing prayers invoke God to bless persons and not just things. At the same time, however, the structure and content of these prayers reveal that their theological basis is a sacramental view of the world and that they concern the praise of God for creation, particular fruits of that creation, for the covenant and particular high points in the history of salvation when God acted to lead, save, and redeem the chosen people. These stated motivations are called the *mirabilia Dei* or the *magnalia Dei*, Latin terms for the awe-inspiring, mighty deeds God has done in history. In proclaiming these "wondrous deeds of God" in the liturgical assembly, we ask God to continue to care for every generation of believers who invoke these deeds of salvation.

In sacramental liturgy specifically, we acclaim and bless God who gives life and value to all creation, and in specifying certain elements from creation such as water and bread and wine, we then ask God to bless these gifts for the sake of those very persons who bless him through the prayer. The theological point to be made here from the perspective of the Catholic sacramental imagination is that liturgical symbols do not lose their reality content as natural or manufactured symbols. Rather, precisely as symbols that occasion the act of blessing God, they become more truly what they are natively— bearers of God's presence and images of God's goodness.

CONSECRATION OF SACRED CHRISM

Traditionally, the ceremony to consecrate chrism and to bless oils takes place at the Chrism Mass, which is celebrated at the diocesan cathedral on the morning of Holy Thursday unless circumstances dictate otherwise (see chapter 12).

The bishop adds balsam or another kind of perfume and then invites all to pray,

> Let us pray
> that God our almighty Father
> will bless this oil
> so that all who are anointed with it
> may be inwardly transformed
> and come to eternal salvation.

It is notable that, in addition to asking that the oil be blessed, "all who are anointed" are specially cited and their "inward transformation" by the sacraments of initiation and ordination may lead them "to eternal salvation," an appropriate eschatological reference.

The rubrical direction then states, "Then the bishop may breathe over the opening of the vessel of chrism," recalling, among other things, how the risen Jesus breathed on the apostles in his resurrection appearance in the Gospel of St. John (20:22).

> God our maker,
> source of all growth in holiness,
> accept the joyful thanks and praise
> we offer in the name of your Church.

This names God's attributes as *maker, source of holiness* to whom we offer "thanks and praise" (recall the notion that this is what liturgical "blessing" means) in the gathered assembly.

> In the beginning, at your command,
> the earth produced fruit-bearing trees.
> From the fruit of the olive tree
> you have provided us with oil for holy chrism.

As is customary in the revised blessing prayers, this recounts salient moments of salvation history, here referring to olive oil.

> The prophet David sang of the life and joy
> that the olive would bring us in the sacraments of your love.

Following the patristic practice known as typology, Old Testament references are applied to New Testament references and church usages in the sacraments:

> *After the avenging flood,*
> *the dove returning to Noah with an olive branch*
> *announced your gift of peace.*

This refers to Genesis 9:11, where the dove released from the ark returns with an olive branch, signaling that the water had subsided.

> *This was a sign of a greater gift to come.*
> *Now the waters of baptism wash away the sins of men,*
> *and by the anointing with olive oil*
> *you make us radiant with your joy.*

Here is another example of Old Testament typology referring to baptism, specifically washing with water and the joy that comes from sacramental initiation.

> *At your command,*
> *Aaron was washed with water*
> *and your servant, Moses, his brother,*
> *anointed him priest.*
> *This too foreshadowed greater things to come.*

This is a combination of Leviticus 8:6 and Exodus 29:4 about washing, and Leviticus 8:12 and Exodus 30:30 about anointing as background for anointing with oil today.

> *After your Son, Jesus Christ, our Lord,*
> *asked John for baptism in the waters of the Jordan,*
> *you sent the Spirit upon him*
> *in the form of a dove*
> *and by the witness of your own voice*
> *you declared him to be your only, well-beloved Son.*
> *In this you clearly fulfilled the prophecy of David,*
> *that Christ would be anointed with the oil of gladness*
> *beyond his fellow men.*

This includes a significant reference to Jesus' own baptism in the Jordan (e.g. Matt 3:13–17) and the endowment of the Spirit, one of the results of the sacrament of baptism. The declaration of being "the beloved Son" echoes not only Jesus' baptism but also his transfiguration (Matt 17:1–13), both called "theophanies" or "manifestations" of God among us, in Christ.

> *And so, Father, we ask you to bless [sign of the cross] this oil you*
> *   have created.*
> *Fill it with the power of your Holy Spirit*
> *through Christ your Son.*

As already noted, God the Father is asked to send the Spirit to bless the object. The technical term for this invocation is *epiclesis*.

> *It is from him that chrism takes its name*
> *and with chrism you have anointed*
> *for yourself priests and kings,*
> *prophets and martyrs.*

The lexical reference to *Christ* and *chrism* reiterates that we all are anointed in initiation to be "priest, prophet and king," as were the biblical priests, kings, and martyrs. This is made even more explicit in what follows.

> *Make this chrism a sign of life and salvation*
> *for those who are to be born again in the waters of baptism.*
> *Wash away the evil they have inherited from sinful Adam,*
> *and when they are anointed with this holy oil*
> *make them temples of your glory,*
> *radiant with the goodness of life*
> *that has its source in you.*

The explicit references here to the Book of Genesis and the fall of Adam are especially important to recall when celebrating the Easter Triduum and the overturning of the fall in the resurrection of Christ, the second Adam. The "born again" metaphor is from the dialogue of Jesus with Nicodemus in John 3, reiterated again in what follows.

Through this sign of chrism
grant them royal, priestly, and prophetic honor,
and clothe them with incorruption.
Let this be indeed the chrism of salvation
for those who will be born again of water and the Holy Spirit.
May they come to share eternal life
In the glory of your kingdom.
We ask this through Christ our Lord.
Amen.

Familiar liturgical structure is adhered to here in referring to eschatology ("share eternal life," "glory of your kingdom") and the mediatorship of "Christ our Lord."

PRAYERS ACCOMPANYING THE USE OF SACRED CHRISM

After water baptism, sacred chrism is anointed immediately on those so baptized. The prayer that accompanies the anointing when confirmation is not celebrated is as follows:

God the Father of our Lord Jesus Christ has freed you from
sin, given you a new birth by water and the Holy Spirit, and
welcomed you into his holy people.

This echoes the important theological assumption and experience that in baptism God the Father acts through his Son in the power of the Holy Spirit, and that the Spirit is received in baptism, as well as appreciating baptism as an experience of the paschal mystery.

He now anoints you with the chrism of salvation. As Christ
was anointed Priest, Prophet, and King, so may you live
always as members of his body, sharing everlasting life.

The explicit ecclesiological reference to "his people" is welcome to underscore that sacramental initiation and church belonging are so intrinsically connected as to presume one another. The language of

"Priest, Prophet and King" seen in the prayer to consecrate chrism recurs when the chrism is so used at the Easter Vigil. It designates both the dignity and the responsibility of those so baptized.

If confirmation follows instead of the previous postbaptismal anointing (which is actually more common and is presumed to occur according to the rite for adult initiation at the Easter Vigil), the celebrant invites the assembly to attention and prayer using these exact or "similar words":

> My dear newly baptized, born again in Christ by baptism, you have become members of Christ and of his priestly people. Now you are to share in the outpouring of the Holy Spirit among us, the Spirit sent by the Lord upon his apostles at Pentecost and given by them and their successors to the baptized.
>
> The promised strength of the Holy Spirit, which you are to receive, will make you more like Christ and help you to be witnesses to his suffering, death and resurrection. It will strengthen you to be active members of the Church and to build up the Body of Christ in faith and love.

While fairly generic in terms of describing what the Spirit will enable the baptized to do (for example, "make you more like Christ" and "active members of the Church"), these are among the major themes for confirmation that come to us from the Western church's teaching on confirmation.

(The priests who will be associated with the celebrant as ministers of the sacrament now stand next to him.) The celebrant continues,

> *My dear friends, let us pray to God our Father, that he will pour out the Holy Spirit on these newly baptized to strengthen them with his gifts and anoint them to be more like Christ, the Son of God.*

In the classical style and format of such invitations to prayers invoking the Holy Spirit, we pray that God the Father would send the Spirit among us.

This is followed by a generous period of silence at the end of which

282

the celebrant extends his hands on those to be confirmed and prays,

> *All-powerful God, Father of our Lord Jesus Christ,*
> *by water and the Holy Spirit*
> *you freed your sons and daughters from sin*
> *and gave them new life.*

The first part of this prayer echoes the first part of the postbaptismal prayer above.

> *Send your Holy Spirit upon them*
> *to be their helper and guide.*

The verb *send* adds urgency to this special event of invoking the Holy Spirit once more in this initiation liturgy.

> *Give them the spirit of wisdom and understanding,*
> *the spirit of right judgment and courage,*
> *the spirit of knowledge and reverence.*
> *Fill them with the spirit of wonder and awe in your presence.*
> *We ask this through Christ our Lord.*
> *Amen.*

The third section lists the traditional seven gifts of the Holy Spirit, which were originally articulated in Isaiah 11:1–2. Since then, there have been several lists and interpretations of these gifts starting with the patristic period.

PRESIDENTIAL PRAYERS

THE COLLECT

This prayer is now found among the "Introductory Rites" of the Mass, the purpose of which "is to ensure that the faithful who come together as one establish communion and dispose themselves properly to listen to the Word of God and to celebrate the Eucharist worthily" (*GIRM* 46).

The *GIRM* then goes on to describe the meaning and function of the collect prayer itself (no. 54):

> Next the Priest calls upon the people to pray and everybody, together with the Priest, observes a brief silence so that they may become aware of being in God's presence and may call to mind their intentions. Then the Priest pronounces the prayer usually called the "Collect" and through which the character of the celebration finds expression.

There are at least three things that are worth mentioning about this text, the first two of which can be applied to all liturgical prayers:

1. *Silence.* That the collect is preceded by a brief period of silence is important liturgically and pastorally simply because that silence is meant to invite the gathered assembly to realize that they are engaged in the act of liturgy at which our whole lives are brought before the Lord in a special and unique way. Some commentators will go so far as to say that this silence *is* the prayer that occurs at this time and that the text of the collect simply gives some shape in words to what is being celebrated and to conclude this part of the Mass. A number of recent Roman documents have emphasized that distinct silences should occur during the liturgy. That it is an intrinsic part of the liturgy itself is evident in the *GIRM*'s statement that the "collect" is not a substitute for the silence; rather, it is part of the ritual dynamic that consists in the invitation to pray, the silence, and the praying of the collect.

2. *Character of the celebration.* That the prayer contains the "character of the celebration" is one way of describing its importance as part of the church's *lex orandi* and therefore of its *lex credendi.* In some ways, the word *character* is vague. In another way, it is to be preferred to a word such as *theme* simply because the very multivalence of the liturgy (that is, words, signs, and gestures often have more than one meaning) prevents us from asserting that there is a single "theme" to a particular liturgy. The use of *character* also suggests that we

should not look for more from this prayer than that—it is one lens through which to view the celebration, noting what a particular liturgy celebrates and how this celebration affects those who celebrate it.

3. The term *collect*. In addition to being the term by which this prayer is customarily known, the word *collect* has a number of meanings. First, it refers to the actual gathering (or "collecting") of the assembly for the liturgy. Even here, there are at least two ways to understand this. One is the actual gathering for the celebration in the place of celebration. Another, as described repeatedly in the ancient Gregorian Sacramentary, is the use of the term (literally *ad collectam*) to describe the prayer prayed when the people assembled in one place begin to walk in a procession to another church where the liturgy is to be celebrated. This is from the ancient "stational liturgy," celebrated even today in the city of Rome, where the faithful followed a relic of the true cross in procession from church to church on each of the forty days of Lent.

This is to suggest that at least two of the possible meanings of *collect* refer to the actual geographical and physical act of assembling.

A third meaning is that the assembly "collects" their petitions for this particular celebration—in other words, it is here that we reflect on the "intentions" we bring to the liturgy. (Another obvious place where we reflect on our own intentions is during the prayer of the faithful.) Hence the value of silence as noted in the *GIRM*.

A review of the texts of collect prayers indicates that they follow more or less the same structure and pattern. The following illustration is from the collect of the Christmas "Mass during the Day" (authored by St. Leo the Great in the fifth century; that it has "survived" so long in our prayer is an attestation to its theological value) and exemplifies this structure:

> *O God, who wonderfully created the dignity of human nature*
> *and still more wonderfully restored it…*

This names God, God's attributes, and God's saving action: here, his restoring of human nature after the fall of Adam.

> grant, we pray,
> that we may share in the divinity of Christ,
> who humbled himself to share in our humanity.

This cites the gathered assembly's need for God most usually in light of the attributes noted—to become like God. Human and divine interchange (sometimes referred to when the term *exchange* is used in liturgical prayers).

> Through our Lord Jesus Christ, your Son,
> who lives and reigns with you in the unity of the Holy Spirit,
> one God, for ever and ever. Amen.

This is the final, full trinitarian doxology.

The *GIRM* (no. 54) indicates that the doxologies used to conclude the collects are trinitarian. However the more literal translation of the Latin *in unitate* rendered as "in the unity of the Holy Spirit" invites the possibility that something more is involved here than referencing the Trinity at the end of this prayer.

The renowned liturgical scholar Josef Jungmann argues that the phrase *in unitate* ("in the unity of") at the end of these prayers derives from a usage in the Roman Rite as it developed in the fourth and fifth centuries, which is taken from the doxology that ended the Eucharistic Prayer in the *Apostolic Tradition* ascribed to Hippolytus (third century). In Hippolytus's text, the doxology emphasizes Christ and the church, not the Trinity alone. The text reads,

> Through him, glory to thee and honor,
> to the Father and to the Son, with the Holy Spirit,
> in the holy Church,
> now and for ever.
> Amen.

Jungmann's point is that the Eucharistic Prayer ends with an explicit doxology of the Trinity, but that our naming of the Trinity here and our prayer through Christ is a reminder that this is the Godhead in which *the church* abides and takes its life. He argues that the phrase "in the holy Church" is assumed when we pray "in the unity of the Holy Spirit…" (*in unitate*). In effect, he combines belief in the Trinity with an emphasis on the church's participation in the life of the Trinity as expressed in this doxology and as presumed through the whole prayer. (See chapter 16.)

If we apply these insights to the words of doxology at the end of the Roman Canon, we have an emphasis on Christology ("through him…") on the Trinity, "holy Spirit," "almighty Father" and on the church "in the unity of…." (*in unitate*). This is multivalence at work.

While scholars debate the exact lineage of the doxology—that is, whether it really derives from Hippolytus—and whether the doxology that ends the Canon and the collect are from the same time in history and are of the same genre, the very fact that the assembly is invited to pray the response *Amen* to these doxologies is evidence enough that the liturgy is the prayer of the assembled church, that it is always the church's prayer as it abides in and is ever more fully assimilated into the life of the triune God.

THE COLLECT FOR THE EASTER VIGIL

Note the cosmic reference to "night," the title *Lord*, the reference to the Church, and "adoption" as a result of baptism leading to consequences in daily life. It comes from the previous Roman Missal but is attested as early as the "Verona manuscript," the earliest source of liturgical prayers that have been preserved (which is commonly dated to the sixth century):

O God, who make this most sacred night radiant
with the glory of the Lord's Resurrection,

Naming God and God's attributes, cosmic reference and resurrection are explicitly stated.

> *stir up in your Church a spirit of adoption,*
> *so that, renewed in body and mind,*
> *we may render you undivided service.*

This cites the gathered assembly's need for God in light of the attributes stated and, in this case, an explicit reference to the implications of living lives of service.

> *Through our Lord Jesus Christ, your Son,*
> *who lives and reigns with you in the unity of the Holy Spirit,*
> *one God, for ever and ever. Amen.*

This is the final doxology, the title *Christ* and pronoun *our* signifying relationship in the triune God and relationship with each other in the church.

PRAYER OVER THE OFFERINGS

In comparison with what the *GIRM* says about the collect and the prayer after communion, its assertions about the prayer over the offerings is comparatively brief (no. 77):

> Once the offerings have been placed on the altar and the accompanying rites completed, by means of the invitation to pray with the Priest and by means of the Prayer over the Offerings, the Preparation of the Gifts is concluded and preparation made for the Eucharistic Prayer.

What is said reiterates our thesis that texts should be interpreted in context—here it is the context of having presented the offerings on the altar. The immediate liturgical context is the procession by members of the assembly with the gifts of bread and wine and monetary offerings (see *GIRM* 73).

This hearkens to an early and well-established custom in the Roman liturgy when gifts to be distributed to the poor were brought forward and then distributed after Mass. The very dynamic of liturgical participation—that we gather in order to be dispersed—is exemplified in this ritual action. What we received at this part of the Mass as part of our offering of our resources and the goods of this earth are then in turn shared with those without resources. Interestingly, these actions take place without accompanying words. This is another example of a way in which the church's *lex orandi* need not be textual. Sometimes it is the actions of the liturgy that "say" what the liturgy does.

The texts of the prayer over the offerings "name" God and ask for something for us, which is the result of the celebration of the Eucharist. Again, the use of the term *offerings* here is also deliberately multivalent.

Offerings can refer to the bread and wine, the result of human productivity—"fruit of the earth and work of human hands" (see chapter 12). *Offerings* can also refer to these gifts as they will be transformed into the one, single, perfect, and unique sacrifice that has reconciled us with the Father through the cross of his Son, Jesus Christ. The bread and wine presented on the altar are already understood to be the gifts that, when transformed, become the sacrifice of Christ and, especially when received in holy communion, become the sacrament of our salvation.

Unlike the doxology that concludes the collect, the doxology that concludes this prayer is explicitly (and simply) christological—"through Christ our Lord." But even here, there is a theological lesson. The Roman Rite never cites or calls on the name *Jesus* without a modifier—more often than not adding *our Lord* or *the Lord*. This is because the liturgy is our continual and continued appropriation of the paschal mystery of Christ after his resurrection, ascension, and exaltation to the Father's right hand in glory. The use of *Jesus* without a modifier can place us back to the time when he walked this earth. But the liturgy does not do that. It recalls all that Christ said and did on this earth through the lens and from the perspective of his resurrection and ascension. In effect, calling on "Christ our Lord" means that we invoke and rely on his action among us in light of his exalted state and his interceding for us at the right hand of the Father. Or consider the precise title used at the invitation to communion: "Behold the Lamb of God, / behold him who takes away the sins of the world...the supper of the Lamb." He does not say, "Behold Jesus..."

THE PRAYER OVER THE OFFERINGS AT THE EASTER VIGIL

Like the collect, the prayer is found in the previous Roman Missal and is attested as early as the Verona manuscript:

Accept, we ask, O Lord,
the prayers of your people

Note the ecclesiology of the prayer: "we ask" and "your people."

with the sacrificial offerings,

"Sacrificial offerings" can mean the bread and wine and the consecrated body and blood of Christ.

that what has begun in paschal mysteries

"Paschal mysteries" refers to all that Christ accomplished in his incarnation, obedient life, suffering, death, resurrection, and ascension experienced here and now in the liturgy.

may, by the working of your power,
bring us to the healing of eternity.

This acknowledges God's infinite power in that it is celebrated here and now as it looks to the fullness of life in heaven, imaged here as "healing," which is always experienced in the liturgy.

Through Christ our Lord.

This is a (brief) doxology.

PRAYER AFTER COMMUNION

As with the prayer over the offerings, the *GIRM* is decidedly brief when it describes this prayer. It gives two instructions for what occurs after the assembly has received communion:

> When the distribution of Communion is over, if appropriate, the Priest and faithful pray quietly for some time. If desired, a Psalm or other canticle of praise or a hymn may also be sung by the whole congregation.
>
> To bring to completion the prayer of the People of God, and also to conclude the whole Communion Rite, the Priest pronounces the Prayer after Communion, in which he prays for the fruits of the mystery just celebrated. (nos. 88–89)

Note that the liturgy again insists on time for silence. The rhythm of the liturgy requires that actions and spoken prayer also be accompanied by generous time for silence—for personal prayer. The option of singing a "canticle of praise" indicates what ought to be sung—a song of praise and thanks, not one of adoration. Already in the liturgy, words of adoration (in the "Glory to God") and acts of adoration (before the consecrated species become the body and blood of Christ) have occurred. If a song is sung here, it should not limit the silence after communion; it ought to express the reality of "communion" (our being one in Christ through our communion in the eucharistic gifts) and it ought to be of praise and thanksgiving.

The *GIRM* indicates that the prayers after communion concern "the fruits of the mystery just celebrated." One such fruit often mentioned at this point is for the eucharistic action to bear fruit in our daily lives. This accords with the words of the dismissal rite, which, as directed by Pope Benedict XVI, are "go forth, the Mass is ended," "go and announce the Gospel of the Lord," "go in peace, glorifying the Lord by your life," and "go in peace." The dynamic of the liturgy is that we assemble to be dispersed. These dismissal texts make that explicit.

THE PRAYER AFTER COMMUNION AT THE EASTER VIGIL

This prayer from an eighth century collection of prayers called the "old Gelasian Sacramentary" reads,

Pour out on us, O Lord, the Spirit of your love,

Note the divine name *Lord*, and attribute *your love*.

*and in your kindness make those you have nourished
by this paschal Sacrament*

This explicitly references the Eucharist as the Vigil ends, reminding us that every Eucharist is the ongoing sacrament of what began in baptism and confirmation.

one in mind and heart.

This is an explicit petition for the church with a subtle reminder that we are not yet the perfect expression or fulfillment of Christ's intention that "all may be one" (John 17:21).

Through Christ our Lord.

The doxology.

PREFACES

From the earliest evidence we have from St. Ambrose in the fourth century to Vatican II, in the Roman rite we prayed one Eucharistic Prayer—the Roman Canon. It is generally observed that it is a "fixed" prayer from the "Holy, Holy, Holy" through to the Great Amen. But that is not entirely true. The first part of the Canon was called "the Preface." Liturgical history reveals hundreds of examples of prefaces, despite the fact that in the Missal published after the Council of Trent, the number had been reduced to a dozen. One of the chief aims of the revision of the Roman Canon after Vatican II was to add three additional Eucharistic Prayers and several more Prefaces, most of which come from traditional sources. We now have over

ninety Prefaces to use with the Roman Canon, three Eucharistic Prayers added after Vatican II based on classical sources and usages, as well as two Eucharistic Prayers for Masses for reconciliation, three Eucharistic Prayers for Masses with children with their own Prefaces, and a prayer for Various Needs and Occasions. The variety and number of Prefaces reflects the particular "genius" of the Roman Rite. In what follows, we will pay close attention to what the Prefaces reveal about the theology and spiritual meaning of these feasts and seasons.

The *GIRM* indicates how important the Eucharistic Prayer is in the Mass, and therefore for our study of the liturgy's *lex orandi*:

> Now the center and high point of the entire celebration begins, namely, the Eucharistic Prayer itself, that is, the prayer of thanksgiving and sanctification. The Priest calls upon the people to lift up their hearts towards the Lord in prayer and thanksgiving; he associates the people with himself in the Prayer that he addresses in the name of the entire community to God the Father through Jesus Christ in the Holy Spirit. Furthermore, the meaning of this Prayer is that the whole congregation of the faithful joins with Christ in confessing the great deeds of God and in the offering of Sacrifice. The Eucharistic Prayer requires that everybody listens to it with reverence and in silence. (no. 78)

This very tersely worded and theologically rich text serves as an important reminder that the Eucharistic Prayer, like most other liturgical prayers, articulates what God has done in history to save and redeem us. Through the proclamation and the enactment of the paschal mystery specifically enacted through that proclamation, we today experience that saving mystery anew. This recounting of events in saving history is meant to be *paradigmatic*. The fact that we recount them in liturgical prayers is a history lesson about God's gracious will to save and sanctify us, but it is also an experience of grace and life here and now. Our attentiveness to what God did once through the Christ's saving death and resurrection invites the entire assembly here and now to offer that sacrifice back to the Father through, with, and

in Christ. The spark that makes the liturgy so important is that it is the church's privileged experience of the once for all act of Christ's redemption for us.

The Preface of the Eucharistic Prayer is normally the place in particular where we offer our thanks for these deeds of salvation:

> The *thanksgiving* (expressed especially in the Preface), in which the Priest, in the name of the whole of the holy people, glorifies God the Father and gives thanks to him for the whole work of salvation or for some particular aspect of it, according to the varying day, festivity, or time of year. (*GIRM* 79)

For some liturgical seasons, there is more than one Preface—for example, five for Easter. In all, the present Roman Missal contains close to one hundred Prefaces. (No one prayer says it all.)

The first Preface for the Easter season is assigned for the Easter Vigil (and day) Mass:

> *It is truly right and just, our duty and our salvation,*
> *at all times to acclaim you, O Lord....*

The first phrase, "right and just," in all the Prefaces of the Roman Rite parallels the preceding response of the people to the priest's exhortation, "Let us give thanks to the Lord our God": "It is right and just." This is called a "couplet," where one phrase is repeated in the next, from two different voices, the assembly and the presider. The word *duty* should be understood as a responsibility and a privilege, not a burden. That our praise of God and the act of Eucharist is for our "salvation" reiterates the importance of this term and our need to name how and where "salvation" is operative for us.

> *but (on this night / on this day / in this time) above all*
> *to laud you yet more gloriously,*
> *when Christ our Passover has been sacrificed.*

In the liturgy, the words *hodie* and *hodierna* ("today") as well as the phrase *haec dies / haec nox est* ("this [is the] day" or, as in the case of

the Easter Vigil, "this [is the] night") refer specifically to what the liturgy enacts and why the liturgy is so important. As noted above, St. Leo the Great said everything that Christ has accomplished has passed over into the sacraments. It is here in all of its uniqueness and fullness that we experience these saving mysteries. It is *"this* day," *haec dies*, for which the season of Lent prepares this and to which the liturgies of the Triduum lead. Each and every liturgy is unique, never repeated, and never the same. While we may pray the same texts, hear the same readings, sing the same music, and engage in the same ritual gestures and symbols, each and every act of the liturgy is unique, a uniqueness affected by the different needs, wants, and things that we wish to thank God for; the church itself is always a pilgrim, on the move and never the same, and world events change. Hence the value of the phrase "on this night" with the subtle cosmic reference to "night." The collect for Easter Day states,

> O God, who on this day,
> through your Only Begotten Son,
> have conquered death
> and unlocked for us the path to eternity,
> grant, we pray, that we who keep
> the solemnity of the Lord's Resurrection
> may, through the renewal brought by your Spirit,
> rise up in the light of life.
> Through our Lord Jesus Christ...

That Christ is acclaimed as "our Passover" in the Preface combines two key terms—*our* and *Passover*—the point being that (1) we, as a body, the church community (as opposed to each of us singularly) (2) partake, through the liturgy, in Christ's passing over from death to new life so that Christ's Passover becomes our Passover. The plural should always be kept in mind: it is *we* who do these things; the liturgy is a communal act. The liturgy is where we always take part in the "Passover" of Christ, making it our Passover.

> For he is the true Lamb
> who has taken away the sins of the world;

295

This explicit reference recalls the invitation to communion (noted above, "Behold the Lamb of God...") acclaiming the true "Lamb," whose sacrifice surpasses all of the Passover lambs sacrificed in the first covenant. The reference to taking away "the sins of the world" is a particularly Western liturgical way of proclaiming that Christ's saving mysteries are all encompassing and make us whole.

> *by dying he has destroyed our death,*
> *and by rising, restored our life.*

The liturgy is always the celebration of the ecclesial, church community (see chapter 17), and liturgy always enacts the paschal mystery of Christ (see chapter 16.) This sentence is one of the clearest and most succinct summaries of what the liturgy accomplishes: it draws us into the saving mysteries, inviting us to acknowledge the defeats and sufferings we experience and to take part, through the liturgy, in the resurrection and life. A prayerful meditation that accompanies this and any liturgical text should consider how it invites us in ever new ways to experience personally what we celebrate liturgically.

> *Therefore, overcome with Paschal joy,*
> *every land, every people exults in your praise*
> *and even heavenly Powers, with angelic hosts,*
> *sing together the unending hymn of your glory*
> *as they acclaim...*

Each preface leads into the singing of the "Holy, Holy, Holy," often by reiterating something about the feast or season celebrated, as in the reference here to "Paschal joy." The universal and cosmic references to "every land, every people" exulting in praise reiterates that the genre of the Eucharistic Prayer is one of praise and thanksgiving for what we are drawn into by the liturgy. The reference to "heavenly Powers, with angelic hosts" is clearly eschatological in that all that we proclaim in the liturgy joins us to all those heavenly beings who continually stand in God's eternal presence in heaven. We take part in the mystery of their continual intercession on our behalf in the heavenly kingdom while we here on earth share in the same saving sacrifice of Christ on our behalf.

PROPER PARTS OF THE ROMAN CANON

Another distinction of the Roman Rite is that for certain liturgies or sacramental celebrations, such as Christian initiation, confirmation, ordination, or funerals, as well as for special feasts, there are proper parts to be proclaimed during the Roman Canon. For feasts and seasons, there are two occasions when this occurs.

The first is before the phrase *in communion with those whose memory we venerate* and happens on five occasions: the Nativity and its octave, the Epiphany, the Easter Vigil and its octave, the Ascension, and Pentecost. These particular sections of the Canon offer important insights about the feast being celebrated. They each begin by referring to the particular feast being celebrated and refer to the day or night of the feast specifically.

The theology of such texts is that what is celebrated on a particular day is unique, yet also part of the entire paschal mystery of Christ. While through the liturgy we always "make memory together" of the saving mysteries of Christ's salvation, on particular feasts, such as those with their proper sections, the commemoration is specified in order to distinguish one feast from another and to raise up particular aspects of the same Christ event as experienced through the liturgy.

The proper part of the Roman Canon for the Easter Vigil (and the season) is the following:

> *Celebrating the most sacred night (day)*
> *of the Resurrection of our Lord Jesus Christ in the flesh*
> *and in communion with those whose memory we venerate,*
> *especially the glorious ever-Virgin Mary,*
> *Mother of our God and Lord, Jesus Christ…*

The word *celebrating* clearly indicates what the liturgy does: namely, in a public and structured way, we take part in the very life of God through the paschal mystery in the power of the Holy Spirit and in the communion of the church. *Celebration* underscores festivity and joy; it does not connote ebullience or anything that is unbridled or trivial.

The reference to the "Resurrection of our Lord Jesus Christ in the flesh" joins a number of important christological terms. The word

297

Jesus is not used without the faith-filled modifiers *Lord* and *Christ*. That Christ rose from the dead "in the flesh" is a subtle reiteration of traditional Christian belief in what happened that first Easter "day." The exalted terminology used to describe "the glorious ever-Virgin Mary, Mother of our God and Lord, Jesus Christ…" exemplifies how in and through the liturgy, terms not associated with the Virgin Mary in the Bible are added by way of affirming traditional Catholic faith in who she is in her fullness.

The second place in the Canon in which there is a proper part is after "Therefore, Lord, we pray…" and it occurs on the Easter Vigil and during the octave of Easter. That this section is particular to Easter indicates the singular nature of this feast. The text reads,

> *which we make to you*
> *also for those to whom you have been pleased to give*
> *the new birth of water and the Holy Spirit,*
> *granting them forgiveness of all their sins…*

This insertion refers to the rites of sacramental initiation undertaken at the Vigil through "the new birth of water and the Holy Spirit." That the Holy Spirit is noted here is important theologically because any and all liturgical rites are carried out only because of the power and action of the Holy Spirit in the midst of the church ("which we make to you"). "The new gift of water" refers to the use of the primal element of water in order to convey entrance into divine life in and through Christ. "Granting them forgiveness of all their sins" reflects the totally new nature the baptized receive from initiation into Christ.

SOLEMN BLESSINGS

Solemn blessings were not part of the Mass as revised after Trent. They were added to the post–Vatican II reform of the Mass to elaborate on aspects of the feasts and seasons being celebrated. Most of these come from ancient and traditional sources. While these are not required, they are offered in the Missal as options for the priest to choose. Like the prefaces, they are assigned to particular seasons, feasts, and sacramental celebrations. In the Roman Missal, they include solemn blessings at the end of ordination rites, religious profession, marriage, the blessing of an abbot/abbess, and other special occasions.

The solemn blessing for the Easter Vigil is the following:

> *May almighty God bless you*
> *through today's Easter Solemnity*
> *and, in his compassion,*
> *defend you from every assault of sin.*

Note, again, the importance of *today* in the text.

> *And may he, who restores you to eternal life*
> *in the Resurrection of his Only Begotten,*
> *endow you with the prize of immortality.*

"Only-Begotten Son" refers to the uniqueness of Christ's incarnation and being begotten by the Father from all time and to the church's being similarly "begotten" in Christ, especially through his death and resurrection, celebrated uniquely at Easter.

The phrase "the prize of immortality" refers to life's goal, even though the word *prize* has a more ephemeral meaning in common parlance.

> *Now that the days of the Lord's Passion have drawn to a close,*
> *may you who celebrate the gladness of the Paschal Feast*
> *come with Christ's help, and exulting in spirit,*
> *to those feasts that are celebrated in eternal joy.*

This contains a somewhat premature reference to the end of the Triduum, which occurs at Evening Prayer on Easter Sunday itself. "The Paschal Feast" refers to the entire sweep of the paschal mystery, not just Easter or the resurrection. We never celebrate one aspect of the paschal mystery without celebrating all of it, even though we might emphasize one or another part of it on a given day. It is all of a piece. The reference to "those feasts in eternal joy" uses our familiar speech about liturgical "feasts and seasons" and applies it to the eschatological banquet in heaven (note "the supper of the lamb" reference in the invitation to communion from Rev 19:9).

CONCLUSION

No one liturgical text can say all that can or should be said about the liturgy. Liturgical texts describe the attributes of the God we worship and why we need to worship this God. Liturgical texts never define what is occurring or what should result from worship. Liturgical texts "tether the imagination" simply because, in the end, one's imagination in worship can never be controlled.

DISCUSSION QUESTIONS

1. Review the liturgical prayers that are assigned to next Sunday's Mass and discuss their theological meanings in light of the exercise of this chapter.
2. One of the advantages of the Roman Missal as revised after Vatican II is the number of Prefaces it contains. Review the texts of the Prefaces in the Missal for a particular season, for example, Advent, Christmas, Lent, or Easter, and reflect on the theological meanings about this season that these Prefaces describe.
3. Choose two of the Eucharistic Prayers in the Missal and compare and contrast their theological emphases and content.

15

EXPERIENCES OF THE TRINITY

The purpose of this chapter is to emphasize that the celebration of sacramental liturgy is an experience of the life and action of the Trinity. It discusses (1) that the biblical God in whom we believe in is a God of relationships and relatedness, (2) that "naming God" in liturgical prayers repeatedly emphasizes this through the use of a number of metaphors and names for God, and (3) that the structure and content of liturgical prayers is important to understand in terms of what they say about God and us.

A GOD OF RELATIONSHIPS AND RELATEDNESS

Fundamentally, the biblical God is a God of relationships and relatedness. God's overarching concern is to invite us, followers and fellow believers, into a relationship with him. The Old Testament repeatedly recounts how God's chosen people relate to the "God of Abraham, Isaac and Jacob" and thereby underscores the abiding union into which God invites his followers.

Some of the names assigned to God in the Old Testament are not nouns, but really verbs. For example, in the Book of Exodus 3:14, God says that his name is "I am who I am." The often-used name *Emmanuel* means "I will always be there for you." Jesus came to put a face on God, and the New Testament authors give us a variety of names, including *Christ, Lord, Messiah*, and *Son of God*. That same New Testament gives us a number of names for the Holy Spirit, including *Paraclete* and *Advocate*. As early as the mid-second century, Christians were engaged in searching for appropriate names for the God of the Scriptures to carry over to ever new cultural circumstances in which the church found itself.

The work of "naming God" makes its way into every liturgy that the Christian church celebrates by calling upon God as *Father, Son, and Holy Spirit*, and by countless other terms describing the three persons in God and the attributes of the triune God. This approach to naming God in personal ways and as three persons in one God stands alongside an approach that "names" God in terms of functions—for example, *Creator, Redeemer, Sanctifier*. Such terms, while regularly used in the liturgy alongside terms that are persons and person-oriented, are functions and particular expressions of the way God is experienced. First and foremost is the reality that God is a mystery and that the Church chose to use *Father, Son*, and *Spirit*, and other personal names to emphasize that the God we believe in is a "three-personed God." In addition, in naming the persons in God, we also proclaim that we, human persons, have a personal relationship with God.

The Old and New Testaments are filled with references to all that God has done and continues to do for us, his chosen people, to save, redeem, sanctify, and liberate us from sin and death. As noted in chapter 14, the Latin terms for these acts of God are *magnalia Dei*—God's mighty and wonderful deeds for us—and *mirabilia Dei*—the miraculous and inspiring works of God. Every prayer in the revised liturgy that we use to bless God and by which we ask God to bless people or things recounts these deeds of salvation and miraculous events in order to remind us that it is through the liturgy, uniquely and in a privileged way, that we become partakers in what God has accomplished and still now accomplishes for us and for our salvation. At the same time, the recounting of the *magnalia Dei* has as one of its aims to draw us human beings into the very life and being of the Trinity. What we pray in the liturgy about all that God has done for us is what we experience still through the very words and actions of the liturgy. And this is accomplished through the active presence and work of the triune God, "in [whom] we live and move and have our being" (Sunday Preface VI, from St. Paul's speech on the Aeropagus, Acts 17:28).

Because the Trinity is the heart of our faith and yet also the profoundest of mysteries, it is important to reflect on the church's received theological wisdom about how we try to understand this mystery. Often a distinction is made between the *economic* and the *immanent* Trinity: the "economic" Trinity expresses what God does; the "immanent" Trinity is the three persons in God in relation to one another.

The word *economic* is from the Greek *oikonomikos*, which means relating to arrangement of activities (not a financial metaphor, which we would expect in today's English use of the term). Each person—Father, Son, and Holy Spirit—has different roles within the Godhead, and each has different roles in relationship to the world (some roles overlap).

The Father sent the Son (John 6:44; 8:18). The Son came down from heaven to do not his own will, but the will of the Father (John 6:38). The Father gave the Son, who is the only begotten (John 3:16), to perform the redemptive work of our salvation (2 Cor 5:21; 1 Pet 2:24). The Father and Son sent the Holy Spirit. The Father, who chose us before the foundation of the world (Eph 1:4), predestined us (Eph 1:5; Rom 8:29) and gave the elect to the Son (John 6:39).

Thus the Son did not send the Father. The Father was not sent to do the will of the Son. The Son did not give the Father, nor was the Father called the only begotten. The Father did not perform the redemptive work that his Son accomplished. The Holy Spirit did not send the Father and Son. It is not said that the Son or the Holy Spirit chose us, predestined us, and gave us to the Father.

For a single verse that shows differences in roles, see 1 Peter 1:2: "According to the foreknowledge of God the Father, by the sanctifying work of the Spirit, that you may obey Jesus Christ and be sprinkled with His blood." You can see that the Father foreknows. The Son became man and sacrificed himself. The Holy Spirit sanctifies the church.

The economic Trinity refers to the acts of the triune God with respect to the creation, history, salvation, the formation of the church, the daily lives of believers, and describes how the Trinity operates within history in terms of the roles or functions performed by each Person of the Trinity—God's relationship with creation. The immanent (or essential or ontological) Trinity speaks of the interior life of the Trinity, the reciprocal relationships of Father, Son, and Spirit to one another without reference to God's relationship with creation.

"NAMING GOD" IN LITURGICAL PRAYERS

If we take the Prefaces to the Eucharistic Prayers at Mass, we notice that they all begin by addressing God the Father, and many almost immediately invoke Jesus Christ as our mediator with the Father:

It is truly right and just,
our duty and our salvation,
always and everywhere to give you thanks,
Lord, holy Father, almighty and eternal God,
through Christ our Lord....

What is very important, however, is the way these Prefaces "name" God as *Father*—through the use of very important words that together invoke and articulate a host of meanings about God in the Scriptures. The words are "Lord, holy Father, almighty and eternal God."

This cluster of names surrounding the title *Father* reflects a number of aspects about God at the beginning of this great prayer of thanksgiving as articulated in the Scriptures:

Genesis 12:4—we pray along with Abraham, who obeyed God's call and whom we acclaim as "our father in faith" in the Roman Canon;

Genesis 18:8—we pray with the mysterious visitors to Abraham who shared the food Sarah prepared for them;

Exodus 19:20—we pray with Moses who received the Torah;

John 1:1, 14—we pray with Jesus named the (incarnate) Word of God who was made flesh and dwelt among us;

Luke 24:13–35—we pray with the disciples on the road to Emmaus on that Sunday night when they recognized the risen Lord in the breaking of the bread (the Eucharist).

These metaphors are collected and articulated as we begin the prayer in the Eucharist that recounts the *magnalia Dei*.

Some other factors of these biblical names are worth noting, especially because "God language" and "naming God" has been and is an important preoccupation of theologians, especially when it comes to the term *Father*.

Scripture scholars tell us that in almost every instance in the Old Testament, the title *Father* is only available to the specially "chosen ones" of God. Like other monarchies in the ancient Near East, the Davidic dynasty is called into unique relationship with God (Ps 89:19–37); the king is chosen as a son of God; by implication, God is father. When Israel repents and turns to God, the title *Father* is invoked (Isa 63:16) because in a patriarchal culture, sonship functions as a metaphor for covenant. The Book of Wisdom states that God, a severe king to the sinner, is a father to the righteous.

In the New Testament, the covenant relationship is articulated in a new way by Jesus in order to express the intimate relationship between human and divine: Jesus called God *Abba*, "Father." When Paul uses the name *Father* as the acceptable translation of *Abba*, he usually links it grammatically with the name *Lord Jesus Christ* (Eph 1:2, 3). That is, the covenant relationship begun in Israel and manifested in Jesus is made available to the believer through baptism. Because of our baptism, we are bold to say *Abba*. *Father* is not a natural name for God, or we would not need to be "bold" and dare to call God *Father*. It is a term of the biblical covenants as we now experience them in the liturgy.

The liturgy invites us to appreciate and experience anew the breadth and depth of what God has already accomplished for us and for our salvation. To offer praise and thanks by naming three persons in God is crucial to the whole enterprise of our salvation simply because deeds and names are part of each other in the Scriptures and they are intrinsically connected in what we experience in and through the liturgy (again, through "prayers and rites").

Naming the Trinity as three persons is a continual reminder that the triune God is a mystery to be pondered and appropriated. While the privileged place to do this is at the liturgy, it should also be part of other kinds of prayer and provide a corrective when our prayer approaches God as unreachable or unapproachable or when we become so comfortable with naming God's attributes that we forget that our God is a God of relationship, not a God who in his transcendence is divorced from our world and from our lives as believers.

In the celebration of the liturgy, we experience a kaleidoscope of images and likenesses for God revealed through the texts of the Mass. For example, the presidential prayers for the Evening Mass of the Lord's Supper on Holy Thursday evening provide the following excellent examples:

> *Only Begotten Son*—this important term in the collect describes at least two things: who Jesus is in relation to God the Father and who we are as children of God (similarly "begotten" of the Father). The term *only* reflects the truth that Jesus is the unique Son of God and as such the unique mediator of our salvation from God. The term *begotten*, when applied to the church, recalls what occurs to us at Baptism—that we are made sharers in the divine life and partakers in the mystery of God. This is to say that to "name" the second Person of the Trinity in this way in the liturgy refers both to Jesus and to the community of the redeemed who are intrinsically related to and live in relationship with God—the Father, Son, and Spirit.
>
> *The memorial of this Victim is celebrated*—this phrase in the prayer over the offerings puts a sacrificial cast on the paschal mystery. While we can never separate cross from resurrection, humiliation from exaltation, or dying from rising, the Latin term used here (*hostia* = victim) really refers to the sacrifice that Christ uniquely accomplished once and for all. The subject "memorial of..." describes the liturgy as uniquely the commemoration of this once for all sacrifice, our experience of its entire saving effects here and now in our lives. Again, what surfaces here is the way a term on one level refers to Christ, and on another level refers simultaneously to the community of the church and the way the church is drawn into the mystery of the divine life of God through the liturgy.

O God, almighty Father, in the unity of the Holy Spirit. This phrase is from the final doxology at the end of every Eucharistic Prayer. What it does is to recap how the Eucharistic Prayer begins by addressing God, delineates the way Christ redeemed us and its benefits, and concludes with a reference to the Holy Spirit. This classical formula is an important statement of our faith in the Trinity and the way the Trinity acts to enable the saving work of our redemption to be accomplished through the liturgy. The phrase "in the unity of…" refers, on one level, to the three Persons who comprise God. On another level, however, it refers to the community of the Church as it is incorporated into the Trinity. In classical liturgical language, "in the unity" is a reference both to God and to the church as drawn into and receiving life from the Trinity. It is a reassertion that what was accomplished in baptism—our partaking in the mystery of the divine life—is renewed and strengthened in and through the Eucharist, understood as baptism's renewal.

The richness of "God language" as found in liturgical texts might well encourage our personal prayer to be similarly precise in order to sustain in our personal prayer the same dynamic at work in the liturgy. The variety of images and likenesses we use to describe God in the liturgy can help enliven our personal prayer so that it can always be a personal conversation with and in the three-personed God.

TRINITARIAN STRUCTURE AND CONTENT OF LITURGICAL PRAYERS

Almost all of the classical and the reformed Roman Rites have a trinitarian structure. We address God the Father, pray through the Son, in the power of the Holy Spirit. A prime example of this is the structure of the Eucharistic Prayers as revised and used in the Roman Rite today. (Recall that the three Eucharistic Prayers added to the Roman rite in 1968 were from ancient sources.)

According to the *General Instruction of the Roman Missal*, the Eucharistic Prayer has a trinitarian structure (as quoted in the previous chapter):

> Now the center and high point of the entire celebration begins, namely, the Eucharistic Prayer itself, that is, the prayer of thanksgiving and sanctification. The Priest calls upon the people to lift up their hearts towards the Lord in prayer and thanksgiving; he associates the people with himself in the Prayer that he addresses in the name of the entire community to God the Father through Jesus Christ in the Holy Spirit. Furthermore, the meaning of this Prayer is that the whole congregation of the faithful joins with Christ in confessing the great deeds of God and in the offering of Sacrifice. The Eucharistic Prayer requires that everybody listens to it with reverence and in silence. (no. 78)

Then the *GIRM* delineates the parts of this prayer (again, as quoted in the previous chapter):

> The main elements of which the Eucharistic Prayer consists may be distinguished from one another in this way:
>
> a) The *thanksgiving* (expressed especially in the Preface), in which the Priest, in the name of the whole of the holy people, glorifies God the Father and gives thanks to him for the whole work of salvation or for some particular aspect of it, according to the varying day, festivity, or time of year.
> b) The *acclamation*, by which the whole congregation, joining with the heavenly powers, sings the Sanctus (Holy, Holy, Holy). This acclamation, which constitutes part of the Eucharistic Prayer itself, is pronounced by all the people with the Priest.
> c) The *epiclesis*, in which, by means of particular invocations, the Church implores the power of the Holy Spirit that the gifts offered by human hands be consecrated, that is, become Christ's Body and Blood, and

that the unblemished sacrificial Victim to be consumed in Communion may be for the salvation of those who will partake of it.

d) The *Institution narrative and Consecration*, by which, by means of the words and actions of Christ, that Sacrifice is effected which Christ himself instituted during the Last Supper, when he offered his Body and Blood under the species of bread and wine, gave them to the Apostles to eat and drink, and leaving with the latter the command to perpetuate this same mystery.

e) The *anamnesis*, by which the Church, fulfilling the command that she received from Christ the Lord through the Apostles, celebrates the memorial of Christ, recalling especially his blessed Passion, glorious Resurrection and Ascension into heaven.

f) The *oblation*, by which, in this very memorial, the Church, in particular that gathered here and now, offers the unblemished sacrificial Victim in the Holy Spirit to the Father. The Church's intention, indeed, is that the faithful not only offer this unblemished sacrificial Victim but also learn to offer their very selves, and so day by day to be brought, through the mediation of Christ, into unity with God and with each other, so that God may at last be all in all.

g) The *intercessions*, by which expression is given to the fact that the Eucharist is celebrated in communion with the whole Church, of both heaven and of earth, and that the oblation is made for her and for all her members, living and dead, who are called to participate in the redemption and salvation purchased by the Body and Blood of Christ.

h) The *concluding doxology*, by which the glorification of God is expressed and which is affirmed and concluded by the people's acclamation Amen. (no. 79)

In the first part of the Eucharistic Prayer, the thanksgiving, the Roman Rite offers a number of variable texts.

Because the season of Easter expands our celebration of Christ's paschal mystery into one fifty-day event, the following Preface texts, which are used repeatedly in this season, are worth particular reflection.

Easter Preface One: (from the Old Gelasian sacramentary)

> *It is truly right and just, our duty and our salvation,*
> *at all times to acclaim you, O Lord,*
> *but (on this night/ on this day / in this time) above all*
> *to laud you yet more gloriously,*
> *when Christ our Passover has been sacrificed.*

(This introduction is used in all the following Prefaces.)

Note the use of the names *Lord* and *Christ*, to affirm our faith in his resurrection. Notable, too, is the way *Passover* is now ascribed to Christ's paschal mystery.

> *For he is the true Lamb*
> *who has taken away the sins of the world;*
> *by dying he has destroyed or death,*
> *and by rising, restored or life.*

The Liturgy of the Eucharist repeatedly uses *Lamb* to refer to Christ and his sacrificial death. The invitation to communion recalls its use in the Gospel of John 1:29, "Behold the Lamb of God," which follows the singing (or saying) of "Lamb of God you take away the sins of the world, have mercy on us / grant us peace."

The concluding couplet is an insightful and memorable summary of the way the liturgy incorporates us into Christ's paschal victory.

Easter Preface Two: (from the Old Gelasian sacramentary)

> *Through him the children of light rise to eternal life*
> *and the halls of the heavenly Kingdom*
> *are thrown open to the faithful;*

The liturgy often describes the baptized as "children of the light" who have overcome darkness and sin through Christ. This cosmic symbolism is noted as far back as the New Testament and has been repeatedly used in liturgical prayers. (Recall how central it is in the mystagogic catechesis in chapter 3.)

> *for his Death is our ransom from death,*
> *and in his rising the life of us all has risen....*

Again, this is a powerful insight into the heart of what sacramental liturgy enacts and accomplishes.

Easter Preface Three: (from the Missale Gothicum)

> *He never ceases to offer himself for us*
> *but defends us and even pleads our cause before you:*

As in the words of institution and consecration in the revised Eucharistic Prayers, the use of the phrase "for you" is an important statement about how Christ's death is sacrificial, for our sakes and for our salvation. That he pleads our cause is a reference to his continuing intercession on our behalf at the Father's right hand in glory.

> *he is the sacrificial Victim who dies no more,*
> *the Lamb, once slain, who lives for ever.*

Again, a reference to Christ's sacrifice, here imaged as a "Victim" for our deliverance, recalling the scapegoat image in the Old Testament. Then we immediately turn to acclaim "the Lamb" whose once for all death is experienced again and again in and through the Eucharist.

Easter Preface Four: (from the Old Gelasian Sacramentary)

> *For, with the old order destroyed,*
> *a universe cast down is renewed,*
> *and integrity of life is restored to us in Christ.*

This is a succinct summary of what is proclaimed at the Easter Vigil in the Exsultet. The "old order" is replaced forever by the "new order" in Christ. Note, too, the cosmic reference to the "universe" once cast down, now renewed forever. This leads to our personal appropriation of this cosmic and universal event in our lives being restored in Christ.

Easter Preface Five: (from the Old Gelasian Sacramentary)

> By the oblation of his Body,
> he brought the sacrifices of old to fulfillment
> in the reality of the Cross
> and, by commending himself to you for our salvation,
> showed himself the Priest, the Altar, and the Lamb of sacrifice.

The familiar themes from the other Easter Prefaces are reiterated here. The juxtaposition of *Priest, Altar,* and *Lamb* are poignant reminders of the way this unique sacrifice of Christ's death and resurrection continue to be experienced in their fullness, uniquely through the liturgy.

While many of the elements noted in the *GIRM* contained in the Eucharistic Prayer are well-known and self-explanatory, the *epiclesis* deserves special attention because it had been somewhat neglected in the Roman Rite and now features prominently in the revised liturgies after Vatican II. As regularly noted previously, the Greek term *epiclesis* means "invocation." In classical liturgical prayer structures, we ask God to send the Holy Spirit on us and on what we ask to be blessed (such as the bread and wine at the Eucharist).

While the Roman Canon contains no explicit verbal *epiclesis* (thus "somewhat neglected"), the structure and contents of the Eucharistic Prayers added after Vatican II refer twice to the Holy Spirit.

> The first is to ask God the Father to send the Holy Spirit on the offerings:

> Make holy, therefore, these gifts, we pray,
> by sending down your Spirit upon them like the dewfall,
> so that they may become for us
> the Body and Blood of our Lord Jesus Christ.
> (Eucharistic Prayer II)

> Therefore, O Lord, we humbly implore you:
> by the same Spirit graciously make holy

these gifts we have brought to you for consecration,
that they may become the Body and Blood
of your Son our Lord Jesus Christ.
                              (Eucharistic Prayer III)

Therefore, O Lord, we pray:
may this same Holy Spirit
graciously sanctify these offerings
that they may become
the Body and Blood of our Lord Jesus Christ.
                              (Eucharistic Prayer IV)

Look, we pray, upon your people's offerings
and pour out on them the power of your Spirit,
that they may become the Body and Blood
of your beloved Son, Jesus Christ,
in whom we have become your sons and daughters.
                    (Eucharistic Prayer for Reconciliation I)

And now, celebrating the reconciliation
Christ has brought us,
we entreat you:
sanctify these gifts by the outpouring of your Spirit,
that they may become the Body and Blood of your Son,
whose command we fulfill when we celebrate these mysteries.
                    (Eucharistic Prayer for Reconciliation II)

Note the important specifying of the persons in the Trinity—
Father, Son, and Holy Spirit—in the part of the Eucharistic Prayer for
Various Needs and Occasions right before the institution narrative:

You are indeed Holy and to be glorified, O God,
who love the human race
and who always walk with us on the journey of life.
Blessed indeed is your Son,
present in our midst
when we are gathered by his love,
and when, as once for the disciples, so now for us,
he opens the Scriptures and breaks the bread.

313

Therefore, Father most merciful,
we ask that you send forth your Holy Spirit
to sanctify these gifts of bread and wine,

With these rich texts as background, we can then appreciate what the *Catechism of the Catholic Church* says about the *epiclesis*:

The *Epiclesis* ("invocation upon") is the intercession in which the priest begs the Father to send the Holy Spirit, the Sanctifier, so that the offerings may become the body and blood of Christ and that the faithful, by receiving them, may themselves become a living offering to God. (no. 1105)

It then goes on to specify the consecrating and sanctifying nature of the central part of the Eucharistic Prayer:

Together with the anamnesis, the epiclesis is at the heart of each sacramental celebration, most especially of the Eucharist:

> You ask how the bread becomes the Body of Christ, and the wine...the Blood of Christ. I shall tell you: the Holy Spirit comes upon them and accomplishes what sur-passes every word and thought....Let it be enough for you to understand that it is by the Holy Spirit, just as it was of the Holy Virgin and by the Holy Spirit that the Lord, through and in himself, took flesh. [John Damascene] (no. 1106)

The second instance of an epicletic prayer in the revised Eucharistic Prayers in the Roman Rite occurs after the *anamnesis* ("memorial") section of the Eucharistic Prayer. This prayer asks the Spirit to draw the gathered liturgical assembly more firmly and fully into the unity that Christ wills for us.

Humbly we pray
that, partaking of the Body and Blood of Christ,
we may be gathered into one by the Holy Spirit.
(Eucharistic Prayer II)

*Look, we pray, upon the oblation of your Church
and, recognizing the sacrificial Victim by whose death
you willed to reconcile us to yourself,
grant that we, who are nourished
by the Body and Blood of your Son
and filled with his Holy Spirit,
may become one body, one spirit in Christ.*
(Eucharistic Prayer III)

*Look, O Lord, upon the Sacrifice
which you yourself have provided for your Church,
and grant in your loving kindness
to all who partake of this one Bread and one Chalice
that, gathered into one body by the Holy Spirit,
they may truly become a living sacrifice in Christ
to the praise of your glory.*
(Eucharistic Prayer IV)

*Look kindly, most compassionate Father,
on those you unite to yourself
by the Sacrifice of your Son,
and grant that, by the power of the Holy Spirit,
as they partake of this one Bread and one Chalice,
they may be gathered into one Body in Christ,
who heals every division.*
(Eucharistic Prayer for Reconciliation I)

*Holy Father, we humbly beseech you
to accept us also, together with your Son,
and in this saving banquet
graciously to endow us with his very Spirit,
who takes away everything
that estranges us from one another.*
(Eucharistic Prayer for Reconciliation II)

The Easter season is brought to a close by the Solemnity of Pentecost, a feast that notes the power and work of the Holy Spirit in the communion of the church. Hence its Preface, from two texts combined from the Old Gelasian Sacramentary, is worth special note:

> For, bringing your Paschal Mystery to completion,
> you bestowed the Holy Spirit today
> on those you made your adopted children
> by uniting them to your Only Begotten Son.

The celebration of a special solemnity for Pentecost both affirms the prominence of the paschal mystery as *the* mystery of faith and the way the Holy Spirit enables us continually and repeatedly to participate in it. The phrase "adopted children" reminds us that we are not children of God by flesh but by baptism, and through baptism are adopted sons and daughters.

> This same Spirit, as the Church came to birth,
> opened to all peoples the knowledge of God
> and brought together the many languages of the earth
> in profession of the one faith.

The universality of Christ's redemption is extended in the naming and acclaiming of the Holy Spirit. One of the Scripture texts that can be used for the Liturgy of the Vigil of Pentecost relates the story of the tower of Babel (Gen 11:1–8) and the confusion that ensued. Babel is overturned by Pentecost in Acts 2:1–11 by the breath and power of the Holy Spirit.

DISCUSSION QUESTIONS

1. What "names" and "metaphors" for God did you learn about in this chapter that touched you most personally and why?
2. Read and pray over the Scripture texts assigned for the Vigil of Pentecost and the Day of Pentecost. What do these have to say about the power and role of the Holy Spirit in the life of the church today?
3. Review the Scripture and prayer texts for the Vigil of Pentecost and reflect on how this might be a suitable occasion for the celebration of the sacraments of initiation as was common in the patristic era.

16

PASCHAL MEMORIAL

The purpose of this chapter is (1) to return to our working understandings of the terms *paschal* and *memorial* and to use them to establish meanings for our understanding of how "memorial" time
functions in sacraments, (2) to illustrate the ways that sacramental
liturgy uniquely incorporates us into Christ's paschal mystery, and (3)
to emphasize how "participation" is the preferred way to describe our
involvement in sacraments.

WORKING DESCRIPTIONS

PASCHAL

The English term *paschal* is almost a transliteration of the Greek
word from which it is derived—*pascha*. In turn, *pascha* derives from
the Hebrew word for Passover as an event in saving history (Exod 14)
and as an annual feast commemorating Passover.

MEMORIAL

Memorial is from the Greek work *anamnesis*, whose root letters
mne refer to this particular kind of biblical and liturgical "remembering" (*amnesia* is its opposite). Our usual understanding of "remembering" is ensuring we are attentive to and responsible about something or
someone, such as a birthday or an appointment, or a mental exercise in
which we recall events of the past. However, the biblical and liturgical
notion of remembering is always about an event that encapsulates the
past, the present, and the future, and by its unique nature, it is something in which we can "take part in" here and now. The saving event of

the Exodus in the Old Testament and Christ's "paschal mystery" in the New are precisely these kinds of events.

The liturgy makes memory of Christ's paschal mystery and, in sacramental liturgy through the proclamation of the word and sacramental rites, causes us to participate in that same paschal mystery. This is why we can assert that each and every liturgy is both a commemoration of the saving deeds of salvation that occurred once in human history and a new experience of grace here and now as we always look for its fulfillment ("next year in Jerusalem," or "come, Lord Jesus").

This lays out the basis for the argument in this book for a liturgical theology of the sacraments. At the same time, there are other approaches to the liturgy and sacraments that can help us flesh out what "paschal memorial" means.

It is often said that there are two kinds of time: *sacred* and *secular* or *profane*. Given this premise, liturgy becomes our stepping out of profane time to enter into the sacred time in which we encounter God, or more precisely, to encounter God more and more fully. Others will argue this approach by distinguishing between *chronological* time (Greek *chronos*, meaning day-to-day, quotidian time) and *kairetic* time (Greek *kairos*, meaning "a special moment," "a moment in which something occurs that has a lasting impact").

While these distinctions can be understood as separations, in sacramental liturgy they are combined. This is to say that we never really "leave" chronological time ("time marches on"), but that within day-to-day time, there are times, events, seasons, and celebrations that are the most sacred experiences possible this side of heaven. This is the essence of the liturgy and the sacraments. From another perspective, we can say that we celebrate paschal memorial in quotidian time, and in celebrating, all of time is put in proper perspective and all of human life is sanctified.

Another description of sacramental liturgy is that when we celebrate it, we are *at the threshold of heaven*. That is, while we are here on earth, the celebration of the liturgy is the closest we can come to experience the vision of God in heaven, which is life's goal. The liturgy is "heaven on earth." This is to suggest that there is always a "not yet" quality to the liturgy and sacraments. They always make us yearn for their fulfillment in the kingdom of heaven. Phrases such as *the heavenly liturgy* (from the Letter to the Hebrews) capsulize this idea. In the meantime, the "earthly liturgy" is foretaste and promise. When this world ends, there will be no more need for the earthly liturgy because we then will participate in the heavenly liturgy forever.

We also believe that God sent his Son as a human to live like one of us, flawed and fallible human beings in all things but sin. God's own Son underwent humiliation, passion, and death, and was raised in his resurrection in order to ascend to the Father's side in glory. We always need to combine this thoroughly incarnational outlook with the paschal way of understanding who Christ is and who we are in and through him. This suggests that sacramental liturgy is always incarnational and paschal. It is always about our identifying with Christ's humanity and his dying and rising.

One of the poignant phrases of the Christmas liturgy that combines these is Christmas Preface I (from the eighth-century Hadrianum sacramentary):

> *For in the mystery of the Word made flesh*
> *a new light of your glory has shone upon the eyes of our mind,*
> *so that, as we recognize in him God made visible,*
> *we may be caught up through him in love of things invisible…*

Again the first Easter Preface reflects our participation in Christ's paschal mystery:

> *…by dying he has destroyed our death*
> *and by rising, restored our life…*

That incarnation and second coming are also intrinsically related is reflected in Advent Preface I (taken from a combination of two texts from the Verona manuscript of the sixth to seventh century).

> For he assumed at his first coming
> the lowliness of human flesh,
> and so fulfilled the design you formed long ago
> and opened for us the way to eternal salvation,
> that, when he comes again in glory and majesty
> and all is at last made manifest,
> we who watch for that day
> may inherit the great promise
> in which we dare to hope.

The pattern of our human life and death is reflected in Christ. And it is through the resurrection that we need never fear death ever again. Sacramental liturgy always invites us into this same central saving mystery of the incarnation and paschal triumph of the risen Christ for our sakes and on our behalf, until Christ comes again in glory.

Underlying these three approaches to liturgy (among many others) is that memorial time is not chronological time. While we know and believe that Christ came in human history and died and rose in Jerusalem at specific dates and times, the celebration of the liturgy does not send us back in time. Rather, memorial time means that we, here and now in the present, through all the means at our human disposal (see chapters 11 to 14) summon the past and the future in the present. To "summon the past" means that we do recall and experience all that Christ accomplished in the past, especially his dying and rising. We also "summon the future" in the sense that we yearn for the fulfillment of the paschal mystery when Christ comes again to bring an end to time and to draw us to eternity forever. But it is in between the past and the future—the present—that God invites us to participate in "memorial" time. Through what we celebrate, we ourselves are those who live out the paschal mystery in our lives.

Sacramental liturgy is always about the past (which we summon together in celebration), the present (when we experience everything

God accomplished in Christ for us and our salvation), and the future (when what we experience here and now will be fulfilled and our life's journey complete). As noted above, the words of St. Thomas Aquinas in the antiphon for the Magnificat (Canticle of Mary) on the Solemnity of the Body and Blood of Christ (*Corpus Christi*) state, "How holy this feast in which Christ is our food; his passion is recalled; grace fills our hearts; and we receive a pledge of the glory to come, alleluia."

One of the nuances that memorial time brings out is that the liturgy is always "paschal" and not *just* about the passion and death of Christ. The liturgical text that most clearly reflects memorial is the memorial section of the Eucharistic Prayer:

> The *anamnesis,* by which the Church, fulfilling the command that she received from Christ the Lord through the Apostles, celebrates the memorial of Christ, recalling especially his blessed Passion, glorious Resurrection and Ascension into heaven. (*GIRM* 79e)

The Eucharistic Prayers themselves say,

Therefore, O Lord,
as we celebrate the memorial of the blessed Passion,
the Resurrection from the dead
and the glorious Ascension into heaven
of Christ, your Son, our Lord...

(Roman Canon)

Therefore as we celebrate
the memorial of his Death and Resurrection...

(Eucharistic Prayer II)

Therefore, O Lord, as we celebrate the memorial
of the saving Passion of your Son
his wondrous Resurrection
and Ascension into heaven,
and as we look forward to his second coming...

(Eucharistic Prayer III)

Therefore, O Lord,
as we now celebrate the memorial of our redemption,
we remember Christ's Death
and his descent to the realm of the dead,
we proclaim his Resurrection
and his Ascension to your right hand
and, as we await his coming in glory…

(Eucharistic Prayer IV)

Recall, too, that as in the rest of the Roman liturgy, the titles referring to Christ are *Christ* and *Lord*, not *Jesus*. Note the "mystery of faith" acclamations:

We proclaim your Death, O Lord
and profess your Resurrection
until you come again.

When we eat this Bread and drink this Cup,
We proclaim your Death, O Lord,
until you come again. [note past and future]

Save us, Savior of the world,
for by your Cross and Resurrection
you have set us free.

Note also how the paschal mystery is articulated in the prayer to bless water at the Easter Vigil (for the whole prayer, see chapter 11). It links the passion of Christ with the blood and water that came from the wounded side of Christ and then our participation in Christ's paschal mystery:

and, as he hung upon the Cross,
gave forth water from his side along with blood,

These references to John 19:34 and 1 John 5 have become very important because they have been used in a number of ways, especially by patristic authors, to describe the saving effects of Jesus's death and resurrection as commemorated in the sacraments. The classic reference is Augustine's comment that the church is born from the wounded side of Christ. The prayer continues,

> and after his Resurrection, commanded his disciples:
> "Go forth, teach all nations, baptizing them
> in the name of the Father, and of the Son
> and of the Holy Spirit,"

This reference to the end of the Gospel of St. Matthew (28:18–20) offers a number of interpretations, including that the baptized now share in the life of the Trinity and that all the baptized are to be evangelizers and are to go forth and witness in the world to the life-giving saving mysteries of the ascended Christ who intercedes for us at the Father's right hand, principally through the liturgy.

> so that all who have been buried with Christ
> by Baptism into death
> may rise again to life with you.

This explicit reference to Romans 6 recalls the first New Testament reading from the Easter Vigil and reiterates a classical understanding of what baptism accomplishes. The use of the word *may* is interesting, again because of its possible multivalence. One meaning is that we ask that God accomplish this now, namely, that we have new life with Christ here and now. But when read against the actual text of Romans 6, there is an eschatological motif here, namely, "that we shall also live with him," not only here and now, but in heaven forever. A play on the *already* and *not yet* of all Christian liturgy is operative here.

LITURGY AS UNIQUE EXPERIENCE OF PASCHAL MEMORIAL

A MEMORIAL HEARING OF THE WORD

As noted earlier, the Sacred Scriptures, when proclaimed in the liturgy, are anamnetic. Among other things, this is to distinguish them from being a chronological reading in the sense that they are much more than accounts of what happened in saving history. They are unlike "historical records," "chronicles," "journal entries," or "historical accounts." Rather, the proclamation of the scriptures in sacramental liturgy means that they are events during which the telling of the stories of saving history are happenings now of salvation in and through their being proclaimed.

The often-used phrase to begin the gospel, *at that time*, does not mean what it appears to say. In fact the Latin phrase *in illo tempore* means "once upon a time" in the same sense that the Book of Genesis begins with "in the beginning," or any cosmogonic myth begins with this or a similar introduction. These invite us to the retelling of familiar stories of faith through which our ancestors, we ourselves, and all those who come after us in the faith will be saved, redeemed, and sanctified. Over time, we will have heard these stories in the liturgical assembly so frequently that they should become second nature, if not almost memorized. The fact that we know what will happen does not affect their power and effect in the liturgy. We hear them again and again so that through rehearing them, they *happen* again and again in and through the liturgy. The veracity of these texts and their impact on us today is not based on whether the authors' accounts are historically accurate or whether we can date them or locate precisely where they happened. The compelling truthfulness of sacred texts in the liturgy is that they are from the Bible, whose books are varied in terms of genre and literary value. (The Pentateuch is not a Gospel and the Acts of the Apostles is not a historical book such as 1–2 Kings in the Old Testament.) But the complementarity of these genres inside the canonical Bible means that they are declared true for proclamation and that in their proclamation, they save, sanctify, and make us free. They were written down by authors whose intent was to take note of them and draw implications for our faith. The variety of biblical witnesses about the same event, like the passion of our Lord, attests to the foundational importance of these events and to the truth that one account cannot say everything that can or should be said about those events. The readings take place: what is said occurs in their being proclaimed in the liturgy.

Certain parts of the Scriptures are also raised up for emphasis when they are used as part of the prayers for consecration and of blessing. (Recall chapters 11 and 14, about the prayer to bless water and about the rite of consecrating chrism and blessing oils.) The same is true for antiphons at the entrance and communion processions in the Mass, as well as at other places in the liturgy. It is especially clear that these phrases and passages are meant to underscore how the Scriptures are part and parcel of liturgical memorial.

MEMORIAL ENACTED, NOT REENACTED

The liturgy is not a reenactment of saving events of salvation history. We do not engage in a drama based on past events. Rather, the liturgy is a set of commemorative events through which we (literally) "make memory together" of the central saving events of Christ's life, death, and resurrection through the means described earlier, namely, sacramentality, human action and word, word enacted, and prayer events. These are the ways in which sacramental liturgy functions. We make memory of Christ by doing in liturgy what we do in human life in daily and domestic things, not by staging a play that tries to reenact what happened once and for all in human history. We begin and end the day by naming light and darkness in the Liturgy of the Hours, and thus we rely on the cosmos and human words to commemorate Christ's paschal triumph. Baptism is the water bath through which we are freed from sin. This combines the cosmic element of water with the Scriptures and blessing prayers. Taken together, they are the means to "make memory" of Christ's paschal mystery and through which we are incorporated into it. We do not go to the river Jordan. Rather, all the events of salvation using water (reflected in the blessing prayers) are experienced in the sacramental liturgy of baptism.

We make memory of the risen Lord at table by recounting stories of faith from the Scriptures and praying that bread and wine might become sacred food, just as we dine three times a day for food ingestion and sustenance. The daily domestic ritual of eating food is the basis for our making memory of the whole paschal mystery and not just of the Last Supper. We do not go to the Upper Room in Jerusalem for the

Eucharist. Rather, the liturgical commemoration of the Eucharist relies on all the passages about feeding in the Scriptures and our hungering for the bread that will last forever. This has been done in every era of world history, at every place on the globe. We do not "play act" and try to reenact or reminisce on what it must have been like when Jesus dined in the houses in Palestine.

All the other sacraments function in a similar way. We anoint with oil to salve the bodies of the sick and weary in rites of healing (if not necessarily of curing). We anoint with sweet smelling chrism to pass on the messianic character and the meaning of sharing in messiahship.

The events of which we make memory are always paschal. They always concern human life, suffering, death, and resurrection. This was the way God chose to save us—through these saving events. The narrative recounting of the events from the Scriptures become the grammar of our relationship with God in sacramental liturgy. By "words and rites"—not staging and drama—we take part in the once-for-all events of our redemption.

That there are dramatic elements of the liturgy is clear—for example, to sing the Song of Zechariah as the sun rises during Morning Prayer or the blessing of new fire out of doors and following a candle in procession into church. In addition there are certain (optional) ritual gestures that can take place in the liturgy that may appear to be a historical reenactment. A first example occurs on Palm Sunday of the Lord's Passion, which offers three options for a procession with the gathered assembly holding palm branches. This was actually a late (tenth-century) addition to the Roman liturgy, originally from Gaul, where the liturgy was always far more expressive than the Roman liturgy. (Note that after the procession itself, the Mass texts for this Sunday never refer back to the procession with palms. They all focus on the death and resurrection of Christ.) A second example is the washing of the feet during the Evening Mass of the Lord's Supper on Holy Thursday. That it is optional (the Missal says, "where a pastoral reason suggests it") tells us that the liturgy as a public event of prayers and rites should not be diminished in any way by the foot washing. The accompanying direction that at this Mass there may be a collection of gifts for the poor reflects the regular Roman custom of collecting gifts for the poor at Mass and delivering them afterward. Otherwise, the Roman liturgy is fairly straightforward and does not reenact. It makes paschal memorial in common by word, "rites and prayers."

One example that Robert Taft, SJ, regularly uses to describe the liturgy is from the famous fresco in the Sistine Chapel in Rome of the creation of Adam. This fresco painting by Michelangelo illustrates how God breathes life into man. The image is of nearly touching fingers— God's and Adam's. One interpretation of this image for our purposes would be that there is a "spark" between them that gives life. The "spark" of the paschal memorial in sacramental liturgy is that when all that is of God is offered to us through Christ, we respond with all that is in us that needs healing, redirection, and reconciliation. This means that for sacramental liturgy to be our appropriation of the paschal mystery, we need to be as humble and honest as we can in acknowledging our need for God in that particular sacramental rite. The way in which sacraments function is that they are particular expressions and commemorations of the paschal mystery celebrated in common through which we experience all that the paschal mystery offers us. Some are once-for-all commemorations—baptism, confirmation, and orders (each of which gives us a sacramental character). Others are received more frequently, such as (in descending order of frequency) the Eucharist, penance, anointing of the sick, and (depending on circumstances) marriage. Each in its own way is a commemoration of the paschal mystery to reflect and respect the changes in human needs. But for the "spark" to occur, it requires honesty and humility. Then our lives can be expressions of the paschal mystery in our own day and age.

Going back to the distinction between memorial and reenactment, this is to suggest that the only way paschal memorial really happens is when we are drawn into it through the liturgy. Liturgical memorial always incorporates us into what is being celebrated to the degree that there is no liturgical celebration without the gathered assembly's humble and honest openness to what occurs in the liturgy. We are always "active" participants in the liturgy. But we can be

327

"passive" participants for reenactments that can never touch us on that deep level.

FROM "RECEPTION" TO "PARTICIPATION"

One of the stated goals of the Constitution on the Sacred Liturgy is the "active participation" of the gathered assembly in the celebration of the sacred liturgy, with all its ministers understood to be part of the assembly. That those who revised the liturgy had this in mind is clear in the design and contents of the reformed rites. Among other ways, active participation is evidenced by everyone "taking part" in the liturgy according to their roles, with their gifts and talents at the service of the gathered assembly. Sometimes this means movement, speaking, gestures, being engaged in the signs and symbols of the liturgy, listening, and silence.

But there is a more fundamental level confirming that the celebration of the liturgy of the sacraments means that we "participate" in the very being of God through "participation" in (sacramental) liturgy. This is part of the essence of what *memorial* means. The description that we "receive" sacraments had served the church well, especially when liturgical assemblies were silent in what happened before them and on their behalf. It was also a part of the schema that St. Thomas Aquinas designed to describe how sacraments operate. He distinguished "minister" from "recipient." This accorded with his use of Aristotelian philosophy, which sustained such distinctions in a binary way.

Yet the language of the Constitution on the Sacred Liturgy describes the way sacraments operate in a different way:

> The Church, therefore, earnestly desires that Christ's faithful, when present at this mystery of faith, should not be there as strangers or silent spectators; on the contrary, through a good understanding of the rites and prayers they should take part in the sacred action conscious of what they are doing, with devotion and full collaboration. They

should be instructed by God's word and be nourished at the table of the Lord's body; they should give thanks to God; by offering the Immaculate Victim, not only through the hands of the priest, but also with him, they should learn also to offer themselves; through Christ the Mediator, they should be drawn day by day into ever more perfect union with God and with each other, so that finally God may be all in all. (no. 48)

The phrase "by offering the Immaculate Victim" is enormously rich in its theology. It means that both the royal priesthood of all believers and the ordained share in the offering of the Mass.

That the ordained preside over the celebration of the sacraments is clear, with, for example, the Rite for Ordination restricted to bishops. In order to deal with the intrinsic interrelationship of the baptized and the ordained, Vatican II's Dogmatic Constitution on the Church makes two important statements about the distinction in essence between the ordained and the baptized priesthoods (no. 10) and that through baptism, the faithful share in the ability to worship God through the liturgy (no. 11), an idea that was central to St. Thomas Aquinas's understanding of sacramental character (see chapter 5).

This text from the Constitution sustains St. Thomas Aquinas's understanding of the "character" imprinted in baptism, namely that it enables us to join in the worship of the church.

The reference to "taking part in the Eucharistic sacrifice, which is the fount and apex of the Christian life" also asserts the fundamental importance of all liturgy as participation in God through Christ's saving mysteries.

Sunday Preface I commemorates how we, the people of God, became "a chosen race" through our participation in Christ's paschal mystery:

For through his Paschal Mystery,
he accomplished the marvelous deed,
by which he has freed us from the yoke of sin and death,
summoning us to the glory of being now called

a chosen race, a royal priesthood,
a holy nation, a people for your own possession,
to proclaim everywhere your mighty works,
for you have called us out of darkness
into your own wonderful light.

(from 1 Pet 2:9)

Also notable is that, true to the genre of liturgical prayers, what Christ accomplished is not simply described. Rather, through the prayer and rites of the liturgy, the gathered assembly shares in them.

This notion of the priesthood of the baptized was emphasized in the twentieth century "liturgical movement" (see chapter 8). The sharing in Christ's priesthood by all the baptized is mentioned in the rite for infant baptism when the priest anoints the newly baptized with chrism:

> *God the Father of our Lord Jesus Christ has freed you from sin, given you a new birth by water and the Holy Spirit, and welcomed you into his holy people. As Christ was anointed Priest, Prophet and King, so may you live always as members of his body, sharing everlasting life. Amen.*

Because of the complementarity and intrinsic relationship between the two "priesthoods," it is more theologically accurate to speak about *participation* in the sacraments than *reception* of them.

AN EXAMPLE: EVENING MASS OF THE LORD'S SUPPER

The Evening Mass of the Lord's Supper on Holy Thursday is filled with paschal references, starting with the Entrance Antiphon (adapted from Gal 6:14): "We glory in the cross of our Lord Jesus Christ." The paschal motif is carried over into the Collect with its particular refer-ence to Christ's willingness to accept death for our salvation:

> *O God, who have called us to participate*

in this most sacred Supper,
in which your Only Begotten Son,
when about to hand himself over to death,
entrusted to the Church a sacrifice new for all eternity,
the banquet of his love,
grant, we pray,
that we may draw from so great a mystery,
the fullness of charity and of life.

The paschal motif is expanded in the Prayer over the Offerings:

Grant us, O Lord, we pray,
that we may participate worthily in these mysteries,
for whenever the memorial of this sacrifice is celebrated
the work of our redemption is accomplished.
Through Christ our Lord.

It is reiterated in the Preface for the Most Holy Eucharist, with particular emphasis on Christ as eternal High Priest and the offering done as a "memorial":

For he is the true and eternal Priest,
who instituted the pattern of an everlasting sacrifice
and was the first to offer himself as the saving Victim,
commanding us to make this offering as his memorial.
As we eat his flesh that was sacrificed for us,
we are made strong,
and, as we drink his Blood that was poured out for us,
we are washed clean.

Especially in the Roman Canon, the paschal motif of the liturgy is specified in the memorial section of the Eucharistic Prayer:

Therefore, O Lord,
as we celebrate the memorial of the blessed Passion,
the Resurrection from the dead,
and the glorious Ascension into heaven
of Christ, your Son, our Lord,

we, your servants and your holy people,
offer to your glorious majesty
from the gifts that you have given us,
this pure victim,
this holy victim,
this spotless victim,
the holy Bread of eternal life
and the Chalice of unending salvation.

The prayer after communion reminds us of the eschatological ("not yet") dimension of all liturgy:

Grant, almighty God,
that, as we are renewed
by the Supper of your Son in the present age,
so we may enjoy his banquet for all eternity.
Who lives and reigns for ever and ever.

The celebration of the liturgy (in this instance the Eucharist on Holy Thursday evening) is the privileged place and means whereby we are drawn into and appropriate the paschal mystery of Christ in our lives. To do that most effectively, we need to access the strengths and weaknesses in our lives, the successes and failures, the sources of real growth in God and those things that hinder our growth in God, and we need to bring these to the celebration of the liturgy. It is there that the gathered assembly can experience what we pray in the first Preface of Easter (subtitled "The Paschal Mystery"):

For he is the true Lamb
who has taken away the sins of the world;
who by dying destroyed our death,
and by rising restored our life.

IMPLICATIONS

It is precisely in the celebration of the liturgy that the dying and rising of Christ intersects with our very human lives in need of redemption and sanctification. Nothing could be more consoling than to realize that it is through this celebration that *our* deaths and defeats in life have been overcome, and that from the resurrection of Christ comes *our* real life. One of the purposes of celebrating the liturgy is so that we can put life—real life with all its fragility and all of its joys—into proper perspective. That perspective is the paschal mystery of Christ, accomplished once and for all and yet continually appropriated by the church in the celebration of the liturgy.

One consequence of the paschal centeredness of the liturgy is that other kinds of prayer deserve this same paschal quality. The liturgy's linking of death and resurrection, humiliation and glorification, betrayal and reconciliation offer helpful paradigms for personal prayer, which might tend to emphasize one aspect of these profound realities in isolation or as distinct from each other. Put simply, prayer about suffering should always be done from the perspective of the hope that comes from the resurrection. Conversely, prayer about the resurrection should always be grounded in the reality that triumph came about after suffering, humiliation, betrayal, and death. The resurrection does not offer "cheap grace." It offers us enduring hope and a totally new life because it came about after facing into and dealing with the most profound and hurtful of human realities.

But when the resurrection of Christ is appreciated as the center of our faith, it becomes the lens of hope through which we view and deal with our own weakness, sickness, terminal illnesses, humiliations, and defeats in our daily life. When brought to prayer in light of the paschal mystery, they are truly transformed through our participation in Christ's saving death and resurrection.

DISCUSSION QUESTIONS

1. Compare the way Christ's suffering and death are described in the traditional devotion of the Stations of the Cross and the way these same mysteries are described in the prayer texts from the Easter Triduum.

2. Explain the difference between watching movies such as *The Passion* and participating in the liturgy of Good Friday.
3. In what ways can the paschal mystery be a helpful lens through which to evaluate our lives that can always give us hope despite the worst things we might experience in life?

17

COMMUNIO

The purpose of this chapter is (1) to indicate how sacraments are always "epiphanies" of the church, (2) to indicate several meanings for the term *communio*, while illustrating this variety with reference to sacramental rites, (3) to indicate the importance of naming saints in sacramental liturgy, and (4) to note that the church is both holy and an imperfect pilgrim church.

AN EPIPHANY OF THE CHURCH

The word *epiphany* is from the Greek word *epiphaneia*, meaning "manifestation." In the liturgical calendar, the solemnity of the Epiphany is celebrated toward the end of the Christmas season, which normally extends to the Feast of the Baptism of the Lord. That it is an important commemoration of at least three epiphanies is clear from the antiphon to the gospel canticle of Mary:

> *Three mysteries mark this holy day: today the star leads the Magi to the infant Christ; today water is changed into wine for the wedding feast; today Christ waits to be baptized by John in the river Jordan to bring us salvation.*

That the solemnity of the Epiphany was an important day on which to celebrate baptism is evident from the testimony, again from the patristic era, of keeping vigil the night before Epiphany (the way we keep vigil for Easter; the other time when baptism can be celebrated with special solemnity is the vigil of Pentecost).

In chapter 1, we indicated that belonging to a "covenanted people" was among the chief characteristics from the Scriptures that we can draw on as a foundation for understanding sacramental liturgy. Baptism brings us into the church as the community of God's people, chosen and immersed forever in the paschal dying and rising of Christ in the "communion" of the church. We are drawn into these sacred realities and relationships by God's gracious invitation and abiding action.

Foundational to this is the fact that we experience God together as a community of believers. We who are related to God in and through covenant religion are ourselves related to one another as fellow believers. The datum of Judeo-Christian revelation and liturgy is that we go to God together.

Covenant religion is always essentially about our relationship with God and the support and challenge that comes from that fact. As noted above, the words of Eucharistic Prayer IV say,

> Time and again you offered them covenants
> and through the prophets taught them to look forward to
>   salvation.

The inner dynamic reflected here is the perennial dynamic of biblical religion—God invites and we respond. But notice that it is the "we" who respond. Essentially, all liturgy is about the enactment of the paschal mystery in and among the community that is the church. The covenants forged with our forebears in the faith—from the Old Testament covenants to the new and eternal covenant in the blood of Christ—coalesce in the communal covenant we experience first at baptism and then as renewed in and through the eucharistic liturgy.

In terms of the life relation derived from this belonging and church consciousness, we who celebrate the sacred mysteries of Christ are then challenged to communal self-transcendence. That is to say, we who are nourished at the altar are then to be members of a community that assumes its proper responsibility to live more fully converted lives in conformity with the gospel in the community of the church before and in the world.

The fundamental given of the Judeo-Christian tradition is that we are so much a part of this "communion" that we are, in fact, never not in communion with one another and with God. While this is the reality in all of life, it is strongly evident in the experience of sacraments in the patristic era (see chapter 3). It is also a foundation for all sacramental liturgy celebrated in all eras of the church's life, even when celebrations were not marked by the kind of "active participation" we can presume today. This is expressed and is clearly evident in the present reformed rites of the sacraments. While some celebrations are still focused on the individual in emergencies (for example, infant baptism, anointing of the sick) or sometimes in the exclusive way we experience a sacrament like penance, it is also to be noted that these sacramental liturgies also have lectionaries and liturgical forms that call for and encourage communal celebrations.

The word *epiphany* can be joined to the phrase *of the church* in the celebration of the sacraments because every time we participate in them, the church is present in all its uniqueness and "grace-filled-ness." As will become apparent in the rest of this chapter, there are many qualities and facets to what "church" means, and all of them are enfleshed and at work whenever sacraments are celebrated.

There are many epiphanies recounted in the Old and New Testaments. Among them are the epiphany of God to Moses in the Book of Exodus (20:1–17), the child Jesus to the visitors from the East (Matt 2:1–12), Christ's baptism (Matt 3:13–17) and transfiguration (Matt 17:1–13) (when, on both occasions, a voice from the heavens declared, "This is my beloved son, with whom I am well pleased"), and Christ's crucifixion on the cross when the earth quaked (Matt 27:45–56). That we call sacramental liturgy "epiphanies of the church" is meant to underscore that what occurred in special times and circumstances in saving history occurs still in the church's celebration of liturgy and sacraments. Every sacrament manifests the power and action of God among us. Every sacrament manifests how we are part of one another in and through the relationship of the covenant.

The reality of church belonging is so strong that we are never, in fact, not in relationship with each other through baptism and church belonging. For example, some authors argue that the distinction often made between "public" and "private" prayer is really not correct because we are always part of each other, we are never on our own. A more proper distinction would be between "public" and "personal" prayer. We are always a part of each other here and now as well as the wider, universal church and the church that came before us in history and that will come after us until the kingdom comes. The term *epiphany* used here emphasizes the fact that sacraments are always acts of God, in Christ, in the power of the Holy Spirit.

COMMUNIO

The term *communio* has been used frequently in the Catholic Church since 1985, when the bishops who gathered for the Extraordinary Synod in Rome judged it to be a way to interpret the documents of Vatican II and many other things in the life of the church. That the term is itself multivalent and carries several meanings is part of its theological value.

Communio is used here primarily to emphasize that any assembly of the church is always gathered at God's invitation and that the church is always a reflection of the *communion* of the Trinity, three persons in one God, and of the church abiding in the triune God. The church is not self-generated. This is especially true at the liturgy. Sacramental liturgy is always an act of the church in a number of ways. The term *communio* reinforces the multivalence of the reality that is the church.

CELEBRATIONS IN COMMON

The Constitution on the Sacred Liturgy states,

It is to be stressed that whenever rites, according to their specific nature, make provision for communal celebration involving the presence and active participation of the faithful, this way of celebrating them is to be preferred, so far as possible, to a celebration that is individual and quasi-private.

This applies with especial force to the celebration of Mass and the administration of the sacraments, even

though every Mass has of itself a public and social nature.
(no. 27)

This was an important reassertion of the kind of presumed ecclesial
dimension of the sacraments that has characterized much of the
church's experience of them (see chapters 1 to 5). The statement that
the Mass always has "a public and social nature" could be extended to
all the sacraments simply because the rhetoric of all the prayers of
sacramental liturgy is plural: "we," "our," "us": "*We* ask this through
Christ *our* Lord," "Lord hear *our* prayer," "Have mercy on *us*." In the
litany of the saints at the Easter Vigil, we sing "pray for *us*," "hear *our*
prayer." This is true of the prayers said at the presentation of the bread
and wine, which state that "we have received" what we offer. In the
present Roman Missal, the only times when the singular is used in
public prayers is before receiving communion: "But only say the word
and my soul shall be healed," and when in the Creed we say, "I
believe."

It is also true that at certain times in the church's history the
sacraments were celebrated in quasi-private settings—for example, the
"private Mass," when infant baptisms virtually replaced adult baptisms
after the patristic era (see chapter 5 for both), and the anointing of the
sick in emergencies. What this paragraph in the Constitution did,
however, was to emphasize the communal nature of the sacraments so
that all the rites, including penance and anointing, have communal
celebrations as well as celebrations when this is either not possible or
not envisioned (as noted above). The *GIRM* now refers to "private"
Masses as a "Mass at which only one minister participates" (no. 252)—
that is, that there should never be a "solitary" Mass, and the church
directs that at least one person may participate and in doing so become
a presence and witness for the whole church, especially by verbal participation in the words and prayers of the liturgy.

THE GATHERED ASSEMBLY

Theologically, the simple phrase *the gathered assembly* carries a
wealth of meaning. The word *church* comes from two Greek words:
ek, meaning "out," and the verb *kaleo*, meaning "to call." Originally,

this was a civic term for a public gathering as a response to the call of the "town crier." In the Bible, the calling of an assembly is often described as done at God's command through the words of another, as in the first reading on Ash Wednesday, Joel 2:1: "Proclaim a fast, call an assembly."

The theological point to be made here is that we come together to celebrate sacraments at God's gracious invitation. More technically, in the light of our treatment of St. Augustine (see chapter 3), this puts the emphasis on God and not ourselves in order that we not be guilty of Pelagianism, the heresy that claims that we can "earn" salvation. Rather what we do is always initiated by, sustained by, and completed by God.

This idea also informs the texts at the presentation of bread and wine at Mass (see chapter 12):

> Blessed are you, Lord God of all creation,
> for through your goodness we have received
> the bread / wine we offer you:
> fruit of the earth and work of human hands,
> it will become for us the bread of life / our spiritual drink.

There always needs to be a delicate balance between emphasizing our involvement and "work" in the preparation for and the celebration of sacramental liturgy and emphasizing that what we do is done as a response to God's invitation who sustains us in doing it.

This is to say that the things we prepare and produce through human ingenuity are legitimately emphasized as the "work of human hands" for the sake of "the work of our redemption." But it also says that all we do is a response to God having created us, given us faculties of mind, will, and heart, and having invited us to call an assembly in which the gathered church celebrates the liturgy.

THE "LOCAL CHURCH"

The term *local church* is used to describe a number of things, but in the documents of Vatican II, it refers to the diocese. When the *GIRM* describes the Eucharist it states,

The celebration of the Eucharist in a particular Church is of utmost importance.

For the Diocesan Bishop, the prime steward of the mysteries of God in the particular Church entrusted to his care, is the moderator, promoter, and guardian of the whole of liturgical life. In celebrations that take place with the Bishop presiding, and especially in the celebration of the Eucharist by the Bishop himself with the Presbyterate, the Deacons, and the people taking part, the mystery of the Church is manifest. Hence, solemn celebrations of Mass of this sort must be exemplary for the entire diocese. (no. 22)

This reflects a patristic example of the liturgy when the local diocese could celebrate with the bishop, presbyters, deacons, and gathered assembly. In one sense, this is quite anachronistic given the size of (arch)dioceses today. From the late patristic era onward, the celebration of the Eucharist came to be led by the priest presiding, not the bishop, in which case "presbyters" became the one "priest." The Eucharist was also celebrated in various communal settings of parishes and religious communities. While sacraments are intended to be celebrated in one's parish, there are times when it is not convenient, for example penance or the anointing of the sick. Marriage is commonly celebrated in the parish of the bride, although exceptions, or "dispensations," can be granted. This is intended to reflect church "belonging" before, during, and after any act of sacramental liturgy.

At the same time, the expression *local church* has come to refer to the place where the liturgy of the sacrament actually takes place, most commonly one's parish church. Parish belonging means that we belong somewhere and can rely on the services of the church in any place for liturgy and sacraments. The Order of the Christian Initiation for Adults is a prime example of the relationship between diocesan and parish belonging and sacramental celebration.

Almost all of the rites associated with the RCIA, as well as the catechumenate, take place in the local parish. But the Rite of Election, when catechumens become candidates for baptism and already baptized candidates are ready for initiation into the Catholic

Church, normally takes place in the diocesan cathedral. This harkens back to the time when mystagogues such as Sts. Cyril of Jerusalem and John Chrysostom delivered catechetical lectures before baptism and mystagogical catecheses after baptism. That sacramental initiation itself now normally takes place in one's parish church reflects the growth of Catholicism from the patristic era.

Records for sacraments are kept in one's parish for baptism, confirmation, first communion, marriage, ordination, and anointing of the sick. This ensures that one can rely on that parish to produce evidence of the sacrament having taken place. Wherever one lives and where the celebration of marriage or ordination takes place, part of the required "paperwork" for these sacraments involves sending a record of those sacraments to the place of baptismal record. It also means that if the marriage is annulled or the priest laicized, that record is also sent to the parish of the baptism. One of the reasons why a couple entering into a marriage must secure a baptismal certificate dated within six months of the wedding is to insure that neither person contracted a prior marriage or was ordained. When a parish is closed or is merged with another, the records about sacraments celebrated in that parish are transferred to the "merged" parish or to another parish as specified by the (arch)diocese.

Note that baptisms and marriages are normally to be celebrated in a parish church, as opposed to a college campus chapel. But when dispensations are given for the celebration of these sacraments outside the parish church, the record of those sacraments must be in the (local) geographical parish where the wedding venue is located and a record sent to the parish of one's baptism. While securing these documents as part of one's preparation for marriage can be tedious (if not, at times, arduous), they are important to reflect the fundamental ecclesiological reality of sacraments and one's "freedom" to enter into these states of life.

THE UNIVERSAL CHURCH

It is often observed that one of the meanings of *catholic* (as we say in the Creed, "one, holy, catholic and apostolic") is "universal." In other words, participation in and belonging to one's local diocese automatically means that one belongs to the church universal, which is comprised of all local churches joined together. This also implies awareness of and respect for the various cultures that together make up the universal church. When it comes to the celebration of sacramental liturgy, this often means that different countries have different customs (and certainly vernacular translations) for the celebration of the liturgy. For example, in countries where Christianity is not the predominant religion, it would be common for the RCIA to be celebrated over a period of time, up to the three years envisioned in the rite itself. However in a culture like the United States, it is more common for the RCIA to last from several months up to a year. The very structure of the RCIA was made decidedly flexible so that such variations and adaptations by local bishops' conferences could be established.

The notion of universal church also means that we belong to a church tradition that has lasted for more than two millennia.

NAMING SAINTS

One particular way of understanding the universal church is to look to our past "family album" of all those who have gone before us marked with the sign of faith.

The naming of saints in the Roman Canon is one way that this is exemplified and practiced. Thus this section of the Canon begins with the following passage:

> *In communion with those whose memory we venerate,*
> *especially the glorious ever-Virgin Mary,*
> *Mother of our God and Lord, Jesus Christ,*
> *and blessed Joseph her Spouse,*
> *your blessed Apostles and Martyrs,*
> *Peter and Paul...*
> *and all your Saints;*
> *we ask that through their merits and prayers,*
> *in all things we may be defended*
> *by your protecting help.*

Toward the end of the prayer we pray:

> *To us, also, your servants who, though sinners,*
> *hope in your abundant mercies,*
> *graciously grant some share*
> *and fellowship with your holy Apostles and Martyrs:*
> *with John the Baptist, Stephen,*
> *Matthias, Barnabas,*
> *Ignatius, Alexander,*
> *Marcellinus, Peter*
> *Felicity, Perpetua,*
> *Agatha, Lucy,*
> *Agnes, Cecilia, Anastasia,*
> *and all your Saints;*
> *admit us, we beseech you,*
> *into their company,*
> *not weighing our merits,*
> *but granting us your pardon....*

In the third Eucharistic Prayer, the insertion of a saint of the day or a patron saint is envisioned when the priest says,

> *May he make of us*
> *an eternal offering to you,*
> *so that we may obtain an inheritance with your elect,*
> *especially with the most Blessed Virgin Mary, Mother of God,*
> *with blessed Joseph, her Spouse,*
> *with your blessed Apostles and glorious Martyrs,*
> *with Saint N. and with all the saints*
> *on whose constant intercession in your presence*
> *we rely for help.*

One of the most poignant ways in which we commemorate the saints in the Roman Rite is when we sing the Litany of the Saints. We sing it for the sacraments of initiation—that is, at baptism and confirmation—and it is sung annually at the Easter Vigil and all other times when baptism and confirmation are celebrated. We sing the litany at ordinations to the diaconate, presbyterate, and episcopacy, with the candidates lying prostrate. We also sing it for the dedication of a church between the profession of faith and the deposition of relics in the altar, which is a particularly graphic and poignant placement. (In cases where no deposition occurs, the prayer of dedication follows the Litany of the Saints.) The Litany of the Saints is also prayed in the sacrament of the anointing of the sick and in the Rite for a Major Exorcism.

To the established list of saints in the litany, other saints may be added. For example, the RCIA states that "the singing of the Litany of the Saints may include...names of other saints (for example, the titular of the church, the patron saints of the place or those to be baptized)" (no. 221).

We invoke the names of the saints as models and examples for us in living the faith, as heavenly intercessors on our behalf before the throne of God, and as reminders that each and every time we celebrate the liturgy we are part of a living faith tradition that goes back to "holy Mary, Mother of God," St. John the Baptist, St. Joseph, Sts. Peter and Paul, all the way to St. John Paul II and beyond.

This emphasis leads to several implications, among which is that church belonging, especially on the local level, is not of our own making. It is also not an assemblage of like-minded people or people who are naturally friends. Part of the mosaic that makes up the church in any (and every) age is the diversity of its members. The history of the church indicates this when in different periods, different groups came to the fore. For example, many of the persons discussed in chapters 2 to 6 spoke from their particular experience to the reality of church belonging as reflected in sacramental liturgy. Examples are Tertullian and St. Justin reflecting the age of the martyrs and the need for careful apologetics about the nature of the church; the influence of St. Benedict and cenobite monasticism (as opposed to hermits; *cenobite* from the Greek term *koinos*, meaning "common" and *bios*, meaning "life"); the mendicant tradition as exemplified by Sts. Dominic and Francis of Assisi. The apostolic communities often emulate the Society of Jesus, founded after the Council of Trent. In our own day, new ecclesial movements have new and emerging roles in the church.

All of these are examples of certain kinds of religious community belonging that should not be regarded as in competition with or apart from dioceses, parishes, and places where evangelization, catechesis, and theological argumentation continue to occur and flourish.

Thus *church belonging* is not a generic term or a generalization. Catholics have belonged to the church in a variety of ways over our entire history.

THE IMPERFECT (PILGRIM) CHURCH ON EARTH

The church is a pilgrim in the sense that it is the community of believers on their way to complete union with and in God in eternity. Before we are called from this life to the next, we are the imperfect, pilgrim church on earth. This means that we who are the church of Christ on this earth must strive to become the *less imperfect* church. For that to happen, we need to be reshaped and reformed in God's image and likeness through the Eucharist and other acts of the sacred liturgy.

It is a classical assertion that one of the main purposes of the celebration of the Eucharist is to build up the church. Hence, there is a church centeredness in every celebration of the Eucharist. Herein lies a challenge—namely, that the church on earth may be seen in the world as the community that lives and exemplifies its identity before the world. No celebration of the liturgy is ever only about itself or closed in on itself. It is always about the wider, universal church and how the church sees itself as a "sacrament of salvation" for the whole world.

In every eucharistic liturgy, there are two points in particular at which the local, gathered assembly prays with and for the universal church. The first is when the pope and bishop are named in the Eucharistic Prayer. Their explicit naming should not be seen to be about them individually, but as shepherds of the universal church and local church (meaning diocese). Every celebration of the liturgy (especially the Eucharist) is always "in communion with the whole Church" (Roman Canon).

Each of the Eucharistic Prayers added to the Mass after Vatican II has explicit requests that the church may grow in holiness:

Communio

Remember, Lord, your Church,
spread throughout the world,
and bring her to the fullness of charity,
together with N. our Pope and N. our Bishop
and all the clergy.

(Eucharistic Prayer II)

Listen graciously to the payers of this family,
whom you have summoned before you:

(Eucharistic Prayer III)

Look, O Lord, upon the Sacrifice
which you yourself have provided for your Church,
and grant in your loving kindness
to all who partake of this one Bread and one Chalice
that, gathered into one body by the Holy Spirit,
they may truly become a living sacrifice in Christ
to the praise of your glory.

(Eucharistic Prayer IV)

Be pleased to keep us always
in communion of mind and heart,
together with N. our Pope and N. our Bishop.
Help us to work together
for the coming of your Kingdom,
until the hour when we stand before you,
Saints among the Saints, in the halls of heaven,
with the Blessed Virgin Mary, Mother of God.

(Eucharistic Prayer Reconciliation I)

May he make your Church a sign of unity
and an instrument of your peace among all people
and may he keep us in communion
with N. our Pope and N. our Bishop
and all the Bishops
and your entire people.

(Eucharistic Prayer Reconciliation II)

Lord, renew your Church (which is in N. [name the location])
by the light of the Gospel.
Strengthen the bond of unity
between the faithful and the pastors or your people,
together with N. our Pope, N. our Bishop,
and the whole Order of Bishops,
that in a world torn by strife
your people may shine forth
as a prophetic sign of unity and concord.
(Eucharistic Prayer Various Needs)

The second point at which the gathered assembly prays with and for the universal church is in the universal prayer (prayer of the faithful). The fact that after the proclamation of the Scriptures and the homily, the assembly is to focus on "general" intercession in the "prayer of the faithful" means that we turn our minds and hearts to the needs of the wider Church and the wider world. The admonition of the *General Instruction of the Roman Missal* (no. 69) in this connection is very helpful when it states that the assembly engages in prayer for the salvation of all, "exercising the office of their baptismal priesthood." This is an explicit naming of what the baptized always do as they engage in the liturgy in communion with the ordained, installed, and other liturgical ministers. The celebration of the Eucharist is always done with and among an ensemble of ministers and ministries on behalf of and as an articulation of the baptismal priesthood of all.

A poignant example of this church consciousness again is the collect from the Evening Mass of the Lord's Supper:

O God, who have called us to participate
in this most sacred Supper,
in which your Only Begotten Son,
when about to hand himself over to death,
entrusted to the Church a sacrifice new for all eternity,
the banquet of his love,
grant, we pray,
that we may draw from so great a mystery,
the fullness of charity and of life.

Entrusted to the Church a sacrifice new for all eternity. —It is rare to find a reference to the church in a collect (unlike the Eucharistic Prayer, which is filled with such references). Hence it is important to note its place in this prayer at the start of the Holy Thursday liturgy. It states in a straightforward way that every act of liturgy is by, with, and for the church. Liturgy is always about the common prayer of the assembly of all believers. It reminds us of what St. Augustine observed about the relationship between the Eucharist and the church, namely, that we who are the body of Christ on earth celebrate the Eucharist to receive the body of Christ in this sacrament in order that we, as the church in the world, might be the more perfect reflection of God.

We offer. —Among the classical phrases used in the Roman Canon to describe the eucharistic action is *we offer* or variations of it, such as *we humbly pray, we ask you to accept and bless, we pray, we celebrate, we ask you.* These phrases are simple, subtle, yet theologically important indications that the entire gathered assembly joins the priest in celebrating the sacred liturgy and in offering this act of praise to the Father. It underscores that in no way is the assembly passive. In fact, *active participation* in the liturgy is to be presumed. The celebration of the liturgy is a celebration by the baptismal priesthood and the ordained priesthood in this act of thanks and praise for God's gifts of redemption and salvation. Even the priest, who is charged to pray and act "in the name of Christ, the head of the church" (*in persona Christi capitis ecclesiae*), does this on behalf of and in the name of the church.

The foundation on which the liturgy is based is the communal, covenantal relationship that the particular gathered assembly enjoys with God and the entire church, universal, diocesan, parochial.

At the same time, this church consciousness is also an enormous consolation in that it reminds us that we are never alone, we always belong, and we are always part of something bigger than we are as individuals. The very gathering of the assembly to celebrate weddings, funerals, baptisms, anointing of the sick, and Mass is a statement of belonging and of relationship. Indeed no one is alone nor can be alone in the church. This truth is never more important than when we experience separation or distance from God. It is then that members of the church are signs and instruments of God with us in the persons and personalities of fellow believers.

The dynamic involved in every sacramental liturgy is that we gather at God's invitation to celebrate sacred realities through which we literally "take part in" the triune God through Christ's paschal mystery in the communion of the church. Then, we celebrate those divine mysteries through the church's designated rites and prayers, called the liturgy of the sacrament. At its end, we are dismissed, sent forth to live more fully converted lives in daily life and in the world. The physical dynamic is that "we come" and "we go." The theological reality is that we gather and are sent forth.

One of the important features of the revised Rite for Baptism for Children is the expanded "Blessing and Dismissal" options, addressed first to the parents and then to the rest of the assembly. For example:

> God the Father, through his Son, the Virgin Mary's child, has brought joy to all Christian mothers, as they see the hope of eternal life shine on their children. May he bless the mothers of these children. They now thank God for the gift of their children. May they be one with them in thanking him for ever in heaven, in Christ Jesus our Lord.
> R. Amen.

> God is the giver of all life, human and divine. May he bless the fathers of these children. With their wives they will be the first teachers of their children in the ways of the faith. May they also be the best of teachers, bearing witness to the faith by what they say and do, in Christ Jesus our Lord.
> R. Amen.

> By God's gift, through water and the Holy Spirit, we are reborn to everlasting life. In his goodness, may he continue to pour out his blessings upon all present, who are his sons and daughters. May he make them always, wherever they may be,

faithful members of his holy people. May he send his peace upon all who are gathered here, in Christ Jesus, our Lord.
    R. Amen. (Rite for Baptism of Several Children 69)

Also, the Prayer over the People for the Rite of Confirmation says,

Confirm, O God,
what you have brought about in us,
and preserve in the hearts of your faithful
the gifts of the Holy Spirit:
may they never be ashamed
to confess Christ crucified before the world
and by devoted charity
may they ever fulfill his commands.
Who lives and reigns for ever and ever.
R. Amen.

    (no. 49)

One of the "Concluding Rites" for the communal celebration of the sacrament of penance ("Form Two") states,

May the Lord guide your hearts in the way of his love
and fill you with Christ-like patience.
R. Amen.

May he give strength
to walk in newness of life
and to please him in all things.
R. Amen.

    (no. 58)

Participants in sacramental liturgy need to know that it is presumed that they realize in life what they have celebrated. That it is admittedly a tall order and it can mean different things for different people is clear. But the intrinsic life relation of sacramental liturgy has been emphasized in Pope Benedict XVI's revisions of the dismissals in the order of Mass: for example, "Go in peace, glorifying the Lord by your life."

DISCUSSION QUESTIONS

1. In the contemporary culture that prizes individuality, the church's emphasis on sacramental liturgy, for example, communal celebrations of baptisms, can be both a challenge and a consolation. Explain.
2. Destination weddings are a phenomenon that puts the emphasis on the couple and (usually only some) family and friends. How does this coincide or clash with the church consciousness and presumed communal celebrations of the sacraments?
3. Given the decline in the number of ordained clergy, some parishes regularly celebrate the Funeral Mass at a regularly scheduled parish Mass. This sometimes occurs for the Nuptial Mass for weddings. What are the advantages of such celebrations?

18

ALREADY AND NOT YET

The purpose of this chapter is (1) to indicate the ways in which all sacramental liturgy is always a *privileged* yet provisional experience of the mysteries of Christ, (2) to note the value of approaching sacraments eschatologically through examples from texts used in the Eucharist and in the sacrament for the anointing of the sick, (3) to demonstrate the relationship between the liturgical calendar and the celebration of sacraments, and (4) to explain the life relation of appreciating sacraments this way.

PRIVILEGED YET PROVISIONAL

We have already seen that the church's experience of the liturgy is always a privileged experience of God, through Christ's paschal mystery, in the power of the Holy Spirit, in the *communio* of the church (in all its many dimensions). Given especially the Western church's emphasis on the reality of Christ's presence in the Eucharist and the emphasis on sacraments as "conferring" or "causing" grace, our present liturgy is legitimately called the "font and apex" of the church's life (again, the Vatican II phrase). The rhetoric of Christ's presence in sacramental liturgy as "real" has the advantage of emphasizing how those who participate in sacramental liturgy experience the paschal mystery at its deepest level.

At the same time, another equally important aspect of all liturgy is encapsulated in the Aramaic term *maranatha* (found at the end of 1 Cor 16:22) that can be understood as the indicative, "The Lord comes," or the imperative, "Come, Lord Jesus." The latter is more to our point here. That many liturgies, especially from the early church, use this as the concluding dismissal tells us how important it is to understand that liturgy leads to its fulfillment in the kingdom of heaven.

St. Paul famously argues in many of his epistles that we need to "become what we are," and that what we will finally be has not yet been revealed or fulfilled. There is an "already" and "not yet" dimension to all liturgy, as there is to the Christian life in general. Even as we acclaim and welcome the Lord's action and presence on our behalf in the liturgy, we also pray for his second coming at the end of time to bring time to an end. The short phrase "as we wait in joyful hope" in the embolism following the Lord's Prayer at Mass encapsulates this reality. The phrase "thy kingdom come" not only gives words to the reality of the Christian life in the Lord's Prayer, but it is also what is celebrated and experienced in every sacramental rite. What is accomplished in and through the liturgy is "the work of our redemption." But this is a foretaste of what is yet to be revealed. Such expressions as "and as we look forward to his second coming" in the third Eucharistic Prayer reflect that all sacraments should be enacted in such a way that the perspective is on manifesting the kingdom here and now until we are called from this life or this earthly life passes away. This is a paradigm for what the whole Christian life is about, watching and waiting in grateful anticipation for the end of time and, in the meantime, living between the already and the not yet as living witnesses in hope before all the world.

As already noted, paragraphs 1–13 of the Constitution on the Sacred Liturgy are the most theological of the entire document. They also provide its foundation. In no. 2, it reflects both the reality of what the church is and the church's destiny.

> It is of the essence of the Church that she be both human and divine, visible and yet invisibly equipped, eager to act and yet intent on contemplation, present in this world and yet not at home in it; and she is all these things in such wise that in her the human is directed and subordinated to the divine, the visible likewise to the invisible, action to contemplation, and this present world to that city yet to come,

which we seek. While the liturgy daily builds up those who are within into a holy temple of the Lord, into a dwelling place for God in the Spirit, to the mature measure of the fullness of Christ, at the same time it marvelously strengthens their power to preach Christ, and thus shows forth the Church to those who are outside as a sign lifted up among the nations under which the scattered children of God may be gathered together, until there is one sheepfold and one shepherd.

What we celebrate in the liturgy is the fullest experience we can have of the triune God through Christ's paschal mystery here and now before the coming of God's kingdom. Yet all of these privileged celebrations are all always provisional in that we are to see beyond them to what they promise and hope for—eternal life. Our participation in God in sacramental liturgy is as good as it gets in human life on this good earth. But one of their chief aims is to help us yearn for their fulfillment in seeing God face-to-face and being united with all redeemed humanity with God forever.

WE WAIT IN JOYFUL HOPE

Every time we pray the Lord's Prayer we say, "Thy kingdom come." Among other things, this means that as long as we remain here on earth, we are awaiting the completion of our redemption in Christ, and we look forward to his coming again in glory at the end of time to bring time to an end.

The Constitution on the Sacred Liturgy puts it this way: "In the earthly liturgy we take part in a foretaste of that heavenly liturgy which is celebrated in the Holy City of Jerusalem toward which we journey as pilgrims and where Christ is sitting at the right hand of God" (no. 8). In other words, while the liturgy is the center of our faith and is our present experience of redemption in Christ, it is also always a provisional experience of that redemption until we see God face-to-face in the kingdom of heaven. The plea *maranatha* underscores how we plead for Christ to come again and for his kingdom to be realized in its fullness. In the meantime, the liturgy is the closest we can come to the perfect experience of that kingdom here on earth.

The technical term that describes this reality is *eschatology*, from the Greek *eschatos*, meaning "end." This aspect of Christian theology deals with what will happen at the "end" of time to us personally and communally, especially at our death. But to focus only on what will happen when we die eclipses the fact that eschatology ought to invite us to appreciate the present, the here and now, as much as possible. Eschatology also gives us hope in the assurance that God is always with us now, and he will lead us to the hereafter. An eschatological emphasis on the liturgy gives us hope, even as we deal with imperfection and incompletion in our own lives. When we hear texts in the liturgy about such incompleteness, we should be encouraged that God has not abandoned us, and we should be challenged to help realize all those things Christ came to bring on earth—peace, reconciliation, solidarity, joy, love. Eschatology also should help us approach death as an undeniable reality. The liturgy of the sacraments, especially the Eucharist and the sacrament of the anointing of the sick, offers us helpful lenses through which to view death.

THE EUCHARIST

A major contribution of post–Vatican II eucharistic liturgy is the eschatological emphasis now present in the Eucharistic Prayers. In the Roman Canon, there is no explicit mention of the second coming. The phrase in the memorial prayer speaks about Christ's death, resurrection, and ascension:

> *Therefore, O Lord,*
> *as we celebrate the memorial of the blessed Passion,*
> *the Resurrection from the dead,*
> *and the glorious Ascension into heaven…*

Compare that with Eucharistic Prayer III, which at that same point says,

> *Therefore, O Lord, as we celebrate the memorial*
> *of the saving Passion of your Son,*
> *his wondrous Resurrection*
> *and Ascension into heaven,*
> *and as we look forward to his second coming....*

Or Eucharistic Prayer IV:

> *as we now celebrate the memorial of our redemption,*
> *we remember Christ's Death*
> *and his descent to the realm of the dead,*
> *we proclaim his Resurrection,*
> *and his Ascension to your right hand;*
> *and, as we await his coming in glory,*
> *we offer you....*

The very same emphasis is found in two of the three memorial acclamations:

> *We proclaim your Death, O Lord,*
> *and profess your Resurrection*
> *until you come again.*
>
> (first memorial acclamation)

> *When we eat this Bread and drink this Cup*
> *we proclaim your Death, O Lord,*
> *until you come again.*
>
> (second memorial acclamation)

We are also reminded of this eschatological aspect of the Eucharist when the priest invites us to communion by saying,

> *Behold the Lamb of God,*
> *behold him who takes away the sins of the world.*
> *Blessed are those called to the supper of the Lamb.*

This text is like many others in the liturgy in that it has more than one meaning. In addition to inviting us to partake in the body and blood of Christ in communion, this text also reminds us that "this supper" in this Eucharist is also an anticipation of being at the eternal banquet with Christ in the kingdom forever. The biblical source for this invitation is Revelation 19:9, where we hear about "the supper of the Lamb" in eternity. This image of intimacy with God through the Eucharist is another way the church reminds us that although we here on earth yearn for a "new heavens and a new earth," nevertheless, for as long as we remain on this good earth, God sustains and supports us at the altar table of the Eucharist with the food of everlasting life.

This same sentiment is found in the prayer at the end of the Order for the Blessing and Sprinkling of Water at Sunday Mass:

> *May almighty God cleanse us of our sins,*
> *and through the celebration of the Eucharist*
> *make us worthy to share at the table of his Kingdom.*

The eschatological meaning is clear. This world will come to an end and our individual lives will come to an end. We face both with the encouragement that comes from our paschal faith that makes us watch for Christ's return at the end of time to bring time to an end. In the meantime, we celebrate the Eucharist in joyful hope and eager expectation. At the Eucharist, in a privileged and unique way, we receive again and again what St. Paul handed on to us that he himself received: belief in the resurrection and the experience of the resurrection through the Eucharist. And we, the liturgy's ministers and faithful gathered assemblies, hand on to each other what we have seen and heard—the unique mystery of Christ himself—and what we have ourselves received from our forebears in the faith.

As noted in chapter 17, we sing the Litany of the Saints at several celebrations of the sacraments, especially at life-shaping or life-changing events, for example baptism, confirmation, anointing of the sick, or ordination. This litany is itself highly eschatological since these members of the church's "family album" have "gone before us with the sign of faith / and rest in the sleep of peace" (Roman Canon).

The preface for the Solemnity of All Saints places this eschatological aspect of the communion of the saints before us as we pray,

For today by your gift we celebrate the festival of your city,
the heavenly Jerusalem, our mother,
where the great array of our brothers and sisters
already gives you eternal praise.

Towards her, we eagerly hasten as pilgrims advancing by faith,
rejoicing in the glory bestowed upon those exalted members of
    the Church
through whom you give us, in our frailty, both strength and good
    example.

Even during the Paschal Triduum, when we commemorate the suffering, death, and resurrection of Jesus Christ and our incorporation into this central, saving mystery of our faith, there are eschatological references in the prayers of these liturgies. These texts reflect the reality that all liturgy is eschatological; it is always the past made present and operative among us, as well as the future present and operative among us.

The prayer after communion at the Evening Mass of the Lord's Supper states,

Grant, almighty God,
that, just as we are renewed
by the Supper of your Son in this present age,
so may we enjoy his banquet for all eternity.

Similarly, the prayer over the people at the end of the Celebration of the Passion of the Lord on Good Friday states,

May abundant blessing, O Lord, we pray,
descend upon your people,
who have honored the Death of your Son
in the hope of their resurrection:
may pardon come,
comfort be given,
holy faith increase,
and everlasting redemption be made secure.

The prayer over the offerings at the Easter Vigil states,

Accept, we ask, O Lord,
the prayers of your people
with sacrificial offerings,
that what has begun in paschal mysteries
may, by the working of your power,
bring us to the healing of eternity.

In the prayer after Communion on Easter Day, we pray,

Look upon your Church, O God,
with unfailing love and favor,
so that, renewed by the paschal mysteries,
she may come to the glory of the resurrection.

PASTORAL CARE OF THE SICK: RITES OF ANOINTING AND VIATICUM

At Vatican II, the council fathers (in the Constitution on the Sacred Liturgy 72–74) called explicitly for the revision of the sacrament of "extreme unction," now more properly termed the sacrament of the "anointing of the sick" and the rite of viaticum (the last reception of communion before one's death). The new ritual provides texts for the celebration of the anointing during Mass. Also notable is that the first chapter concerns visitation to the sick, sometimes with the reception of communion, and the last chapter contains (especially beautiful) prayers to be said with and for the dying. It is noteworthy that the title of this rite is Pastoral Care of the Sick: Rites of Anointing and Viaticum. In summary form, we can say that the three parts of this rite concern the following:

1. Pastoral Care of the Sick

The various chapters here concern pastoral visits to the sick, communion of the sick (with a Liturgy of the Word and a brief rite of reception), and the rite of the anointing with a Liturgy of the Word or within Mass. There are specifications for what to do when the sick person is in the hospital.

2. Pastoral Care of the Dying

These chapters include viaticum within Mass or are preceded by a Liturgy of the Word, the commendation of the dying, prayers for the dead and a continuous rite of penance and anointing, and lastly, a rite for emergencies (with penance, anointing, and viaticum).

3. Texts for Use in the Rites for the Sick

This chapter contains a number of additional biblical readings, greetings, litanies, and prayers.

Understandably, the rite contains many allusions to eschatology, the kingdom of heaven, and the reality of Christian death. Among the most poignant are found in the preface for a Mass at which the anointing takes place:

for you have revealed to us
in Christ the healer
your unfailing power and steadfast compassion.

In the splendor of his rising
your Son
conquered suffering and death
and bequeathed to us his promise
of a new and glorious world,
where no bodily pain will afflict us
and no anguish of spirit.

Through your gift of the Spirit,
you bless us, even now,
with comfort and healing,
strength and hope,
forgiveness and peace.

In this supreme sacrament of your love
you give us the risen body of your Son:
a pattern of what we shall become
when he returns again at the end of time.

The words that follow contain an eschatological reference always found at the end of the "Holy, Holy, Holy" acclamation, in that it always unites our prayers with those of the "(arch)angels and saints" already before the throne of God, whom we seek to join when this earthly life comes to an end:

> *In gladness and joy*
> *we unite with the angels and saints*
> *in the great canticle of creation,*
> *as we say (sing)...*

The introduction for the Rite of Viaticum says,

> My brothers and sisters, before our Lord Jesus Christ passed from this world to return to the Father, he left us the sacrament of his body and blood. When the hour comes for us to pass from this life and join him, he strengthens us with this food for our journey and comforts us by this pledge of our resurrection.

The last of the prayers offered as the prayer after communion at the Rite of Viaticum asks,

> *Father,*
> *your son, Jesus Christ, is our way, our truth, and our life.*
> *Look with compassion on your servant N.*
> *who has trusted in your promises.*
> *You have refreshed him/her with the body and blood of*
> * your Son:*
> *may he/she enter your kingdom in peace.*

But even as we, the living Christian community, celebrate these rites, especially of anointing and viaticum, with the sick, the "General Introduction" to the rite asserts,

> the role of the sick in the Church is to be a reminder to others of the essential or higher things. By their witness the

sick show that our mortal life must be redeemed through the mystery of Christ's death and resurrection. (no. 3)

SACRAMENTS AND THE LITURGICAL YEAR

The sacred liturgy is the unique place where we celebrate what has already been accomplished for our salvation and what is yet to occur when we are called from this life to eternity. Liturgy is, in fact, "already and not yet." For that reason, it is useful to indicate the intersection of the celebration of the sacraments with the church's celebration of days, weeks, feasts, and seasons.

One of the documents contained in The Roman Missal, entitled *Universal Norms on the Liturgical Year and the Calendar,* indicates the way the liturgy "tells time" by describing how we celebrate the mysteries of Christ each and every day, but also on specific days, that is, Sunday, solemnities, feasts and memorials, and weekdays. According to these *Norms,* we do this by celebrating daily "the Eucharistic Sacrifice and the Divine Office." We also "tell" liturgical time during "the cycle of the year" when we celebrate the mysteries of Christ "from the Incarnation to Pentecost Day and the days of waiting for the Advent of the Lord" (meaning Christ's second coming). The *Norms* then go on to describe in order of precedence the celebrations of "the Paschal Triduum," which is followed by "Easter Time" and preceded by "Lent" (which are celebrated chronologically as Lent, the Paschal Triduum, and Easter Time).

But, at its center, the liturgical year is not a calendar so much as it is a framework, the setting within which we who celebrate the sacraments are continually drawn into the mystery of God. The liturgical year is not a biography of Jesus of Nazareth but, rather, the pattern according to which we are immersed again and again into the mysteries of Christ's life on earth and his paschal mystery. Understanding the calendar helps us to appreciate how our communal biographies can be continually inserted into the life of the triune God for our sakes and our salvation. Often the liturgical year is presented in a circular diagram with different colors, for example, purple for Advent and Lent, white for

Christmas-Epiphany, green for Ordinary Time, and so forth. In fact, however, it is better to diagram the liturgical year not with a circle but with a spiral. That is to say that while retaining the important circular image of season into season, the purpose of the spiral is to indicate that the same feasts and seasons are also celebrated each and every year, and over time, one year leads to another. We celebrate the church's same liturgical year every year from our baptism to our natural death. In a sense, we celebrate the same liturgy every year, but the liturgy is never the same because we who celebrate it evolve and change, as does the church and the world in which we live. The celebration is always of the same God experienced communally in the liturgy. A spiral would seem to be a better image, for it is meant to demonstrate that one year leads to the next and to the next. This is one of the reasons why at the start of the Easter Vigil, the priest uses a stylus to make the Greek letters *Alpha* and *Omega* on the paschal candle to signify "Christ yesterday and today, the Beginning and the End, the Alpha and Omega." He then traces on the candle four numerals that are the current year of our Lord and says, "All time belongs to him and all the ages. To him be glory and power through every age and for ever. Amen."

LENT–EASTER–PENTECOST

The celebration of the sacraments of initiation at the Easter Vigil accords both with ancient tradition and with these *Norms on the Liturgical Year*. The period of "mystagogy" (initiation into the "mysteries") occurs during the fifty days of Easter Time, which ends on Pentecost Sunday. That Lent is understood to be the premier season to prepare for the Paschal Triduum is clear both in this document and in the assertions found in the Constitution on the Sacred Liturgy (no. 109), which indicates that this season has both baptismal features and penitential features. The gospel readings assigned for the third, fourth, and fifth Sundays of Lent are especially pertinent examples of this understanding of this season.

As noted in chapter 13, in the A cycle, those readings are the following:

Third Sunday—John 4:5–42, the Samaritan woman (water)
Fourth Sunday—John 9:1–41, the man born blind (light)
Fifth Sunday—John 11:1–45, the raising of Lazarus (life)

The use of water at baptism on the Easter Vigil in the light of the paschal candle and the coming of the dawn in nature signify how the newly baptized receive the light of Christ in this liturgy. The Lenten Gospels prepare us for that celebration.

Other sources during Lent that exemplify this connection of Lent, Easter, and initiation at the Easter Vigil are the Prefaces that are prayed on the Sundays when these Gospels are proclaimed at the Sunday liturgy:

Third Sunday (from a combination of texts from the eighth-century Gregorian Sacramentary and the Mozarabic Sacramentary):

> *For when he [Christ] asked the Samaritan woman for water to*
> * drink,*
> *he had already created the gift of faith within her*
> *and so ardently did he thirst for her faith,*
> *that he kindled in her the fire of divine love.*

Fourth Sunday (from the eighth-century Hadrianum sacramentary):

> *By the mystery of the Incarnation,*
> *he has led the human race that walked in darkness*
> *into the radiance of the faith*
> *and has brought those born in slavery to ancient sin*
> *through the waters of regeneration*
> *to make them your adopted children.*

Fifth Sunday (also from the eighth-century Hadrianum sacramentary):

> *For as true man he wept for Lazarus his friend*
> *and as eternal God raised him from the tomb,*
> *just as, taking pity on the human race,*
> *he leads us by sacred mysteries to new life.*

In the C cycle, those Sunday Gospels are the following:

Third Sunday—Luke 13—parable of the fig tree (God's patience)
Fourth Sunday—John 8—the woman accused of adultery (God's forgiveness)
Fifth Sunday—Luke 15—parable of the prodigal son (reconciliation)

Here, the themes proper to a Christian understanding of penance and reconciliation figure prominently. In the patristic era, it was customary for baptized adults who needed to be reconciled because of post-baptismal sin to spend the season of Lent engaged in special penitential practices in order to be reconciled on what we now call Holy Thursday at a mass celebrated by the bishop. In the revised order for the sacrament of Penance, the seasons of Advent and Lent are singled out as particularly opportune times for a communal celebration of the sacrament (see Rite of Penance, appendix, no. 20–24).

While there are no proper prefaces on these Sundays to reflect the Gospel themes of the day, the following Prefaces from the Eucharistic Prayers for Reconciliation state,

For you do not cease to spur us on
to possess a more abundant life
and, being rich in mercy,
you constantly offer pardon
and call on sinners
to trust in your forgiveness alone.

Never did you turn away from us,
and, though time and again we have broken your covenant,
you have bound the human family to yourself
through Jesus, your Son, our Redeemer,
with a new bond of love so tight
that it can never be undone.

Even now you set before your people
a time of grace and reconciliation,

and, as they turn back to you in spirit,
you grant them hope in Christ Jesus
and a desire to be of service to all,
while they entrust themselves
more fully to the Holy Spirit.

(Preface I)

For though the human race
is divided by dissension and discord,
yet we know that by testing us
you change our hearts
to prepare them for reconciliation.

Even more, by your Spirit you move human hearts
that enemies may speak to each other again,
adversaries join hands,
and peoples seek to meet together.

By the working of your power
it comes about, O Lord,
that hatred is overcome by love,
revenge gives way to forgiveness,
and discord is changed to mutual respect.

(Preface II)

This is to suggest that while sacraments can be celebrated at any time, there are certain seasons and times in the liturgical calendar when the liturgical context can help to emphasize the way in which all sacraments are "epiphanies of the church" and the fact that during certain seasons, the church celebrates some sacraments within the rich texture provided by the readings, prayers, and rites of particular seasons. The entire thirteen and a half weeks from Ash Wednesday to Pentecost are thus particularly focused on sacraments of initiation. The celebration of the stages of sacramental initiation on the Sundays of Lent helps to draw this out more fully. Those stages are the Rite of Election on the First Sunday of Lent, normally at the diocesan cathedral celebrated by the bishop, followed by the three prebaptismal "scrutinies" on the third, fourth, and fifth Sundays of Lent, normally in the church or chapel where the liturgical assembly is gathered for worship, many of whom will hopefully be present for sacramental initiation at the Easter Vigil.

ADVENT–CHRISTMAS–EPIPHANY

The *Norms* indicate that second in rank to the celebration of the paschal mystery in Lent and Easter is the commemoration of Christ's coming in the flesh in Christmas Time, which is preceded by the season of Advent, a Latin term that means "coming." The time of Advent–Christmas–Epiphany commemorates Christ's coming in human flesh and at the end of time to bring time to an end. This second coming is particularly celebrated during Advent. The *Norms* state,

> Advent has a twofold character, for it is a time of preparation for the Solemnities of Christmas, in which the First Coming of the Son of God to humanity is remembered, and likewise a time when, by remembrance of this, minds and hearts are led to look forward to Christ's Second Coming at the end of time. For these two reasons, Advent is a period of devout and expectant delight. (no. 39)

Thus Advent can be understood to be the season that emphasizes what all liturgy is—a celebration in time waiting and watching for the end of time. Sacramental liturgy is always celebrated "in between" times, between the first and second coming of our Lord. This is expressed clearly in Preface I of Advent:

> *For he assumed at his first coming*
> *the lowliness of human flesh,*
> *and so fulfilled the design you formed long ago,*
> *and opened for us the way to eternal salvation,*
> *that, when he comes again in glory and majesty*
> *and all is at last made manifest,*
> *we who watch for that day*

may inherit the great promise
in which we now dare to hope.

Another example of a strong eschatological motif to the liturgy is in the rite for the Dedication of a Church. This rite is always celebrated at a Eucharist and has always ranked very high in the church's assessment of liturgies that are not technically among the seven sacraments. A review of its Prefaces to the Eucharistic Prayer can be instructive:

For you have made the whole world a temple of your glory,
that your name might everywhere be extolled,
yet you allow us to consecrate to you
apt places for the divine mysteries.
And so, we dedicate joyfully to your majesty
this house of prayer, built by human labor.
Here is foreshadowed the mystery of the true Temple,
here is prefigured the heavenly Jerusalem.
For you made the Body of your Son, born of the tender Virgin,
the Temple consecrated to you,
in which the fullness of the Godhead might dwell.
You also established the Church as a holy city,
built upon the foundation of the Apostles,
with Christ Jesus himself as the chief cornerstone:
a city to be built of chosen stones,
given life by the Spirit and bonded by charity,
where for endless ages you will be all in all
and the light of Christ will shine undimmed for ever.
(Preface I)

For in this visible house that you have let us build
and where you never cease to show favor
to the family on pilgrimage to you in this place,
you wonderfully manifest and accomplish
the mystery of your communion with us.
Here you build up for yourself the temple that we are
and cause your Church, spread throughout the world,
to grow ever more and more as the Lord's own Body,

369

till she reached her fullness in the vision of peace,
the heavenly city of Jerusalem.

(Preface II)

AN ESCHATOLOGICAL LENS

The final of our four *lenses* (in addition to Trinity, paschal mystery, and *communio*) through which we might want to view the liturgy's texts and rites is *eschatological*. St. Benedict puts it poignantly in his *Rule for Monks*: "Have death daily before your eyes" (or in another translation, "Remind yourself every day that you will die"). The former translation is more akin to the "lens" reference because eschatology does not become the end of life, but the way to measure what matters in life and what life is all about. If the liturgy is viewed as "the future present," we can realize even more fully why we are called to "the heavenly liturgy" for which "the earthly liturgy" is preparation, foretaste, and promise.

DISCUSSION QUESTIONS

1. In light of the contents of this chapter, consider how sacramental liturgy can be described as "the threshold of heaven" and "heaven on earth."
2. Pray over and discuss the prayers for the dying found in chapter 6 of the Rite of Anointing and Pastoral Care of the Sick.
3. Discuss the meaning of the ancient Aramaic word *maranatha* (meaning "the Lord comes" or "come Lord Jesus") and its implications for understanding all sacraments.

CONCLUSION

Sacramental Celebration Is Sacramental Theology

The premise of this book has been that the liturgy can and should be the basis about what we understand the sacraments to be and the way the celebration of sacramental liturgy affects our understanding and living of the Christian life. Taking this premise to be true, three words are in order about the celebration of sacramental liturgy to conclude this text.

BE PREPARED

Especially in light of what has been argued here from a number of sources—including the Scriptures, prayer texts, liturgical rites, and directions—it should be clear that there is a great deal that goes into the design and celebration of sacramental liturgy. To pray over the Scripture readings and the prayer texts and rites before the liturgy can be one way to deepen our appreciation of what takes place in the celebration. The ancient practice of *lectio divina* means that we engage in a holy reading of such texts and allow them to become almost second nature and a part of our lives. The examples given throughout this book from the liturgy's prayers will hopefully provide a guide as to what is contained in the Scriptures, prayers, and rites of the liturgy.

PARTICIPATE

One of the chief aims of the reform of the liturgy after Vatican II has been the active participation of the entire gathered assembly in the liturgy. The careful selection of prayers and rites from the liturgical patrimony of the Western church came to be incorporated in the revised sacramental liturgies, which aim to foster such participation. We participate in the liturgy through our senses in a number of ways. In addition to being attentive to what is occurring, we should also make sure that we engage our bodies and our senses in what is taking place. The celebration of sacramental liturgy is not something we primarily watch. It is something that we are meant to be engaged in by active participation. Sacramental liturgy is not about spectators and actors. It concerns the engagement of all who are gathered for these most sacred rites and, through that engagement, participate in the living God thereby revealed and manifested.

LIFE RELATION

From what has been argued here, it is clear that we can understand the sacraments in a number of ways, especially when we examine the liturgy by which we celebrate them. One of the advantages of the reformed liturgy is that it is normally celebrated in the language of the people celebrating it so that comprehension and engagement in the liturgy is facilitated. Another advantage is that the reformed liturgy repeatedly makes reference to our need for God and our living out in life what we celebrate. This means that the liturgy of the sacraments should really be a lens through which we view life and our foundation for living it. Central to the Christian faith is the paradox that suffering leads to glory, that we need to acknowledge our spiritual poverty to be filled with the riches of God's grace, and that we are our brothers' brother and our sisters' sister. It implies that we live what we celebrate despite contrary cultural pressures or the lack of cultural supports for our faith. We need to celebrate sacramental liturgy to worship God, to be made holy, and to be witnesses in the world to what we celebrate and believe.

Lex orandi, lex credendi, lex vivendi.

BIBLIOGRAPHIES

English Translations of Vatican documents (such as the constitutions, etc., of the Second Vatican Council) can be accessed at the Vatican II Web site, www.vatican.va.

CONTENTS OF LITURGICAL BOOKS

The following outline may be helpful as an introduction and guide to the liturgical books that are presently used in the church's liturgy and to which I have referred in this book.

The Roman Missal (third edition, 2011)
The Missal is really a collection of books whose evolution and history are an important source for scientific and systematic study.

The present Missal contains some introductory documents, including the following:

> *The General Instruction of the Roman Missal*
> *Norms for the Distribution and Reception of Holy Communion under Both Kinds in the Dioceses of the United States of America*
> *Universal Norms on the Liturgical Year and the Calendar*
> *Table of Liturgical Days*
> *General Roman Calendar*
>
> Part One—Proper of Time
> Mass texts (also called a Mass formula) for each day of each liturgical season, almost all of which are derived from what have been traditionally called:

Antiphonal
Verses often from the Scriptures to accompany the entrance and communion processions and suggested verses of Psalms.

Sacramentary
Prayers for the presiding bishop or priest, for example, collects, prayer over the gifts, prayer after communion.

Lectionary and the *Book of the Gospels*
Scripture readings to be proclaimed at Mass.
Sunday structure: Old Testament, psalm, New Testament, acclamation, Gospel (continuous, one evangelist each year, John through Lent and Easter).
Weekday structure: First Reading (Old Testament or New Testament), psalm, acclamation, Gospel (continuous: Matthew, Mark, Luke).

Part Two—The Order of Mass
Texts of the "ordinary" of the Mass.
Rubrics, meaning directions, usually printed in red (from the Latin *rubens*, translated as "red"), in the text of a "Mass formula" that describe what is to be done during the Mass.

Part Three—Proper of Saints
Same sources as for the Proper of Time for all the saints in the Calendar.

Part Four—Additional Masses
Commons, Ritual Masses, Votive Masses, Masses for the Dead.

The Roman Pontifical (liturgies celebrated by the bishop)

Ordinations (bishop, presbyter/priest, diaconate)
Rites of Installation to the Ministries of Reader and Acolyte
Rite of Election
Rite for Confirmation

Rite for the Dedication of an Altar and a Church
"Station" Masses (when the diocesan bishop visits a parish or
other institution in the diocese)

The Roman Ritual (formerly one volume, now several volumes, for
each sacrament)

Rite of Baptism for Children
Rite for the Christian Initiation of Adults
Order for Christian Funerals
Rite for the Pastoral Care and Anointing of the Sick
Rite of Marriage
Rite of Penance

The Liturgy of the Hours (1975)

Four volumes as revised after the Second Vatican Council.
Formerly, "The Divine Office" or "The Roman Breviary."
The Hours

Office of Readings
Psalms, Reading from Scripture, Reading from the Fathers
of the Church, or another source.
Morning Prayer—Lauds
Hymn, Psalms, Scripture, Canticle of Zechariah (Luke
1:68–79), Intercessions, Lord's Prayer, Prayer
Midday Prayer—Terce, Sext, None
Evening Prayer—Vespers
Hymn, Psalms, Scripture, Canticle of the Blessed Virgin
Mary (Luke 1:46–55), Intercessions, Lord's Prayer, Prayer
Night Prayer—Compline
Scripture, Examination of Conscience, Psalms, Canticle of
Simeon (Luke 2:29–32), Marian antiphon (e.g., *Salve Regina*)

Structure of the Book

Proper of the Seasons
Solemnities

Psalter
Proper of the Saints
Commons
Office of the Dead
Appendices

ON THE LITURGICAL REFORMS OF VATICAN II

Bugnini, Annibale. *The Reform of the Liturgy 1948–1975*. Translated by Matthew J. O'Connell. Collegeville: Liturgical Press, 1990.

Marini, Piero. A *Challenging Reform: Realizing the Vision of the Liturgical Renewal*. Edited and translated by Mark Francis, John Page, and Keith Pecklers. Collegeville, MN: Liturgical Press, 2007.

ON SACRAMENTS

Chauvet, Louis-Marie. *The Sacraments: The Word of God at the Mercy of the Body*. Collegeville, MN: The Liturgical Press, 1997 (original), 2001.

———. *Symbol and Sacrament*. Collegeville, MN: The Liturgical Press, 1987 (original), 1994.

Kilmartin, Edward. "A Modern Approach to the Word of God and Sacraments of Christ: Perspectives and Principles." In *The Sacraments: God's Love and Mercy Actualized. Proceedings of the Theological Institute II*, edited by F. A. Eigo, 59–109. Villanova, PA: Villanova University Press, 1979.

———. "Systematic Theology of the Sacraments: Perspectives and Principles." In *Christian Liturgy: Theology and Practice*, 199–376. Kansas City: Sheed and Ward, 1988.

———. "Theology of the Sacraments: Toward a New Understanding of the Chief Rites of the Church of Jesus Christ." In *Alternative Futures for Worship*, vol. 1, edited by Regis A. Duffy, 123–75. Collegeville, MN: Liturgical Press, 1987.

Leeming, Bernard. *Principles of Sacramental Theology.* New York: Longmans Green, 1956.

Osborne, Kenan B. *Christian Sacraments in a Postmodern World: A Theology for the Third Millennium.* New York: Paulist Press, 1999.

———. *Sacramental Theology: A General Introduction.* New York: Paulist Press, 1988.

———. *Sacramental Theology: Fifty Years after Vatican II.* Hobe Sound, FL: Lectio, 2014.

Pourrat, Pierre. *Theology of the Sacraments.* 2nd ed., translated from the 3rd French ed. St. Louis: B. Herder, 1910.

Power, David N. *Sacrament: The Language of God's Self Giving.* New York: Herder and Herder, 1999.

———. *Unsearchable Riches: The Symbolic Nature of the Liturgy.* New York: Pueblo Publishing Co., 1984.

Rahner, Karl. *The Church and the Sacraments.* New York: Herder and Herder, 1966, rev. ed. 1970.

———. "The Concept of Mystery in Catholic Theology." In *Theological Investigations,* vol. 6, translated by Karl-H. Kruger and Boniface Kruger, 36–76. New York: Seabury Press, 1974.

———. "Considerations on the Active Role of the Person in the Sacramental Event." In *Theological Investigations,* vol. 14, translated by David Bourke, 161–84. New York: Seabury Press, 1976.

———. "How to Receive a Sacrament and Mean It." *Theology Digest* 19 (Fall 1971): 227–34.

———. "Introductory Observations on Thomas Aquinas' Theology of the Sacraments in General." In *Theological Investigations,* vol. 14, translated by David Bourke, 149–60. New York: Seabury Press, 1976.

———. "On the Theology of Worship." In *Theological Investigations,* vol. 19, translated by Edward Quinn, 141–49. New York: Crossroad, 1983.

———. "The Presence of Christ in the Sacrament of the Lord's Supper." In *Theological Investigations,* vol. 4, translated by Kevin Smyth, 287–311. New York: Crossroad, 1973.

———. "The Presence of the Lord in the Christian Community." In *Theological Investigations,* vol. 10, translated by David Bourke, 71–83. New York: Seabury Press, 1973.

————. "What Is a Sacrament?" In *Theological Investigations*, vol. 14, translated by David Bourke, 135–48. New York: Seabury Press, 1976.

Ross, Susan. *Extravagant Affections: A Feminist Sacramental Theology*. New York: Continuum, 1998, 2001.

Schillebeeckx, Edward. *Christ: The Sacrament of the Encounter with God*. New York: Sheed and Ward, 1963, 1987. (1987 edition is available in paperback.)

Segundo, Juan Luis. *The Sacraments Today*. Translated by John Drury. Eugene: Wipf and Stock, 2005.

Stringer, Martin. *A Sociological History of Christian Worship*. New York: Cambridge University Press, 2005.

Vaillancourt, Raymond. *Toward A Renewal of Sacramental Theology*. Translated by Matthew J. O'Connell. Collegeville, MN: Liturgical Press, 1979.

ON METHOD

Fagerberg, David W. *On Liturgical Asceticism*. Washington, DC: The Catholic University of America Press, 2013.

Fisch, Thomas, ed. *Liturgy and Tradition: Theological Reflections of Alexander Schmemann*. Crestwood: St. Vladimir's Press, 1990.

Irwin, Kevin W. *Context and Text: Method in Liturgical Theology*. Collegeville, MN: The Liturgical Press, 1994.

————. *Liturgical Theology: A Primer*. Collegeville, MN: The Liturgical Press, 1990.

Johnson, Maxwell. *Praying and Believing in Early Christianity: The Interplay between Christian Worship and Doctrine*. Collegeville, MN: The Liturgical Press, 2013.

Kavanagh, Aidan. *On Liturgical Theology*. New York: Pueblo, 1984. Now available from The Liturgical Press.

McCall, Richard. *Do This: Liturgy as Performance*. Notre Dame: University of Notre Dame Press, 2007.

Schmemann, Alexander. *For the Life of the World: Sacraments and Orthodoxy*. 2nd and rev. ed. Crestwood, NY: St. Vladimir's Seminary Press, 1973.

Vagaggini, Cipriano. *Theological Dimensions of the Liturgy.* Translated by Leonard J. Doyle and W. A. Jurgens. Collegeville, MN: The Liturgical Press, 1976.

Wainwright, Geoffrey. *Doxology: The Praise of God in Worship, Doctrine and Life: A Systematic Theology.* New York: Oxford University Press, 1980.

PREVIOUS WORKS BY KEVIN W. IRWIN

"Sacrament." In *New Dictionary of Theology,* edited by Dermot Lane, Mary Collins, and Joseph Komonchak, 910–22. Wilmington, DE: Glazier, 1987.

"Method in Liturgical Theology: Context is Text." *Eglise et théologie* 20 (1989): 407–24.

"Liturgical Theology." In *New Dictionary of Sacramental Worship,* edited by Peter Fink, 721–33. Collegeville, MN: The Liturgical Press, 1990.

"Sacramental Theology: A Methodological Proposal." *The Thomist* 54 (1990): 311–42.

"The Sacramentality of Creation and the Role of Creation in Liturgy and Sacraments." In *Preserving the Creation: Environmental Theology and Ethics,* edited by Kevin W. Irwin and Edmund J. Pellegrino, 67–111. Washington, DC: Georgetown University Press, 1994.

"Liturgy, Justice and Spirituality: Scholarly Update." *Liturgical Ministry* 7 (Fall 1998): 162–74.

"Sacramentality and the Theology of Creation: A Recovered Paradigm for Sacramental Theology." *Louvain Studies* 23 (1998): 159–79.

"Discovering the Sacramentality of Sacraments." *Questions liturgiques* 81 (2000): 171–83.

"Development of Doctrine in the Sacraments." In *Rediscovering the Riches of Anointing,* edited by Genevieve Glen, 29–81. Collegeville, MN: The Liturgical Press, 2002.

"*Lex Orandi, Lex Credendi*—Origins and Meaning: State of the Question." *Liturgical Ministry* 11 (Spring 2002): 57–69.

"Sacramental Theology." In *New Catholic Encyclopedia*, vol. 12, 465–79. 2nd rev. ed. Washington, DC: The Catholic University of America Press, 2002.

"The Sacramental World—The Primary Language for Sacraments." *Worship* 76, no. 3 (May 2002): 197–211.

"*Lex Orandi, Lex Credendi, Lex Vivendi* in the Rites of Christian Initiation." *Canon Law Society of America Proceedings, Sixty-fifth Annual Meeting* (Alexandria, VA, 2005): 27–55.

Models of the Eucharist. New York: Paulist Press, 2005.

"Sacramentality: The Fundamental Language for Liturgy and Sacraments." In *Per Ritus et Praeces: Sacramentalita della Liturgia*, 131–60. Analecta Liturgica 28. Rome: Studia Anselmiana, 2010.

"The Mystery of the Incarnation: Advent-Christmas-Epiphany." *Assembly* 17, no. 1 (Jan. 2011): 2–10.

Serving the Body of Christ: The Magisterium on Eucharist and Ordained Priesthood. New York: Paulist Press, 2013.

INDEX